# British Cinema and a Divided Nation

# British Cinema
# and a Divided Nation

John White

EDINBURGH
University Press

Edinburgh University Press is one of the leading university presses in the UK. We publish academic books and journals in our selected subject areas across the humanities and social sciences, combining cutting-edge scholarship with high editorial and production values to produce academic works of lasting importance. For more information visit our website: edinburghuniversitypress.com

© John White, 2022, 2023

Edinburgh University Press Ltd
The Tun—Holyrood Road
12 (2f) Jackson's Entry
Edinburgh EH8 8PJ

First published in hardback by Edinburgh University Press 2022

Typeset in Garamond MT Std by
Manila Typesetting Company

A CIP record for this book is available from the British Library

ISBN 978 1 4744 8102 1 (hardback)
ISBN 978 1 4744 8103 8 (paperback)
ISBN 978 1 4744 8104 5 (webready PDF)
ISBN 978 1 4744 8105 2 (epub)

The right of John White to be identified as author of this work has been asserted in accordance with the Copyright, Designs and Patents Act 1988, and the Copyright and Related Rights Regulations 2003 (SI No. 2498).

# Contents

List of Figures ... vii

1 Introduction: Popular Culture and a Shared National Perspective ... 1

**Part I  Reinterpreting Pre-twentieth-century British History**
2 What Chance Sisterhood under Patriarchy? *Mary Queen of Scots* (Josie Rourke, 2018) ... 23
3 What Would it Be to "Turn the World Upside Down"? *Fanny Lye Deliver'd* (Thomas Clay, 2019) ... 35
4 Politics in "The Corridors of Power" Then (and Now): *The Favourite* (Yorgos Lanthimos, 2018) ... 49
5 Class as the Crucial Division in UK Society: *Peterloo* (Mike Leigh, 2018) ... 65

**Part II  Rehearsing Twentieth-century British History**
6 One-nation Conservatism 1920s/2020s: *Downton Abbey* (Michael Engler, 2019) ... 87
7 Defending this "Island Nation": *Darkest Hour* (Joe Wright, 2017) and *Churchill* (Jonathan Teplitzky, 2017) ... 104
8 Identity Politics: *Where Hands Touch* (Amma Asante, 2018) and *A United Kingdom* (Asante, 2016) ... 121
9 Colonialism and the Reshaping of History: *Viceroy's House* (Gurinder Chadha, 2017) ... 138

**Part III  Re-presenting Britain in the Twenty-first Century**
10 Educated Elites and Plebeians: *The Sense of an Ending* (Ritesh Batra, 2017) and *Daphne* (Peter Mackie Burns, 2017) ... 157
11 Migration in an Age of Ideological Confrontation: *God's Own Country* (Francis Lee, 2017) ... 172

12 Rural Poverty: *Dark River* (Clio Barnard, 2017) and *The Levelling* (Hope Dickson Leach, 2016) — 189

13 Urban Poverty: *Sorry We Missed You* (Ken Loach, 2019) — 203

14 Conclusion: Liberal Consensus Politics, Economics, and Class — 218

Bibliography — 231

Index — 247

# Figures

| | | |
|---|---|---|
| 2.1 | The patriarchal entrapment of women in this society emphasized in one shot in *Mary Queen of Scots* | 27 |
| 2.2 | Elizabeth I, a woman elevated above all others and yet utterly alone, in *Mary Queen of Scots* | 29 |
| 3.1 | Fanny repays her husband, John, for the patriarchal violence he has shown her, in *Fanny Lye Deliver'd* | 38 |
| 3.2 | Fanny executes patriarchy in the form of the High Sheriff in *Fanny Lye Deliver'd* | 40 |
| 4.1 | Women in *The Favourite* handle guns as competently as men: here, Abigail Masham | 53 |
| 4.2 | Woman as hysterical: Queen Anne bellows for the musicians to stop playing in *The Favourite* | 58 |
| 5.1 | When we are introduced to Nellie in *Peterloo*, it is her hands we see first | 71 |
| 5.2 | A carefully placed and constructed shot of three generations of working-class women in *Peterloo* | 78 |
| 6.1 | The country house as the culminating representation in a series of images of idealized England in the opening to *Downton Abbey* | 88 |
| 6.2 | The upper class and the servant class, Lady Mary and Anna Bates, working together to lay out the chairs for the royal visit in *Downton Abbey* | 94 |
| 7.1 | In early scenes from *Darkest Hour*, Churchill is repeatedly framed in such a way as to suggest he is trapped | 109 |
| 7.2 | Marcus Peters with Churchill on the London Underground in *Darkest Hour* | 113 |
| 8.1 | Miscegenation: black and white bodies next to each other in *Where Hands Touch* | 122 |
| 8.2 | Boxed in a tight space, Lenya and Lutz look up as planes fly overhead in *Where Hands Touch* | 130 |

| | | |
|---|---|---|
| 9.1 | The administrator of the Viceroy's household, Ewart, expresses the colonial attitude towards Indian independence within the opening minutes of *Viceroy's House* | 139 |
| 9.2 | A world of absolute privilege: the indoor staff assembled to greet the Mountbattens in *Viceroy's House* | 145 |
| 10.1 | Tony waking to the morning light coming into his bedroom in *The Sense of an Ending* | 164 |
| 10.2 | In *Daphne*, we repeatedly find Daphne alone within boxed spaces inside the frame | 166 |
| 11.1 | Gheorghe responds to the provocations of Johnny and pins him to the ground in *God's Own Country* | 175 |
| 11.2 | With Gheorghe's guidance, Johnny is able to look up and see the beauty of the landscape around him for the first time in *God's Own Country* | 183 |
| 12.1 | In *Dark River*, Alice, here walking her sheep through a market sales-ring, appears well able to hold her own in a man's world | 191 |
| 12.2 | Clover prepares to shoot a young calf in *The Levelling* | 198 |
| 13.1 | In *Sorry We Missed You*, from a quite distant observational camera we frequently see Ricky driving his white delivery van through heavy traffic | 211 |
| 13.2 | A static shot from behind his boss, Maloney, means we are forced to watch Ricky as he almost begs for time off in *Sorry We Missed You* | 213 |

CHAPTER 1

# Introduction: Popular Culture and a Shared National Perspective

## I

At the end of *Dunkirk* (Leslie Norman, 1958), a narrator summarises the significance of the historical event on which this film is based.[1] He says:

> This was Dunkirk. Over a third of a million men were lifted from the mole[2] and the beaches but for others there was no escape, some thousands mainly the sick and the wounded were held in a captivity that was to last five long years. Many remained never to return. Those that were saved straggling ashore dazed and resentful found almost to their astonishment a new reality waiting for them. Dunkirk was a great defeat and a great miracle. It proved if it proved anything, that we were alone and undivided, no longer were there fighting men and civilians, there were only people. A nation had been made whole.

The shadow of this single event and of the entire war and the legends created around both, have hung over Britain ever since 1945. The narrator's words (and the whole film) demonstrate the way in which dominant versions of history are shaped through the structuring of the popular cultural narrative. This process is happening all the time: the creation of a shared, collective culture which is a depository of a society's "knowledge" and understanding of the past constructed in such a way as to be relevant to the present. Most obviously the British story (or version) of "Dunkirk" might be seen to be different if viewed from a German perspective, or from a French perspective; but equally there might have been a range of possible perspectives on this event that would have been offered by others from within Britain when this film was made in 1958. The choice of which particular events to present and the writing of the narrative around each of those events are political acts, interventions contributing to the weave of the fabric of a society that is eventually collectively achieved. Julian Thompson clarifies exactly how in the creation of a unifying national myth the media and their political sources employed the idea of heroic little civilian-crewed boats saving the British army during the early summer of 1940:

> To boost national morale and cohesion, the story of the "little ships" was milked as hard as it could be. The facts are that more than two and a half times as many troops were taken from Dunkirk harbour as from the beaches, and of those taken off the beaches the majority were transported in destroyers or other ships, albeit in many cases ferried out to these larger vessels, either by "little ships" or by ships' boats.[3]

In the film the key concept embodied in the narrator's words about "Dunkirk" is that this event moulded "a new reality." "We" were now "undivided": "a nation had been made whole." The "great miracle" of which the narrator speaks is the saving of the men from the beaches of Dunkirk but it is also the uniting of the nation. The obvious implication is that before this moment Britain was a divided nation. The narrator specifically mentions the divide between "fighting men and civilians" but this is also a nation previously divided along lines of class between those living in (or, on the brink of) poverty and those living a well-provided-for life of wealth and privilege. This was, and is, an ever-present fault line within British society but it was also one that was exacerbated by the economic depression of the 1930s. The crucial question would be whether such divisions in society genuinely disappeared in the wake of the "miracle" of Dunkirk as the narrator suggests, or whether this is no more than the "spin" the film is putting on events? Certainly, the film itself—made eighteen years after the event—remains full of class divisions within the representations we are given of both the military and civilians, something demonstrated most forcefully through the language use of officers and men.

In considering examples of more contemporary British filmmaking, one question we might ask would be whether it is no more than a coincidence that audiences have more recently been presented with another version of the Dunkirk story, *Dunkirk* (Christopher Nolan, 2017), and that in the same year this film was made there were two further British films focusing on this period of British history, *Darkest Hour* (Joe Wright, 2017) and *Churchill* (Jonathan Teplitzky, 2017)? Do these films, like the 1958 version of "Dunkirk," contain a similar interest in the notion of Britain as a divided nation and do they too wish to promote greater national unity? Beyond this, in considering both the 1958 and 2017 versions of *Dunkirk*, we might ask whether the dominant interest of each is the period in which the film is set or the period in which the film is made, since if cultural representations are concerned with shaping the past with relevance to the present, the period of production and exhibition is clearly critical to our understanding of the film.

Widening the scope of our investigations, it is worth recognizing at this point that what we have to say here does not apply only to British cinema, nor only to films, but rather to all media representations. The questions we will be asking will be posed within the specific context of recent British cinema but will have a critically important application with regard to the media as a whole. Were we to consider, for example, media representations of the Covid-19 pandemic, we would be able to identify the same debates around the question of "the nation" and "the unity of the nation" as have been highlighted in relation to films dealing with "Dunkirk." For example, in terms of the creation of a dominant perspective within popular culture, what was happening within newspaper reports of "the nation" stepping outside on to balconies and doorsteps on 26 March 2020 in order to applaud frontline NHS workers and other key workers for their efforts in the face of the Covid-19 crisis? *The Telegraph* claimed the event "brought the nation together"[4] and, according to the *Daily Mirror*, "Britain came to a standstill . . . as we paid tribute to our brilliant NHS carers."[5] The reality, of course, was that *some* UK citizens applauded while others took no notice. There most certainly was a media representation in both words and images of Britain as a united nation but the reality may have been that the country remained divided in a variety of ways.

## II

Since our title is *British Cinema and a Divided Nation* we probably ought to question from the outset whether the term "divided nation" is not a truism: has Britain not always been a divided nation? To investigate further we might try to consider to what extent, where, and when within British cinema history the country has been presented as either divided or united? As has been implicitly suggested, the most obvious time the representation of a country as united is seen of critical importance is during time of war when film (inevitably) tends towards being propaganda. Classically this might be seen to be the case during the Second World War, blatantly for example in a film like *The Lion Has Wings* (Michael Powell, Brian Desmond Hurst, and Adrian Brunel, 1939), and perhaps slightly more subtly in a film such as *49th Parallel* (Powell, 1941). At such times, because of a singular external threat, the media including the film industry is motivated to produce representations of the world that might be described as propaganda.[6] On the other hand, Britain has also often been portrayed as a divided nation, so the keynote parameter of this book is certainly nothing new within film studies. Charles Pattie and Ron Johnston, for example, point out that:

> It was frequently contended during the 1980s that Britain was becoming increasingly divided . . . Further, because throughout that decade the government of the United Kingdom was provided by the Conservative party, led by Margaret Thatcher, the growing divide was commonly attributed to that government's policies; the divided nation was a consequence of Thatcherism.[7]

This notion of a divided land could be traced back much further. For example, in the mid-1800s the divide between the middle classes and the poorest sections of the working class "was widely perceived as one of the main social problems facing Victorian society and was encapsulated by Disraeli in 1845 in his claim that England had become a country of 'two nations', rich and poor."[8] Gerry Mooney quotes Friedrich Engels describing the situation in Manchester in the 1840s:

> The town itself is peculiarly built, so that a person may live in it for years and go in and out daily without coming into contact with a working people's quarter or even with workers, that is, so long as he confines himself to his business or to pleasure walks.[9]

And yet, despite the fact that the concept of division is nothing new, it is also the case that in recent years some contemporary commentators have viewed Britain as "an increasingly divided nation" in which "access to the basics, a decent job and a house can seem like a pipe dream."[10] According to Mark Garnett and Philip Lynch, "the most important socio-economic features of contemporary Britain can most usefully be introduced by exploring its contemporary divisions."[11] Taking its cue from this sort of perspective, this book will attempt to identify divisions within society that are given narrative shape and cultural form within a selection of recent British films. However, this will not prevent us from continuing to question the idea of "the nation." For example, reflecting further on the notion of division in relation to the concept of nationhood, we might ask whether any nation can ever be said to be truly united. Is it not the case that unity always exists in a tenuous, parlous relationship to disunity? Extending the debate much further, we might question whether there is any such thing as a nation? Mary Fulbrook suggests:

> Nations are themselves myths. There is no such "real entity" as a nation: only a social reality . . . when enough people are prepared to believe in the salience of a certain set of characteristics as attributes of nationhood.[12]

Benedict Anderson famously defines "the nation" as "an imagined political community."¹³ "It is imagined," he says, "because the members of even the smallest nation will never know most of their fellow-members, meet them, or even hear of them, yet in the minds of each lives the image of their communion."¹⁴ Attempting to give some general basis to our discussions, maybe we can at least speak about periods when the divisions within a society have lessened and the unity intensified. Fulbrook asserts that "a sense of nationhood is more likely to occur under certain conditions than others."¹⁵

A further set of questions might present themselves around the issue of whether we should see each division, either within a society or as presented within a film, as distinct and different or whether all divisions—political divisions, social divisions, gender divisions, racial divisions, religious divisions, etc.—should be viewed as being linked in some way. An additional difficulty is that the notion of "Britishness" implicit in the concept of "British cinema" automatically carries within it the divisions of England, Scotland, and Wales, and (even more problematically) the further division of Northern Ireland (and potentially, within a geographical interpretation of the concept of the British Isles, Ireland as a whole, that is including Éire). Furthermore, within all of this internal national division, according to some, "English national identity has been studied much less extensively than its Scottish and Welsh counterparts."¹⁶

Many of the divisions briefly outlined here are frequently seen as being of critical importance in determining the outcome of the Brexit referendum of 23 June 2016, when almost 52 percent of voters came out in favour of leaving the European Union. The result left "the nation" split pretty much 50:50. Breaking down the voting into the component countries of the United Kingdom,¹⁷ both England and Wales voted reasonably decisively to leave, while both Scotland and Northern Ireland voted even more decisively in favour of staying in the EU. However, the divides revealed by the vote were also regional and generational. Analysing the data, Paul Welfens says:

> With the exception of London, most English regions returned a pro-Brexit vote. Beyond the regional perspective, there is a clear distinction between younger and older generations, the elderly being in favour of Leave.¹⁸

On the face of it, the UK election three years later in December 2019 showed Britain to be a rather more united nation. There was a landslide Conservative victory; effectively, a rejection of liberalism and socialism, and an endorsement of conservatism and nationalism. The Conservative Party acquired a majority of eighty in the House of Commons, winning almost 44 percent of the votes overall and more than 47 percent in England, the highest percentages seen since the 1970s. Analysts, however, suggested what this election actually demonstrated was the entrenched nature of the divides revealed by the Brexit vote of three years earlier. According to Rob Ford, a politics professor at Manchester University, the election results showed "huge swings to the Conservatives in older, white, working-class urban seats" and that "Brexit was a key driver of these shifts."[19] His analysis demonstrated that: "The higher the Leave share, the greater the Tory gain, rising from a modest two-point swing in seats with a Leave vote below 45% to a whopping eight-point swing in seats where 60% or more voted Leave in 2016."[20]

Alongside this political activity and the divisions this seems to reveal, other analysts have studied social and wealth inequality in Britain and concluded the country to be a divided nation. *Health Equity in England: The Marmot Review 10 Years On*, a report written by a team working under Professor Sir Michael Marmot and Dr Jessica Allen, was released early in 2020. The report concluded health was getting worse "for people living in more deprived districts and regions" and highlighted the fact that in some areas of England more than one child in two was growing up in poverty.[21] In *Breadline Britain: The Rise of Mass Poverty*, published in 2015, the authors asked in their preface: "Why, with the country twice as rich as it was thirty years ago, have poverty rates doubled? What are the forces that have turned Britain into one of the most unequal and socially fragile countries in the rich world?"[22] Other analysts have suggested there is a direct link between the wealth gap in British society and the political divisions exposed by the Brexit vote:

> In the immediate aftermath of the EU referendum, the Joseph Rowntree Foundation analysed voting patterns across the UK and found that support for Brexit was strongest in the poorest households, . . . in those areas with higher unemployment . . . and in areas where a large percentage of the population had few or no qualifications . . .[23]

We will consider these political tensions through an examination of contemporary British cinema, exploring the ways in which the contest of ideologies always at work within media representation played out after 2016. Film presentations of the nation will be examined against a backdrop of rising political tension and deepening social division following the "Brexit" referendum.[24] Summing up the post-Brexit situation, James Harvey suggested this vote signaled that, "The transnational promise of fluid borders and co-mingling cultures was being forced out of the geopolitical landscape by a rejuvenated nostalgia for a singular, native identity."[25]

## III

*British Cinema and a Divided Nation* will focus on historical and contemporary drama films, with each chapter offering a reading of either an individual film, or pair of films. In considering the chosen films, part of the interest will be to see ways in which they might be said to deal on the one hand with concepts of "fluid borders and co-mingling cultures," and on the other hand with ideas of "a singular, native identity." All in all, the aim will be to analyse a nation's contested understandings of its past, present, and future, probing the various ways recent mainstream films have approached the concept of nationhood and constructed narratives in relation to ideas of borders and boundaries between places and groups of people. Part of our focus will be on considering whether there has been a new or renewed emphasis on the competing ideological perspectives that confront each other around the issue of nationalism: to what extent we are witnessing the negotiation of a new relationship with the world for a new age and to what extent we are simply seeing a reiteration of a long-standing British, or English, understanding of national identity. A crucial aspect of this approach will necessarily be the assessment of the relative importance of this issue in relation to other socio-economic concerns found in the films under discussion. Are there socio-economic drivers around the issue of nationalism that might be seen to be operating? In this regard, certain commentators remind us of the importance of taking account of the economic base to nationalism. Tim Vlandas and Daphne Halikiopoulou, for example, emphasize "the importance of economic insecurity as a driver of far right party support."[26] They suggest, "factors such as immigration tend to be treated as cultural, thus often overlooking their economic dimension."[27]

The idea of the nation—viewing nationalism and the nation state from a variety of perspectives—will be central to the investigation undertaken in this book. Against this ever-present backdrop, the effort will be to see each of the films under discussion within four key contexts: the historical, the political, the economic, and the social. These contexts are deemed important in relation both to the period in which the film is set, and to the time and place in which each film is made and screened; and these contextual elements are seen as critical in understanding meaning. It will be contended that to live within the UK today is to live within an intensely divided society. The question being asked will be how contemporary films might be seen to be responding to, or reflecting, the nature of this society. The linkage between films (and the media in general) and society is clear. Plenty of film critics have taken this approach. In considering films made in the United States, for example, Robin Wood says: "what happens in the cinema will clearly depend upon what happens in American society and politics."[28] According to Dudley Andrew, within this framework films go beyond constituting either a response to or a reflection of particular cultural context. "The cinema", he suggests, "literally contributes to a culture's self-image, inflecting, not just capturing, daily experience."[29] John Belton feels,

> the movies assist audiences in negotiating major changes in identity; they carry them across difficult periods of cultural transition in such a way that a more or less coherent national identity remains in place . . .[30]

However, despite these sorts of assertions it is fair to say the question remains as to whether film is able to position itself in such a way as to shape society, or whether it can only ever respond to, or reflect, what has happened in society. Looking at Hollywood but with a general position relevant to our considerations here, Robert Hilliard writes: "While many filmmakers believe that films reflect society and should be responsive, rather than proactive, in regard to social issues, others take the opposite view."[31] Hilliard quotes George Clooney as believing film reflects rather than leads society, and Steven Spielberg as thinking films can make a much more direct contribution to helping audiences to understand "the world and human rights issues."[32] The issue at stake is what audiences take away from watching films. A recent BFI report concludes audiences are "able to distinguish between the art of film, the entertainment it provides, and the reflection and insight it prompts."[33] This report says for "the broad public" there is "no distinction between 'meaningful' and entertaining films"; instead, "the medium and the message" are seen as "two sides of the same coin" and people are "able to appreciate the value of both."[34] In a review for the *Journal of British Studies* that looks at a range of investigations, Kelly Boyd explains that what the historian finds most interesting about films is "how the film illuminates the context in which it is created."[35] Key questions, she suggests, are: "What does British film tell us about the society from which it emerged? What themes spring from them, and how do they illuminate our understanding of events of the era?"[36] She points out historical films have always "used the past to illuminate contemporary problems."[37]

According to Patricia Hill Collins and Sirma Bilge, major axes of social division in a specific society at a given time operate not "as discrete and mutually exclusive entities, but build on each other and work together."[38] This book will in effect set out these major axes of social division within the UK and consider the various ways in which these defining aspects of society receive cultural and ideological expression in a range of contemporary films. Attention will be given to economic divisions of wealth and poverty, differential access to culture and education, and issues relating to gender, sexuality, ethnicity, race, and religion, as well as national (and regional) identity. In essence, these areas of concern are nothing new. Earlier patterns of representation in British cinema would suggest the UK has always been divided along the fault lines of class, gender, race, sexuality, and "local" nationalisms created as a result of having Scotland, Wales, and Ireland existing alongside England within the same geographical space of the British Isles. Books on British cinema have often assessed themes in films against the backdrop of "social context" and contemporary "social discourses";[39] and in relation to issues of migration and immigration, colonialism and nationalism, and wealth and poverty. Fundamentally, we are currently seeing little more than the contemporary period's filmic expression of the same factors of division. And, although there may be much less discussion of "class" in direct terms during the present phase of British history, when we discuss the growing gulf in wealth and health between rich and poor this is, of course, actually what is at stake.

Looking at contemporary British cinema in 2009, Sarah Street suggested a range of important themes to be considered: "nostalgia—'heritage' past and present; youth culture—matters of life and death; experiences of ethnicity and asylum, and place, space and identity."[40] Her interest in the ways in which British films offered "cultural commentary about contemporary mobilisation of the past"[41] summarizes the key line of approach taken by this book. Street pointed out many British films had "become hybridised as generic forms, capable of conveying a range of complexities that centre on narrative, setting and mise-en-scene that defy reductive or generalised categorisation."[42] Here care needs to be taken. It is absolutely true we should recognize the existence of nuanced complexity. However, it is crucial this recognition should not be allowed to operate as a means of preventing generalized conclusions from being made. Generalization should not be seen as a difficulty per se, since this is the means by which the essence of a problem is revealed in its starkest terms.

The concept of British cinema as a "national" cinema has been explored by a range of writers. In their book, *British Historical Cinema*, Claire Monk and Amy Sargeant see historical dramas as burdened by being viewed as "projections of 'the nation'"[43] and by the belief that "the central duty of films set in the past is to document historical fact."[44] Again, this is fair enough, in that what this genre offers is fiction. However, going on to support the idea that "a 'historical' film will often be a work of pure entertainment and pure fiction"[45] is a step too far. While historical films and dramas set in a contemporary period are always "fiction" and will always aim at some level to "entertain," they are never "pure" within either of these dimensions. To assert this once more, films exist in relation to history; and while it is true there is a sense in which history is unknowable, there is also a sense in which it is very definitely knowable, and not just in terms of the factual details of dates. At the same time, Justine Ashby and Andrew Higson are right to highlight the importance of thinking carefully about history, which amounts to the "facts" being "mobilised into a story" in some way by somebody,[46] and about interpretation, which amounts to the creation of meaning by somebody.[47]

Higson tells us that what he calls "the quality costume drama" has found itself to be "both critically successful and of significant box-office interest in Britain but also in other markets, especially the USA."[48] He describes these as films "set in the past, telling stories of the manners and the proprieties, but also often the transgressive romantic entanglements of the upper and upper-middle class English, in carefully detailed and visually splendid period reconstructions."[49] What he calls the "heritage industry" is, he says, "a potent marketing of the past as part of the new enterprise culture, a commodification of museum culture."[50] These ideas will be relevant to a range of films being examined in this book. Higson also recognizes the nature of the audience for these "heritage films," which he says "operate at very much the culturally respectable, quality end of the market, and are key players in the new British art cinema, which straddles the traditional art-house circuit and the mainstream commercial cinemas."[51] He identifies a large proportion of the audience for these sorts of films as middle class and says they are "significantly older than the mainstream cinema audience."[52] He is particularly interested in the way in which although some members of an audience may read these films "as articulating nostalgic, conservative versions of Englishness" others will read them "as critiques of heritage Englishness."[53] His focus is, therefore, on how the makers of a film will "interpret" history and how the audience will then "interpret" the film with which they are presented. Again, this is so far so good. However, Higson ends by suggesting the films he has considered "are rarely about politics in any conventional sense, and are much more frequently about romance and desire, narrative and spectacle, history and tourism."[54] Again, this simply will not do. In fact, what he has to say here is totally meaningless: everything about every film an audience watches is political. The political is inescapable. All of which is not to say that insights such as that offered by Monk when she suggests that rather than the more usual objectification of women, what we see in so-called "heritage films" is that "it is often the men on screen who are displayed as the spectacle to be looked at"[55] are not extremely interesting and absolutely valid. Monk is correct to question claims "about the political conservatism of heritage film texts and their complicity with the Thatcherite project of national unity."[56] Similarly, Julian Petley argues quite correctly that, whether we are thinking about English history itself or British historical dramas, "it is quite possible to imagine multiple, diverse, heterogeneous English heritages and not one English heritage."⁵⁷

## IV

In each of these discussions of UK film production the terms "British" and "English" are repeatedly employed, and we have already suggested how important the idea of the nation will be for this book. Benedict Anderson, among others, has pointed out how the concept of the nation state has come under increased pressure during the second half of the twentieth century and into the twenty-first century. He is interested in the way in which, on the one hand, "huge migrations from impoverished ex-colonial states into the rich capitalist cores got under way"⁵⁸ while at the same time:

> The electronic revolution created communications systems that escaped the control of even the most powerful nation states, permitting movement of finance capital on a scale and a speed unimaginable even thirty years earlier. Transnational systems of production came into increasing dominance, and old-style Fordism began to give way to decentralized, out-of-country production systems and sophisticated, highly flexible niche-marketing.⁵⁹

As Michael Ignatieff explains things, although "we assumed that the world was moving irrevocably beyond nationalism, beyond tribalism, beyond the provincial confines of the identity inscribed in our passports towards a global market culture," we got it wrong and actually what has happened is that "the repressed has returned and its name is nationalism."⁶⁰ Writing around the time of the catastrophically violent break-up of the former Yugoslavia, he says that with the break-up of the Soviet Union in 1989 he thought like many others "we were about to witness a new era of liberal democracy."⁶¹ Similarly, Stuart Hall describes "the resurgence of nationalism" alongside the increasing pace of globalization as "a remarkable reversal, a most unexpected turn of events" that had not been foreseen from any political perspective.⁶² It had been assumed, he says, that "the attachment to the local and the particular would gradually give way to more universalistic and cosmopolitan or international values and identities."⁶³ Fifteen years after his book, *There Ain't No Black in the Union Jack* was first published, Paul Gilroy could still assert in a preface to a new edition of his book in the early 2000s that "Britain's nationalism and racism are still routinely and symptomatically articulated together."⁶⁴

In reflecting on what we are calling "British cinema" we obviously need to be aware of ideas of nationhood in relation to England and the English, Scotland and the Scottish, Wales and the Welsh, and Ireland and the (Northern) Irish. And the final country on this list reminds us of the complexities and the permutations of history with which we are dealing, since there would seem to be a profound difference (and potential antagonism) between ideas of being Catholic Northern Irish and Protestant Northern Irish. This, in turn, reminds us of the depths of differences plastered over by the use of the blanket terms "English," "Scottish," and "Welsh."[65] Paul Ward reminds us of the intricacies at stake when, in considering the supposedly all-enveloping term of "Britishness," he points out this theoretical identity "is mediated by other identities, of place, of class, of religion," and even by "identities of gender."[66][67] Demonstrating the link between nationalism and racism identified by Gilroy, Ward points out that during the late 1960s the politician Enoch Powell "saw black immigration as destructive of the very existence of Britain."[68] More recently, according to Andrew Gamble and Tony Wright:

> Many British people have become much more aware of their separate identity as Scottish, or English, or Welsh, and for an increasing number of them this other national identity has come to be regarded as a primary identity, and their British identity only as a secondary identity, or even an identity they no longer want.[69]

They suggest there is "a new urgency to the conversation about Britishness"[70] caused by "the impact of immigration and multiculturalism" alongside "the assault from Islamic fundamentalism" and "the new political assertiveness from the constituent nations."[71] At the same time: "Shared British enterprises (notably empire and war) have disappeared from view. Globalisation has removed traditional anchors. Europe as a political enterprise has challenged national solidarity. International mobility has quickened."[72]

While the recent pandemic has made obvious the necessity of taking account of the inescapable nature of global contexts, it is also clear that within the nation state of the United Kingdom a variety of nationalisms continue to operate sometimes in parallel and sometimes in confrontational opposition to each other. In the preface to a book on nationalism in the twenty-first century published in 2012, Claire Sutherland felt "migration and diaspora" now created "cultural, economic and social networks" which bound people "across entire continents, let alone countries" but she was also clear that "nationalist ideology" continued to shape global politics.[73] However, in this regard it is the traumatic nature of mass migration that has been most immediately apparent in recent years. As Marcelo Suarez-Orozco describes the situation:

> In the twenty-first century, catastrophic migrations flow from regions plagued by war and terror, rachitic states, unchecked climate change, extreme weather patterns, environmental dystopia, and rampant criminality... Catastrophic migrations are putting millions of human beings at grave risk the world over.[74]

*Introduction* 13

According to Paul Collier, "Migration has been politicized before it has been analyzed. The movement of people from poor countries to rich ones is a simple economic process, but its effects are complex."[75] Again, we find the idea of the complexity of a lot of what is being dealt with here but also the belief that at root something quite simple and easy to understand is taking place.

## V

Following this introductory chapter, this book will be divided into three parts with Part I assessing dramas set within pre-twentieth-century historical periods, Part II looking at dramas set within the twentieth century, and Part III reviewing dramas set in the period after the year 2000.

Part I will comprise four chapters, with a chapter devoted to each of: *Mary Queen of Scots* (Josie Rourke, 2018), *Fanny Lye Deliver'd* (Thomas Clay, 2019), *The Favourite* (Yorgos Lanthimos, 2018), and *Peterloo* (Mike Leigh, 2018). *Mary Queen of Scots* is set during a period of heightened religious tension and fanaticism. In a highly divided society, a struggle for power is occurring within a political elite that is also a socio-economic elite. Issues of gender and sexuality drive both the film's narrative and events within the nation(s) as conceived on screen. Clearly, both English and Scottish nationalisms are at stake. However, axes of social division that are absent may be as significant as factors given prominence at the surface, and so we will also consider the lack of interest shown in issues of class, wealth, and privilege. *Fanny Lye Deliver'd* challenges the conventional boundaries of the period drama more strongly than the other films in this section. The historical context positions us at a dramatic moment of tension between radical ideas and conservative values: Charles I has been executed less than ten years before but a few years later there will be the restoration of the monarchy. Patriarchy, such a dominant force in *Mary Queen of Scots*, is challenged in *Fanny Lye Deliver'd*, and freedom of personal (sexual) expression is set against oppressive religious strictures. This film is conscious of its place both within the context of a particular genre in British cinema and within the lineage of auteur-work in British cinema that has challenged conventional cinematic form. The third film, *The Favourite*, considers the ways in which in this period foreign (and domestic) policy was determined via elite personality clashes and sexual intrigue. Religious differences were the professed determining factor in political decisions during the period but are given little consideration in the film. What is being explored, as with *Mary Queen of Scots*, is the struggle for power within a socio-economic elite. Historically, insurrection (as in the Monmouth Rebellion of a few years previous) is a constant threat. However, the film's focus is on machinations between Tories and Whigs, and between factions within these parties, creating a continual source of intrigue within both the court and the wider government. The final film in this part, *Peterloo*, is set against a backdrop of foreign wars in which as cannon fodder the working class risk death, physical maiming, and psychological trauma. The action again takes place within a divided nation, with a socio-economic and political elite living in comfortable detachment from the everyday experience of ordinary people. Through its narrative, the film envisages the classic operation of a state's repressive apparatuses and the defeat of attempted hegemonic intervention. This film is an exploration of the operation of power within society, and views politics not as a site of potential consensus but as a nexus of conflict.

Part II also comprises four chapters. The films to be considered will be: *Downton Abbey* (Michael Engler, 2019), *Darkest Hour* (Joe Wright, 2017) with *Churchill* (Jonathan Teplitzky, 2017), *A United Country* (Amma Asante, 2016) with *Where Hands Touch* (Asante, 2019), and *Viceroy's House* (Gurinder Chadha, 2017). *Downton Abbey* exists within a genre with a long TV and film history. This "upstairs-downstairs"-style drama is set against a backdrop of Empire, a rigid British class structure, and a system of attitudes built on a supposedly distinctive set of British values, norms, and expectations. What is revealed is a conceptualized nation that even in its "lower" reaches believes in its difference from other nations, European or otherwise. At the same time, this early-twentieth-century fiction plays out against a backdrop of contemporary twenty-first-century issues relating to class, gender, sexuality, and servitude. *Darkest Hour* and *Churchill* will be examined alongside each other in one chapter. Both films look at what are often seen as high points in the life of a controversial figure in British history, Winston Churchill. There might be said to be a return to the historical context of the Second World War in British films produced around the time of these films. Similarities and differences between *Darkest Hour* and *Churchill* (and between these films and *Dunkirk* (Christopher Nolan, 2017)) will be touched on, and we will explore how such films might be said to work towards defining, or redefining, Britain's relationship to continental Europe; after all, there is a clear focus here on the Channel as a border, defensive line, or boundary between contesting ways of seeing the world. Part of our interest will be in what values and beliefs we find asserted, or reasserted, in each of these films. As with other films in this book, we will assess how *Darkest Hour* and *Churchill* might relate to issues of nationalism, how they work to renegotiate British identity, and how they deal with issues of class. The third chapter in this part looks at two films with the same director, *A United Country* and *Where Hands Touch*. In each of these historical dramas, Asante focuses on the story of an interracial relationship, the first between a black African man and a white British woman, and the second between a young biracial black woman in Germany towards the end of the Second World War and a young white German who is the son of a Nazi officer. The second of these films in particular challenges not only notions of racial purity but also simplistic notions of national identity. The final film in this part of the book considers *Viceroy's House*, a film dealing with the dividing of the Indian subcontinent into India, and East and West Pakistan, at the moment of Britain's handing over of independence to this part of the British Empire in 1947. This was a crucial episode in determining the contemporary politics of the region, and a complex historical subject. In part, the film attempts to address the fraught question of who should be held accountable for the horrors of Partition. Inevitably questions will be raised regarding not only the authenticity of any single interpretation of history but also who is able to write (and rewrite) history.

The four chapters in Part III consider six films set during the twenty-first century. The films will be: *Daphne* (Peter Mackie Burns, 2017) with *The Sense of an Ending* (Ritesh Batra, 2017), *God's Own Country* (Francis Lee, 2017), *Dark River* (Clio Barnard, 2017) with *The Levelling* (Hope Dickson Leach, 2017), and *Sorry We Missed You* (Ken Loach, 2019). The first chapter here looks at *Daphne* and *The Sense of an Ending* and considers the nature of an art-house audience as an educated, middle-class elite defined by its self-absorption. Both the films and the culture underpinning them might be defined as comfortable, North London leftfield. In cultural terms both films are undeniably rich texts containing a range of approaches aimed at provoking thought and engagement. In both, there is a restless search for something to give meaning to existence. However, in the final analysis, each film leaves us wrapped within the cosy embrace of elite liberal discussion. *God's Own Country* raises the question of whether there might be a new approach to realism beyond a social-realist aesthetic. Director Francis Lee is clear about his obsession with naturalistic detail, and the cinematography is distinctively tight and restricted. The rise of nationalism across Europe and the political divisions occurring in the UK after the Brexit referendum have created space for xenophobia and homophobia to develop. This film places both of these axes of social division on the screen. *Dark River* and *The Levelling* are the subjects of the third chapter in this part of the book. Both these films with female directors follow a central female character returning to the family home in the countryside and facing the need to address those things that made them leave in the first place. The final chapter in Part III looks at *Sorry We Missed You* and is a further expression from Loach and screenwriter Paul Laverty of classical British social-realism updated in order to square up to the current state of the UK. In its political positioning of the filmmakers' art, this film follows on from *I, Daniel Blake* (Loach, 2016). We are presented with an in-your-face, confrontational political stance and with a film that is both direct and forthright in what it has to say. It takes on the neo-liberal global economy at the site of its most intensely personalised impact, within the life of the individual and their family.

One final chapter will reflect not only on what we have seen in the selected films explored here but also on the ways in which the political struggle between Right and Left has escalated during the past decade. A key element in understanding this confrontation lies in considering the relationship of the nation state to the wider world. Over the past twenty years, or more, economic and political tensions between the West and the rest of the world have significantly intensified. Taking place within the context of globalization, the drive towards neo-liberalism in the West has been paralleled by the emergence of progressively more competitive economies in other parts of the world, and the resulting frictions have been heightened by the potent legacies of imperialism and colonialism. Inevitably within an increasingly interlocked world, global economic developments quickly impact on the lives of ordinary people and as such are rehearsed in media fictions. Direct reference to the concept of the nation, and/or to establishing borders, or crossing borders, or defending borders, is to be found in several of the films considered here. Even more so, the politics of identity and belonging recurs time and again. Unavoidably, the very concept of the independent nation state has been challenged in recent decades by the increasing pace of globalization. At the same time, increased economic competition has resulted in regional destabilization and a variety of military interventions and stand-offs. In response to all of this, within a global context of increasing economic interdependence there has been a resurgence of nationalism and a deepening of political antagonisms. In the face of such a situation, Chantel Mouffe has counseled against believing "collective identities which always entail a we/they discrimination" can be avoided.[76] She suggests such identities continue to "play a central part in politics,"[77] believes this situation has to be addressed head-on, and advises it is unwise to take up the liberal rationalist position which thinks reason is able to eradicate the "archaic 'passions'" of collective identities.[78] Instead, she recommends group identification should be constructed in such a way as to *energize* the democratic confrontation. We cannot aim for consensus, she says, but instead must accept "the conflictual nature of politics."[79]

**Notes**

1. The British and their French allies had been thoroughly defeated by the rapidly advancing German army, but the majority of Britain's troops had evaded capture by being ferried across the Channel from Dunkirk on the French coast to England by the Royal Navy and a flotilla of smaller boats, many of them manned by civilians.

2. The sea wall protecting the harbour.
3. Julian Thompson, *Dunkirk: Retreat to Victory* (London: Pan Macmillan, 2009), p. 296.
4. Verity Bowman, "Clap For Our Carers: How Britons thanked NHS with nationwide round of applause," *The Telegraph*, 27 March 2020. Available at https://www.telegraph.co.uk/news/2020/03/27/thank-nhs-clap-carers/ (accessed 30 March 2020).
5. Jamie Hawkins, "Coronavirus: Britain comes to standstill as millions join Clap for Our Carers," *Daily Mirror*, 26 March 2020. Available at https://www.mirror.co.uk/news/uk-news/breaking-coronavirus-britain-comes-standstill-21761321 (accessed 30 March 2020).
6. Which is not to say British filmmakers during the Second World War were not (increasingly as the war progressed) offering challenges to the pre-war status quo and probing national expectations of what the future should hold for the country. Both full-length feature films such as *Love on the Dole* (John Baxter, 1941) and shorts such as *Tyneside Story* (Gilbert Gunn, 1943) explicitly stated that after the war there should be no return to the economic depression of the 1930s and implicitly asked the audience to imagine a new future.
7. Charles J. Pattie and Ron J. Johnston, "Changing Geographies of Prosperity and Representation: The Role of the Local State," in Richard T. Harrison and Mark Hart (eds.), *Spatial Policy in a Divided Nation* (London: Jessica Kingsley, 1993), p. 37.
8. Gerry Mooney, "'Remoralizing' the Poor?: Gender, Class and Philanthropy in Victorian Britain," in Gail Lewis (ed.), *Forming Nation, Framing Welfare* (London and New York: Routledge, 2017/1998), p. 60.
9. Ibid., and see Friedrich Engels, *The Condition of the Working-Class in England in 1844* (New York: Cosimo, 2008/1892), p. 45. We might also consider the layout of aristocratic country houses that often had underground passageways and hidden stairs allowing the servants to move around unseen by the family and their guests.
10. Hugh Ellis and Kate Henderson, *Rebuilding Britain: Planning for a Better Future* (Bristol: Policy Press, 2014), p. 37.
11. Mark Garnett and Philip Lynch, *Exploring British Politics*, 4th edn. (London and New York: Routledge, 2016), p. 69.
12. Mary Fulbrook, "Myth-Making and National Identity: The Case of the GDR," in Geoffrey Hosking and George Schöpflin (eds.), *Myths and Nationhood* (London and New York: Routledge, 1997), p. 72.
13. Benedict Anderson, *Imagined Communities: Reflections on the Origin and Spread of Nationalism* (London and New York: Verso, 1991/1983), p. 6.
14. Ibid.
15. Fulbrook, "Myth-Making and National Identity: The Case of the GDR," p. 72.
16. Michael Kenny, *The Politics of English Nationhood* (Oxford: Oxford University Press, 2014), p. 1.

17. The Act of Union of 1707 brought together England with Scotland; the Act of Union of 1801 unified the resulting Great Britain with Ireland to form the United Kingdom; and the partition of Ireland in 1921 created the Irish Free State, or Éire, and left Northern Ireland as part of the UK.
18. Paul J. J. Welfens, *An Accidental Brexit: New EU and Transatlantic Economic Perspectives* (London: Palgrave Macmillan, 2017), p. 50.
19. Rob Ford, "Britain's new political landscape: what the voting numbers tell us," *The Observer*, 15 December 2019. Available at https://www.theguardian.com/politics/2019/dec/15/britains-new-political-landscape (accessed 31 March 2019).
20. Ibid.
21. Michael Marmot, Jessica Allen, Tammy Boyce, Peter Goldblatt, and Joana Morrison, *Health Equity In England: The Marmot Review 10 Years On* (2020). Available at http://www.instituteofhealthequity.org/resources-reports/marmot-review-10-years-on/the-marmot-review-10-years-on-executive-summary.pdf (accessed 31 March 2020), p. 149.
22. Stewart Lansley and Joanna Mack, *Breadline Britain: The Rise of Mass Poverty* (London: Oneworld, 2015), p. x.
23. Stephen Armstrong, *The New Poverty* (London and New York: Verso, 2017), pp. 4–5.
24. Each of the films under consideration completed production after the referendum of 2016. However, it should be stated from the outset that, although the "Brexit debate" held centre stage for a lengthy period from 2016 to 2020, in and of itself this often acrimonious debate is not seen as the cause (or even a cause) of the United Kingdom being "a divided nation." Rather, "Brexit" is both symptomatic of already existing divisions within UK society and revelatory of the nature of those divisions.
25. James Harvey (ed.), *Nationalism in Contemporary Western European Cinema* (London: Palgrave Macmillan, 2018), p. 1.
26. Tim Vlandas and Daphne Halikiopoulou, "What is new and what is nationalist about Europe's new nationalism? Explaining the rise of the far right in Europe," *Nations and Nationalism*, 25 (2), April 2019, p. 430.
27. Ibid.
28. Robin Wood, *Hollywood From Vietnam to Reagan and Beyond* (New York: Columbia University Press, 1986/2003), p. 2.
29. Dudley Andrew, "Cinema and Culture," *Humanities* 6 (4), August 1985, p. 25.
30. John Belton (ed.), *Movies and Mass Culture* (London: Athlone Press, 1996), p. 2.
31. Robert L. Hilliard, *Hollywood Speaks Out: Pictures That Dared to Protest Real World Issues* (Chichester: Wiley-Blackwell, 2009), p. 20.
32. Ibid.
33. Anon, "Opening Our Eyes: How film contributes to the culture of the UK," BFI/Northern Alliance/Ipsos MediaCT, July 2011. Available at https://www.bfi.org.uk/sites/bfi.org.uk/files/downloads/bfi-opening-our-eyes-2011-07_0.pdf (accessed 5 April 2020), p. 89.

34. Ibid.
35. Kelly Boyd, "Moving Pictures? Cinema and Society in Britain," *Journal of British Studies*, 34 (1), January 1995, p. 131.
36. Ibid.
37. Ibid., p. 133.
38. Patricia Hill Collins and Sirma Bilge, *Intersectionality* (Cambridge: Polity, 2016), p. 4.
39. Christine Geraghty, *British Cinema in the Fifties: Gender, Genre and the "New Look"* (London and New York: Routledge, 2000), p. 13.
40. Sarah Street, *British National Cinema* (London and New York: Routledge, 2009/1997), p. 127.
41. Ibid., pp. 127–8.
42. Ibid., p. 128.
43. Claire Monk and Amy Sargeant (eds.), *British Historical Cinema: The history, heritage and costume film* (London and New York: Routledge, 2002), p. 1.
44. Ibid., p. 2.
45. Ibid., p. 4.
46. Justine Ashby and Andrew Higson (eds.), *British Cinema, Past and Present* (London and New York: Routledge, 2000), p. 12.
47. Ibid., p. 13.
48. Andrew Higson, *English Heritage, English Cinema: Costume Drama Since 1980* (Oxford: Oxford University Press, 2003), p. 1.
49. Ibid.
50. Ibid.
51. Ibid., p. 5.
52. Ibid.
53. Ibid., p. 6.
54. Ibid., p. 261.
55. Claire Monk, "The British 'heritage film' and its critics," *Critical Survey*, 7 (2), 1995, p. 120.
56. Ibid., p. 121.
57. Julian Petley, "The Englishness of British Cinema: Beyond the Valley of the Corn Dollies," in John Hill (ed.), *A Companion to British and Irish Cinema* (Chichester: Wiley-Blackwell, 2019), p. 475.
58. Benedict Anderson, "Introduction," in Gopal Balakrishnan (ed.), *Mapping the Nation* (London and New York: Verso, 2012/1996), p. 8.
59. Ibid.
60. Michael Ignatieff, *Blood and Belonging* (London: Vintage, 1994), p. 2.
61. Ibid.
62. Stuart Hall, "The Future of Identity," in Sean P. Hier and B. Singh Bolaria (eds.), *Identity and Belonging: Rethinking Race and Ethnicity* (Toronto: Canadian Scholars' Press, 2006), p. 267.
63. Ibid.
64. Paul Gilroy, *There Ain't No Black in the Union Jack: The Cultural Politics of Race and Nation* (London and New York: Routledge, 2002/1987), p. xxiii.

65. At the same time, the idea of regional differences within England itself has always been a feature of "British" cinema and has, perhaps, experienced a period of increased importance recently in the light of the continual debate about a North–South divide within the country (increasingly expressed as a division between London and the rest of the country).
66. Paul Ward, *Britishness Since 1870* (London and New York: Routledge, 2004), p. 37.
67. One point at stake here is that during the course of history "being British" has required a range of different attitudes and behaviours to be displayed by men to those required to be exhibited by women.
68. Ward, *Britishness Since 1870*, p. 113.
69. Andrew Gamble and Tony Wright (eds.), *Britishness: Perspectives on the British Question* (Malden, MA and Oxford: Wiley-Blackwell, 2009), p. 1.
70. Ibid., p. 5.
71. Ibid.
72. Ibid.
73. Claire Sutherland, *Nationalism in the Twenty-First Century: Challenges and Responses* (London: Palgrave Macmillan, 2012), p. 9.
74. Marcelo M. Suarez-Orozco (ed.), *Humanitarianism and Mass Migration: Confronting the World Crisis* (Oakland: University of California Press, 2019), p. 14.
75. Paul Collier, *Exodus: How Migration Is Changing Our World* (Oxford: Oxford University Press, 2013), p. 12.
76. Chantel Mouffe, *On the Political (Thinking in Action)* (London and New York: Routledge, 2005), p. 5.
77. Ibid., pp. 5–6.
78. Ibid., p. 6.
79. Ibid., p. 13.

# Part I

# Reinterpreting Pre-twentieth-century British History

These chapters examine possible reasons for particular periods of early modern history being chosen as dramatic backdrops to films made in the late 2010s. It is suggested each film considered here has specific resonances for early twenty-first-century Britain. Intrigue, conspiracy, and betrayal within the corridors of power are of perennial interest, but at the same time representations of the past emphasizing a "great men" (and, even, a "great women") historical perspective create a particular ideological context for spectatorship. Key issues taken into account will be the socio-economic conditions of each period portrayed and the ever-present nature of patriarchy.

CHAPTER 2

# What Chance Sisterhood under Patriarchy?
## *Mary Queen of Scots* (Josie Rourke, 2018)

### I

*Mary Queen of Scots* was criticized in some quarters for a lack of historical accuracy. The most obvious departure from historical truth is that near the end of the film there is an entirely fictitious scene in which Elizabeth I (Margot Robbie) and Mary Stuart (Saoirse Ronan) discuss the nature of their antagonism face to face. In fact, the two women never met.[1] The director, Josie Rourke, also deliberately introduced a historically false ethnic diversity into the casting for the film: Lord Randolph, the English ambassador to Scotland, is played by the black actor Adrian Lester, and Bess of Hardwick, a lady-in-waiting to Queen Elizabeth, is portrayed by an English actor with a Chinese ethnic background, Gemma Chan. In addition, the role of Mary's private secretary, David Rizzio, who according to the historical record was white Italian, was taken by a Puerto Rican actor, Ismael Cruz Córdova. The historian Suzannah Lipscomb says:

> There certainly were black Africans living in the British Isles by the end of the 16th century (although Randolph was not one of them and it's harder to justify the Asian presence), but it is true to say that the number of non-white faces is far more representative of modern British society than of the 16th century.[2]

The question at stake here is what the relationship should be between the genre of historical drama and the "reality" of history? How historically accurate should we expect a historical drama to be? Rourke said she made it clear with the studio before taking on the project that she would expect to employ a cast that was ethnically mixed, and would refuse to direct "an all-white period drama."[3]

Robert A. Rosenstone has suggested "inventions of characters, dialogue, and incidents" should be seen as "an inevitable part of the dramatic history film."[4] From this perspective, the imagined scene between Mary and

Elizabeth that never actually happened is perfectly acceptable. Looking at the relationship between history and the history film, Rosenstone proposed the traditional historian "created" facts "by picking out certain traces of the past (people, events, moments) and highlighting them as important and worthy of inclusion in a narrative," whereas film "invented" facts, "making up traces of the past which are then highlighted as important and worthy of inclusion."[5] He advocated we should see the history film

> as part of a separate realm of representation and discourse, one not meant to provide literal truths about the past (as if our written history can provide literal truths) but metaphoric truths which work, to a large degree, as a kind of commentary on, and challenge to traditional historical discourse.[6]

The suggestion is that the historical drama continues to cast light on an earlier period but in such a way as to illuminate a different set of possible truths about that past than those generally available to the rigorously factual historian.

The genre of historical drama demands we should reflect on the nature of history—how we conceptualize it, how we understand it, how we make sense of it. This is something that has been taken up by a range of theoretical approaches. Feminism and postcolonialism, for example, have interrogated traditional historical approaches, working to expose the male-orientation and implicit imperialism of traditional history, while postmodernism has centered on the impossibility of finding an overarching, all-encompassing grand narrative that would make sense of everything. Recognition of the need to move away from any sense of a singularity of truth and towards the notion of the coexistence of a plurality of truths has underpinned all late twentieth-century/early twenty-first- century theory. In the final analysis, any version of history, whether a historical drama film or not, is a representation of a matrix of personal interactions that is gone, is lost, and is ultimately unknowable in any sense of finality. Jeffrey Richards reminds us that, whether they are making a documentary or a fictional film, directors organize and construct events to create "a narrative cohesion and order missing from everyday real life," deploying "lighting, movement, dialogue, music and colour to heighten mood and atmosphere, evoke an emotional response in the audience and to advance the story."[7] Both the historian and the filmmaker (and the novelist and the dramatist) are working to excavate some useful truth, or truths, about the past; and such truths can be "useful" only in the sense that they enable us to see the present and our movement into the future with greater clarity.

Beyond these debates around the functions of history and historical dramas, and most pertinently, in discussing the historical novel, Martin Ryle reminds us the historical text is "addressed to the moment of its writing, not its setting."[8] What those who want a film such as *Mary Queen of Scots* to be historically accurate fail to acknowledge is that a film such as this is not primarily "about" the Tudor Elizabethan period but is "about" the contemporary period through which we are living. That *Mary Queen of Scots* is only nominally about events occurring during the second half of the 1500s is made clear by the casting decisions with which we began this chapter, most obviously that England's ambassador to Scotland, Lord Randolph, is portrayed as black and Queen Elizabeth's maid, Bess of Hardwick, appears to be of Chinese ethnicity. This is a contemporary issue that relates to the desire to ensure productions employ an ethnically varied cast, thereby actively challenging previous approaches followed over decades that limited ethnic minority roles and therefore marginalized their presence within media representations: the film is "about" now. The history—although interesting, in that any attempted reclamation of the past casts intellectual light on that past and socio-political light on the present—is only a hook on which to hang an interpretation of the world that actually deals centrally with contemporary issues. As Suzannah Lipscomb explains it in relation to a particular incident in the film in which Mary's private secretary, Rizzio, is found in bed with her husband, Henry Darnley (Jack Lowden): "This is a film that reflects modern identity politics."[9] In a tight two-shot, Mary says to Rizzio: "You have not betrayed your nature. I cannot fault you for succumbing to his charms as I did but we must be more careful now." Mary not only accepts Rizzio's sexuality but also embraces his difference. The problem, as she identifies it, is the difficulty of revealing your true (sexual) identity within a strongly conservative, patriarchal world. The division is clear between the "sisterhood" of Mary and her ladies-in-waiting, prepared not only to accept but to take pleasure in difference, and the male-dominated, male-structured world that reacts with violence towards any expression of identity that is "other"—Rizzio is brutally knifed to death by a gang of men. The BBC reported in early 2020 that homophobic hate crime had increased by more than 50 percent in the past five years.[10] A few months earlier, *The Independent* reported on a poll that suggested homophobia was increasing among young people in the UK, with 27 percent agreeing with the statement that "being gay, lesbian, bisexual or transgender is immoral or against my beliefs."[11]

## II

Beyond this aspect of identity politics, at its heart this is a film about sisterhood and the difficulties, if not impossibilities, faced by sisterhood within a male-dominated world. The European Institute for Gender Equality has estimated that within the current period "in the UK, 44% of women have experienced violence, which is 11% higher than in the EU overall."[12] While, responding to a Home Office restatement of its strategy for dealing with violence against women and girls, Rachel Krys, co-director of the End Violence Against Women Coalition, said:

> Despite a huge increase in the numbers of women reporting rape to the police over the last 5 years, there has been an alarming recent collapse in the rate of cases being charged.[13]

This film operates not simply as an exploration of two particular women who find themselves in positions of power within a specific Tudor/Stuart context, but as an examination of women's position in society throughout history. And, because any text is more about the time in which it is made than it is about the time in which it is set, even more importantly, *Mary Queen of Scots* is "about" the way in which women have to endure the swamping brutality of patriarchy within contemporary society. It is the all-encompassing, inescapable, ensnaring net of male power that is emphasized time and again in this strongly feminist interpretation of the world.

What we are presented with is a violent society. In particular, it is a society full of male violence against women, which may be physical or verbal. In this respect, with great force and clarity the film opens and ends with Mary's beheading. In the opening, she enters a room packed with men and they part to reveal at the heart of this mass of men the ultimate symbol of violence, the executioner's block. She walks towards it and the men close around her and stand in tight formation in order to witness the final act. There is a shot from the side that shows Mary, in the right-hand half of the frame, kneeling before the block, which occupies the left-hand half of the frame. The out-of-focus bodies of men take up the edges of the screen to left and right, emphasizing the final entrapment of this woman. And standing upright in the middle of the shot is the executioner's axe, with its shaft slicing through the centre of the shot. This scene and this shot summarize the whole film, particularly when a (man's) hand pushes Mary roughly from behind to force her neck down onto the block. This is a film about the division between men and women, about the difference between them, and about the violence done to women in a man's world. Mary has transgressed the boundaries placed by men on what a woman can do and on what she should be, and she must be punished for that. She has sought to operate within the world of men and is to be judged according to male codes, values, and norms. In fact, Mary did not seek this; as she makes clear when addressing one of her ladies-in-waiting, it is rather the case that as a queen she has been given a role to play within a patriarchal world.

**Figure 2.1** The patriarchal entrapment of women in this society emphasized in one shot in *Mary Queen of Scots* (Josie Rourke, 2018).

The nature of male violence against a transgressor that we see Mary finally having to kneel before is echoed in the death of her private secretary, Rizzio. As already mentioned, he is killed in the most brutal fashion in an enactment of the historical death of the historical figure of Rizzio that is also, at least as importantly, a contemporary symbolic enactment of male violence against the LGBT+ community. In the company of women, Rizzio is accepted and valued as themself. When they cross-dress and dance before Mary's inner circle of ladies-in-waiting, she says to them: "Be whoever you wish with us: you make for a lovely sister."[14] Only men find Rizzio's life choices to be an affront and a challenge. Although, of course, if you are not an outsider, a foreigner, as Rizzio is as a Catholic Italian, and therefore doubly other, your sexual proclivities, if not accepted, may at least be tolerated, as in the case of Henry Darnley (Jack Lowden) called out as a "sodomite" by his father the Earl of Lennox (Brendon Coyle).

Investigating this male world further, we might note Lord Bothwell (Martin Compston) announces himself immediately in the film as being driven by "duty, not ambition" and that this word, ambition, comes back time after time in the script. The patriarchal world we see is one of naked, ruthless, and literal cut-throat ambition. The response of James, Earl of Moray (James McArdle), Mary's half-brother, to Bothwell's protestation that he is not driven by ambition is, "And what reward does your loyalty command?" In other words, he is aware that any apparent male code of honour is in fact a cover for more dubious designs. At the same time, Elizabeth's Privy Council is repeatedly shown attempting to work out the motivations and "loyalties" of the main players in the continual politicking that is taking place. The male-dominated world is one of constant intrigue, plotting, and conspiracy. Elizabeth's chief advisor, William Cecil (Guy Pearce), is good at his job because he understands the world in terms of "ambition" and sees something like marriage as nothing more than a functional political chess move ("Mary will seek a marriage that strengthens her claim to your throne and makes her children Catholic"). But he is not alone in having this perspective. On the issue of marriage, for example, Lord Randolph reports Mary "feigns disinterest." He cannot believe this is anything other than pretense. This is a world of incessant scheming and maneuvering. Plotting the downfall of one and the elevation of another is the constant preoccupation of each and every male character. The talk is of loyalty and duty, while the reality is something else. The use of open warfare in order to attempt to take power does take place and we see this happening, but this is the exception rather than the rule.

Both Mary and Elizabeth are well aware of the nature of this male world into which they have been thrust. When Darnley suggests he and his father have come to Scotland because "here we are free to worship as we choose," Mary's immediate response is, "I doubt it is faith that brings you, rather the land your father seeks and even the throne." Later, Elizabeth comments to Robert Dudley (Joe Alwyn), in a simple phrase that sums up both the difference and the distance this film sees as existing between men and women, "How cruel men are." Although both women have their ladies-in-waiting providing a support network of sisterhood, both are—because of their exposed positions as monarchs—"alone." During the meeting between the two women that in reality never happened, the script has Mary say, "I am utterly alone," to which Elizabeth responds, "As am I, alone." Two short, sharp phrases, which mirror each other in the way in which they end with the word "alone," emphasize the position of these women. Again, a single shot works to force home the point that is being made about these monarchs. Halfway through the film we see Elizabeth on a palace rooftop discussing the royal succession with Cecil. When Cecil leaves, Elizabeth remains alone on the rooftop. The camera looks down on her in a long shot as she stands with what we know from earlier shots is a view across the Thames, her capital, and her kingdom. And yet, here she is, as Mary has it later, "utterly alone." In a sense, what we see is someone who is elevated and free, existing above all others, and yet at the same time she is also small within the frame, alone and ultimately trapped in this position.

## III

The concept of "sisterhood" is crucial. In early correspondence between Mary and Elizabeth shown in the film, Mary says, "We are two sisters bound

**Figure 2.2** Elizabeth I (Margot Robbie), a woman elevated above all others and yet utterly alone, in *Mary Queen of Scots*.

in womanhood." Both women at various moments believe it is only through meeting each other face to face and recognizing their shared female bond that any differences might be resolved. "We shall accomplish far more without envoys between us," says Mary; while, in addressing her ambassador but in the terms of the film attacking men in general, Elizabeth says, "What have you produced in all your travels between our kingdoms: discord, war, death?" Consistently, scenes dominated by women are juxtaposed with scenes dominated by men: the relaxed, supportive periods Mary spends in the company of her ladies-in-waiting are contrasted with the confrontational, aggressive atmospheres she encounters in rooms in which she is meeting men. Mary is aware of what is seen in the film as the difference between men and women: "Just be wary of these men," she counsels her maids, "their love is not the same as their respect." Later, she says to Bothwell, who had thought in marrying Mary he would become king: "Were you fool enough to trust these men?" The general position taken by the film is clear: men are not to be trusted since they are constantly scheming to increase their own power and wealth, and they have nothing in their relationships with each other to compare with the solidarity to be found between women. This union of women is given its strongest visual representation in a scene in which, surrounded and supported by the women in her inner circle, Mary gives birth. It is as if the group itself is giving birth. Not only that but through intercutting shots of the birth with shots of Elizabeth writing to Mary, it is even made to appear as if Elizabeth is assisting in bringing the child into the world.

Women are presented as having a natural, or inherent, being that is different to men. While some feminists might emphasize equality between the sexes, this approach stresses what are seen as essential differences between men and women. This line of reasoning suggests that, rather than ideas of sex and gender being social constructions, there are real distinctions to be made between men and women. Rourke seems to be working within a post-feminist field in which it is felt there is a natural difference between the binary sexes of male and female. In this regard, Rosalind Gill, in her essay "Postfeminist Media Culture: Elements of a Sensibility," has suggested what is needed is a straightforward acknowledgement of this difference rather than a denial of it.[15] Both Mary and Elizabeth are surrounded by male nobles and advisers, and both have men around them who, as Mary says to Darnley, "would have us deposed." The men, of course, see things differently. When talking among themselves, one man asks another, "How did the world come to this?" and the response is that the chaos is down to the fact that we have "wise men servicing the whims of women." Men see women as too often guided by "passion" and impulse. Her half-brother, the Earl of Moray, addresses Mary as "reckless child" and advises her, "Do not let your cursed passion rule you." This helps us to make sense of the script and gives a coherent perspective on the history: Elizabeth is cooler, more calculating, and slow to anger, whereas Mary is the opposite. As a result, Elizabeth is the more successful politician. Mary gives good advice to her ladies-in-waiting not to trust men but then in her relationship with Darnley succumbs to conventional notions of romance that Elizabeth stands apart from. The cinematography reinforces the romance by showing them riding together along a moorland ridge in a long tracking shot and then together in long shot within a massive landscape against a soundscape of triumphant music. Elizabeth has found the way to survive within patriarchy: "I am more man than woman now. This throne hath made me so," she tells Mary. As women attempting to live within a male realm, Mary and Elizabeth have to begin to attempt to play the game with as much subterfuge and use of plotting as the men: one of them proves better at this than the other. Mary, like Elizabeth, is willing to compromise and is tolerant, but she is quicker to respond with anger to male assaults. Elizabeth is more calculating and less immediate in her response. In a piece of heavy symbolism early in the film, it is Elizabeth we see moving a chess piece across a board. Mary believes marriage "is a matter of the heart, not of state" and that these things "don't mix well." She explains that when her first husband died she "could have married any number of suitors: Portugal, Denmark, Sweden," but that she "declined them all" because "I would not have a political marriage imposed on me." Elizabeth realizes she has to go a step further; in order to be combative within the male environment she has not only to decline political marriage alliances but to refuse marriage altogether.[16] Both women are attempting to assert their independence within a male world and struggling to find a means to do that. "Sisterhood" within the narrative of the film (and feminism within the conceptual framework of the film) is linked through these two women to tolerance and liberal values. Mary states that people in Scotland will be "free to worship however they so choose: Catholic or Protestant." But within the all-or-nothing confrontational politics of the male world this is an inadequate response, and is, in fact, a response that cannot even be contemplated. As Cecil attempts to succinctly explain it to Elizabeth: "Mary is our foe and a Catholic." Compromise is out of the question; the enemy is the enemy and needs to be recognized as such and defeated as such.

In a logical, reasoned manner the characters of Mary and Elizabeth with which we are presented "make sense." However, the visual and emotional impact of the film on the spectator works to present a powerful expression of woman as the victim of male oppression, as violated, as abused, as marginalized, and as facing the impossibility of escaping the enmeshing net of vicious patriarchy. The immersive quality of film asks us to move beyond the historical figures of Mary and Elizabeth to respond to a series of scenes forcefully showing the female experience of patriarchy and sisterhood. As a representative woman, Mary is supported through menstruation, romantic and violent encounters with men, pregnancy and childbirth by the group of women around her. In contrast, none of the men around her can ever be fully trusted. As a woman, despite outward signs of allegiance, the men around her consistently bypass, override, or ignore her. What is seen as her intrinsic weakness as a woman is attacked particularly vehemently by the religious zealot, John Knox (David Tennant). Her attempt at religious tolerance[17] has no answer to his unshakeable fundamentalism. It is her sexuality (and the sexuality of women) that seems to especially offend Knox: she is "a fornicator with a monstrous lust," a "pleasuring woman," and "a whore of Babylon."[18] This last phrase is used by Knox at the very moment Mary is being raped by Bothwell, thereby identifying the vicious verbal violence of misogyny with the physical abuse of women by men.

The idea that there is some similarity of essence to being a woman that creates an instant sense of connectedness between all women, a feeling of sisterhood, can be seen throughout *Mary Queen of Scots* and is the reason for the inclusion of scenes featuring menstruation, pregnancy, and childbirth. "Sisterhood" has become a highly contested term but for second-wave feminists signaled solidarity in a collective struggle against patriarchy.[19] As Luce Irigaray had it:

> Whatever inequalities may exist among women, they all undergo, even without clearly realizing it, the same oppression, the same exploitation of their body, the same denial of their desire. That is why it is very important for women to be able to join together, and to join together "amongst themselves." In order

to begin to escape from the spaces, roles, and gestures that they have been assigned and taught by the society of men.[20]

## IV

Each of the divisions identified here—between a white Eurocentric (even Anglo-Saxon) outlook and a more ethnically diverse perspective, between straight heterosexuality and queer permutations of sexuality, between the nationalisms of Scotland and England, between religious tolerance and religious fundamentalism,[21] and between the sisterhood of women and the brutal politicking of men—finds its equivalent within contemporary contested tensions within the political make-up of the UK. However, the division most strongly emphasized in *Mary Queen of Scots* is that between men and women. It could be argued this very much echoes the current reality when to be a woman might be to exist within a constant state of danger. Finally, it should also be noted the division between "Britain" and Europe is also an ever-present backdrop in this film: in addition to the use of French by Mary and her ladies-in-waiting at various times, there exists the absent presence of France and Italy/the Pope. What is not found within this film is any strong sense of the division between classes, or any indication of the vast disparities of wealth and privilege to be found in Scotland and England both in the late 1500s and now. We see fishermen on the beach watching Mary's initial landing in Scotland in 1561, we see common serfs in Mary's army, and we see Knox using a sermon to work a congregation into a foot-stamping, jeering audience, but little is made of the differences in rank and status between these people and the nobles that fill the screen in scene after scene. The film ignores socio-economic issues[22] in favour of showing a struggle for power among the members of a political elite involving repeated rounds of conspiracy and betrayal. In contrast to other aspects of the making of this film, viewing history as the outcome of the relationships and exchanges between members of a social elite works to impose a highly traditionalist perspective of history on the spectator, whether the contest is seen to be between "great" men or between "great" women.

As Mary is executed we hear her final thoughts, reflecting that one day her son will unite the two kingdoms into one, "And we shall have peace." This seems a positive note on which to end the film. However, the irony is, of course, that the accession of James I to the throne in 1603 led ultimately to the English Civil War and the beheading of his son Charles I in 1649. Within the ideational framework of the film, the sadness is that even at the point of death Mary is wishing for something that in reality is impossible: under patriarchy, a world of peace is not possible.

## Notes

1. "... although both Mary and Elizabeth wrote lengthy letters to each other throughout their lives, they never met." See Clarisse Loughrey, "*Mary Queen of Scots*: How historically accurate is it?" *The Independent*, 15 January 2019. Available at https://www.independent.co.uk/arts-entertainment/films/news/mary-queen-of-scots-historical-accuracy-meet-queen-elizabeth-margot-robbie-saoirse-ronan-a8666266.html (accessed 20 April 2020).
2. Suzannah Lipscomb, "A Modern Queen of Scots," *History Today*, 69 (2), February 2019. Available at https://www.historytoday.com/archive/making-history/modern-queen-scots (accessed 20 April 2020).
3. "'I was not going to direct an all-white period drama,' explains Rourke. 'It's not a thing that I do in theater and I don't want to do it in film.'" See Anon, "Josie Rourke Diversity Casting Mary Queen of Scots," *Focus Features*, 12 November 2018. Available at https://www.focusfeatures.com/article/josie-rourke-diversity_casting_mary-queen-of-scots (accessed 20 April 2020).
4. Robert A. Rosenstone, *History on Film/Film on History* (Harlow: Pearson, 2006), p. 8.
5. Ibid., p. 8.
6. Ibid., pp. 8–9.
7. Jeffrey Richards, "Film and Television: the moving image," in Sarah Barber and Corinna M. Peniston-Bird (eds.), *History Beyond the Text* (London and New York: Routledge, 2009), p. 74.
8. Martin Ryle, "The Historical Novel?: Novel, History and the 'End of History,'" in Garin Dowd, Lesley Stevenson, and Jeremy Strong (eds.), *Genre Matters: Essays in Theory and Criticism* (Bristol: Intellect, 2006), p. 166.
9. Lipscomb, "A Modern Queen of Scots."
10. "Between 2014–15 and 2018–19 the number of recorded hate crimes based on sexual orientation across England and Wales went up from 5,591 to 14,491—a rise of 160%. Hate crimes against transgender people have nearly quadrupled in the last five years, to 2,333 reports last year." See Sam Francis, "Call for law change over increases in homophobic hate crimes in London," BBC News, 10 January 2020. Available at https://www.bbc.co.uk/news/uk-england-london-51049336 (accessed 28 April 2020).
11. Lizzie Dearden, "Online hate blamed as researchers find homophobia is increasing among young people in UK," *The Independent*, 15 October 2019. Available at https://www.independent.co.uk/news/uk/home-news/homophobia-lgbt-hate-crime-young-people-gay-trans-poll-research-a9157111.html (accessed 28 April 2020).
12. Anon, "Combating violence against women: United Kingdom," European Institute for Gender Equality, 2016. Available at eige.europa.eu/publications/combating-violence-against-women-united-kingdom (accessed 20 April 2020).
13. Anon, "Government sets out key measures to tackle violence against women and girls," GOV.UK, 6 March 2019. Available at https://www.gov.uk/government/

news/government-sets-out-key-measures-to-tackle-violence-against-women-and-girls> (accessed 28 April 2020).

14. The crucial phrase is "with us." Mary is aware that although this behavior is fine within the closed circle of her sisterhood, this is not something Rizzio should display before the patriarchal world that surrounds them.
15. Rosalind Gill, "Postfeminist Media Culture: Elements of a Sensibility," *European Journal of Cultural Studies*, 10 (2), 2006, pp. 158–9.
16. In her face-to-face meeting with Elizabeth, Mary says, "I should have followed your example and never married."
17. On finding two common soldiers fighting for her are not Catholics, she responds, "We all go to the same heaven," i.e. whether Catholic or Protestant, monarch or ordinary soldier.
18. Knox's most famous work is his treatise, *The First Blast of the Trumpet Against the Monstrous Regiment of Women* (1558), attacking government by women and aimed primarily at the Roman Catholic Mary of Guise, who in the absence of Mary Queen of Scots was ruling Scotland as regent in the late 1550s.
19. Elizabeth Evans, *The Politics of Third Wave Feminisms: Neoliberalism, Intersectionality and the State in Britain and the US* (London and New York: Palgrave Macmillan, 2015), pp. 111–12. Evans quotes bell hooks as claiming "the term is fundamentally flawed, because it emerged from women liberationists who did not acknowledge the extent to which women oppress other women" (p. 112).
20. Luce Irigaray, *This Sex Which Is Not One*, trans. Catherine Porter and Carolyn Burke (Ithaca, NY: Cornell University Press, 1985), p. 164.
21. The historical reality is naturally more complex than the film might suggest. For example, Nigel Wheale reports, "123 Jesuit missionary priests were executed in the cruellest way during Elizabeth's reign as they continued to serve the English Catholic community." See Nigel Wheale, *Writing and Society: Literacy, Print and Politics in Britain 1590–1660* (London and New York: Routledge, 1999), p. 76. Christopher Morris reports that, far from being tolerant, after the rebellion in the North of 1569, Elizabeth "ordered hangings in every village green and market place where the rebels had assembled." See Christopher Morris, *The Tudors* (London: Fontana, 1966), p. 155.
22. One threat to Elizabeth lay in the fact the Catholic north of England might potentially ally itself to Mary's cause. Highlighting the economics of the situation in the 1560s (and a division in the country maybe relevant to the contemporary context), the famous historian George Macaulay Trevelyan points out that "... fortunately for Elizabeth, Northern England, like Scotland, was very thinly populated and very poor. Until the Industrial Revolution, wealth and population were concentrated in the South, and most of all in and near London." See George Macaulay Trevelyan, *A Shortened History of England* (Harmondsworth: Penguin, 1965/1942), p. 241.

CHAPTER 3

# What Would it Be to "Turn the World Upside Down"? *Fanny Lye Deliver'd* (Thomas Clay, 2019)

## I

*Fanny Lye Deliver'd* announces its subject matter clearly and directly in its title: the focus is to be on Fanny Lye (Maxine Peake), this will be her story. Within minutes of the opening, the narrator—who, we learn later, is also one of the central characters, Rebecca Henshaw (Tanya Reynolds)—has summarized the whole film for us. Fanny's life is continuing from season to season, Rebecca says in voiceover, "Till the day the strangers came, turned that whole world upside down, and delivered Fanny Lye from one life into the next." The word "delivered" is used primarily in the sense associated with the birth of a child but also carries biblical associations with being "saved" (from sin, from evil, from Satan). The audience will be aware that in religious terms the "next life" generally refers to life after death but also that in accepting the Christian faith, people have commonly spoken of being "born again." It might be useful to note that the word "delivered" echoes the use of this word in the Lord's Prayer, the prayer attributed to Christ in Matthew 6:9–13.

> And lead us not into temptation,
> But *deliver* us from evil.

This is entirely appropriate for a film in which the central characters struggle to decide how ideas from the Bible should be used to organize society and to shape the day-to-day lives of individuals. There is a strong focus on deciding how the concept of "Thy will be done,/On earth," should translate into action in the real world. In the film, and in the period in which the film is set, other concepts found in this prayer, such as "heaven," the "kingdom" of God, and the nature of "evil," become highly contested.

Of course, there does remain a great deal of mystery, uncertainty, and ambiguity attaching to exactly what is meant by Rebecca's initial summary of what is about to happen to Fanny. We immediately have questions, such as who the strangers might be, where they have come from, and what it is they will do to turn Fanny's world upside down. The notion of "turning the world upside down" is commonly linked to the English Civil War (1642–6) and highlights the way in which during that period social norms and expectations were overturned, but it also often carries with it an implication of accompanying chaos. In his groundbreaking book, *The World Turned Upside Down: Radical Ideas During the English Revolution*, Christopher Hill says:

> From, say, 1645 to 1653, there was a great overturning, questioning, revaluing, of everything in England . . . Literally anything seemed possible; not only were the values of the old hierarchical society called in question but also the new values, the protestant ethic itself.[1]

A ballad, "The World Turned Upside Down," was published as a broadside in 1646.[2] It protests against the way in which Puritans in Parliament have attacked the traditional more exuberant Christmas celebrations, and rails against "Our Lords and Knights, and Gentry too" who "do mean old fashions to forgoe."[3] In the following year, a poem with an accompanying woodcut was published using the same phrase. Its full title was "The World turn'd upside down; or a briefe description of the ridiculous Fashions of these distracted Times," and it described "this land" as "the Bedlam of the World."[4] Both of these contemporary publications position themselves in such a way as to suggest the authors are in favour of a return to at least some of the order and stability found before the Civil War.[5] "The Diggers' Song" from the same period, on the other hand, contains the sort of radical sentiment that is in favour of an upside-down reordering of the world: "the gentry must come down, and the poor shall wear the crown."[6] Clearly this is a historical moment of astonishing social upheaval and evidently as viewers we can expect to see people's lives being violently disrupted.

## II

The structure of *Fanny Lye Deliver'd* follows the protagonist's narrative trajectory from a deeply accepted oppression that is seen as normal, natural, and not to be challenged, to full liberation and powerful new-found confidence. When the film opens, Fanny is literally clearing up men's shit, scooping it into a bucket from the outside privy with a wooden spoon. Her husband, John Lye (Charles Dance), a captain in Oliver Cromwell's army, we are told, has "bought her master's farm at auction"; it seems he has more or less acquired Fanny along the way. John is a severe Puritan adhering strictly to God's commandments, although with an ability to shape this to his own patriarchal perspectives. He takes his young son's part against Fanny, for example, saying,

"Never let a woman best you, son, have I taught you nothing?" Into this world come Rebecca and her "husband," Thomas Ashbury (Freddie Fox); and it is these two, or more accurately the ideas and attitudes they bring with them, that turn Fanny's world upside down.

Fanny defies patriarchy—effectively, the norms and values of her society—in a series of increasingly defiant steps as her self-assurance grows. Firstly, when Rebecca reveals she and Thomas are not married ("Thomas ain't my master, no man is. I go where I likes with whom I likes") Fanny keeps their secret from John. Prior to this, we are told, when Fanny is confronted by a world that fails to appreciate her worth, her mind turns to "a verse of Scripture learned her as a child: 'Bears all things, believes all things, hopes all things, endures all things.'" The quotation on which she has been taught to meditate is taken from I Corinthians 13:7, and it is "charity" that in the King James Version of the Bible is said to "Beareth all things, believeth all things, hopeth all things, endureth all things." In other words, she has been taught from childhood that suffering is not only to be borne but it is to be borne in a spirit of love even for those who are causing your misfortune.[7] When Thomas instigates a faux Eucharist, giving the supplicants pork and mead instead of bread and wine, in defiance of her husband Fanny takes both as they are offered to her. In the lead-up to this, Fanny has watched as John's apparent omnipotence has been challenged and then broken by Thomas. Following Thomas' blasphemous mockery of the Last Supper, in front of John, Fanny next engages in sexual pleasure with Rebecca and Thomas. And then, at Thomas' instigation, and being urged by him to "break free" of her "bonds," she repays John for all the beatings she has received by striking him repeatedly across the back with a switch as Thomas forces John to kneel and submit to her retribution. Later, after having been silent for almost all of the film, Fanny finds her voice and further increased confidence in speaking back to the High Sheriff (Peter McDonald), telling him: "I have earned my freedom more times than I can count . . . Ain't nothin' you can do to me I ain't already suffered." It is at this point that Fanny is fully recognizing and acknowledging the extent of her oppression. Verbalizing it in this way puts her into a position to be able to take action in addressing that oppression, so that finally in a frenzied knife-attack on the Sheriff she gives full vent to the anger she has discovered within herself after having—through the interventions of Thomas and Rebecca—explored the full extent of her submission beneath patriarchy. Like a penitent moving between the Stations of the Cross, Fanny meditates on her passage from each new stage of development to the next, not as a progress towards crucifixion and death but as a journey towards rebirth and new life.

Having said all of this, as has been suggested, Fanny does not have a large speaking role. For much of the film her short interjections, often unexpected

**Figure 3.1** Fanny (Maxine Peake) repays her husband, John (Charles Dance), for the patriarchal violence he has shown her, in *Fanny Lye Deliver'd* (Thomas Clay, 2019).

by the men around her, demonstrate her latent strength and potential for self-development but do not allow her to dominate scenes.[8] The narrative trajectory of Fanny Lye—or her journey towards being born as a new person—does provide the film's structural spine but it is also the case that the other three main characters are each given their own importance within the film's ideational framework. As the stern patriarch, John embodies what the opening inter-titles have suggested is the overall position for people in England in 1657: they have been "freed of the King's tyranny only to suffer Cromwell's puritanical law." This is to some extent the point being made by the ballad mentioned earlier, "The World Turned Upside Down." The other main male role is that of Thomas, which has a large speaking part and often drives the action. It is what he says and does that presents to the audience a series of challenging views purporting to come from a time almost four hundred years before the present day. He says, for example, that he does not "look up to the skies for God and Heaven," believing rather that God is to be found within men and women on earth. Later he asserts that the concept of "sin" is used by the rich "to keep poor men in order" and that he puts his faith in "pure freedom and pure libertinism."

The final main character, Rebecca, through her position as the narrator has the power to direct the audience's attention and (effectively) to shape their response. It is Rebecca who tells us from early in the film that with the death of the King in 1649,[9] "It seemed . . . anything was possible for a time." It is Rebecca who points out as Thomas begins to play with John's son that there is "mischief in his eye." In other words, she draws our attention to the fact that at this point Thomas is not simply demonstrating his belief that there should be joy in a child's life but is deliberately setting in motion a chain of events he feels will disrupt the lives of the family with which they are staying. And it is Rebecca who reminds us of the importance for a woman of finding and asserting the validity of her voice. Fanny, we are told, "took to preaching and spoke her truth to many hearts,"[10] and this is followed by a succinct sentence that in its simplicity sums up the end point to which all that has gone before has been leading: "Fanny's voice rang out clear and true." The notion of "her truth" is critically important. Here is "truth" that belongs to "her" rather than "him"; that is, to Fanny rather than John, or Thomas, but also, and more importantly, to woman rather than to man. It is a highly personal "truth," unique to the individual, and yet it also contains within it an impersonal "truth" appropriate to all women (and ultimately a "truth" for all gradations of supposed gender division).

## III

Thematically, this film primarily examines gender roles, exploring relationships between men and women in a relatively straightforward way. For many people watching this as a film by a British auteur, or as an example of art cinema, the question of whether men should treat their wives as John treats Fanny might seem a non-question. To an educated middle-class audience watching an art-house film, John's domination of his wife might (perhaps) seem immediately unacceptable. However, in national or international terms we are forced to admit such subjugation of women is not merely something redolent of an earlier age.[11] More enlightened men and women may be willing to reflect on aspects of their own marriages or partnerships that may carry vestiges of such coercion. If that were the case, would such spectators then align themselves with the position of Thomas, and/or Rebecca, as expressed in the film? Both of these characters would seem to agree on the importance of more open partnerships, in which either party is free to take up sexual and emotional relationships with other people. Yet, at the same time, it might be said that Thomas dominates Rebecca, that Rebecca idolizes Thomas in some way, and that Rebecca panders in various ways to Thomas' moods. In this case, might it not be Fanny who actually demonstrates a stronger sense of freedom and independence in relation to men? This is particularly true in her relationship with Thomas, but could also be argued for her relationship with John. When Fanny keeps the secret that Thomas and Rebecca are not married, Rebecca's appraisal of the situation is that Fanny "was her own person, I knew that now." In other words, despite John's brutal exercise of authority over her, Rebecca realizes Fanny is able to hold onto an inner part of her self that retains its independence. Equally, when Fanny allows herself to become part of a sexual threesome with Thomas and Rebecca, she is willing to admit she wants Thomas' "prick" inside her. However, when Thomas takes the foreplay in a different direction, only returning to it after he has induced her to beat her husband, Fanny (in effect) refuses him. "Go on then, take me. Do what you want?" she says to him, making it clear that whatever may happen to her body, she will be holding her inner self aloof and apart from whatever sexual act may take place. It is at this point that through the voiceover Rebecca says, "I had never seen Thomas beaten before: it was a mixed emotion." The man she has revered as a font of understanding and clarity about the nature of the world has been found to be flawed. "After no small moping," she continues, "we resolved to leave that place and never speak of Fanny again." This is Rebecca as a more universal figure of woman who finds herself observing a man who when he does not get his own way becomes a child. *Fanny Lye Deliver'd* is at heart a film that examines patriarchy in all its forms—when Fanny whips John with a switch she is beating patriarchy, and when she executes the High Sheriff with an abattoir-worker's knife blow between the shoulder blades she is killing patriarchy both practically within her own life and symbolically on behalf of all women; but this is also a film that recognizes the subtlety and complexity of the concept of patriarchy.

In addressing the nature of patriarchy this film brings to the fore a series of related issues because all these matters are interlinked. Debates from the period that underpin the narrative include those relating to the status of women in society, the role of marriage as an institution, what might be deemed tolerable in terms of the expression of sexuality, the prospect going forward for concepts of social rank, and the necessity of maintaining social order. Each of these debates should be seen in relation to disputes over religious

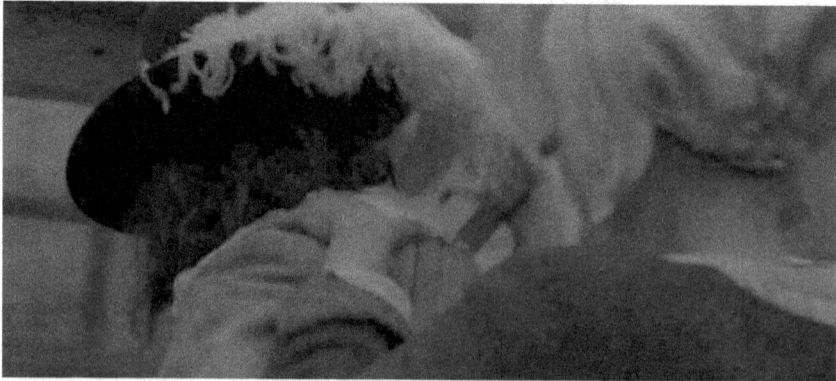

**Figure 3.2** Fanny executes patriarchy in the form of the High Sheriff (Peter McDonald) in *Fanny Lye Deliver'd*.

belief, over concepts of freedom and liberty, and over the importance or otherwise of preserving social order. When Thomas begins to look at the Bible with Fanny, her response from an inculcated position of subjugation is that "Scripture ain't for a woman to touch." Clearly this is about the position of women in society but it is also about the position of ordinary people in relation to religious belief. Is it open to anybody to read and interpret the Bible, or is this the preserve of an educated elite and/or a trained clergy?[12] The most obvious sex scene is that in which Fanny, Rebecca, and Thomas are in bed together and John is tied up so that he has to watch what is happening, but there are other crucial moments for the audience in this regard. For example, in the opening section of the film we see a shot of someone on their knees in a nightshirt moving forward, left to right across the screen. We are not shown a face but could assume this is Fanny. We then cut to John standing with his hands clasped in prayer. What are we to understand by this? There is no wide shot to provide us with a definitive image of what is happening. The reader is forced to construct in her own mind the wide shot that will explain how these images relate to each other. At the same time, we have Rebecca's voiceover telling us, "There was a kind of love between them, some shared affection, I suppose." In other words, the narration labels the images we have seen as relating to "love" but at the same time works to moderate any tendency we might have towards being judgemental.

The two men, John and Thomas, offer us polar opposites in terms of religious belief. John is a religious fundamentalist, equally zealous in his hatred of what he describes as "the Popish swine" and extreme libertarians such as Thomas and Rebecca, who he sees as having "trifled with Satan." Thomas is a complete anathema to John because Thomas believes we should recognize not the heavenly nature of Christ but rather his "earthliness," and in parallel with this "the eternal majesty in each and every one of us." Thomas' religious opinions cannot simply be tolerated as a modified way of worshipping the same Christian God because they turn conventional Protestant belief upside down and offer a direct threat, not just to the social order but more fundamentally to political order. What he is looking towards is total freedom and absolute equality. Just before his major speech outlining his views, Rebecca describes Thomas as a prophet who offers "words of blistering, shining power."[13] And in that speech Thomas essentially asserts this is political:

> Those who live by the law of priest or tyrant beware for a great levellin' is coming... King Charles and the Lords have had their turn, so Cromwell and his great ones are next in line, for they have made themselves as tyrannical as ever the king in his reign.

## IV

In the 1640s and 1650s a range of radical groups emerged straddling the great arenas of debate for the period—religion and politics; and frequently these topics merged since it was generally impossible to proclaim a particular perspective on religion that did not carry with it political ramifications. Underpinning each advocated religious transformation, or political modification, stood what was seen depending on your perspective as either the threat or the promise of social change. The nation was not simply split between followers of the King and supporters of Parliament but was instead splintered into an array of sects and looser groupings with each either promoting various degrees of religious, political, and social change or battling to maintain continuity and stability across these areas of communal life. The largest and most influential group with a strong base in the Army and in London was the Levellers. They agitated for a more representative Parliament, for freedom of conscience and religious toleration, and for an end to all discrimination on grounds of "tenure, estate, charter, degree, birth or place."[14] The Diggers were more radical, calling themselves the True Levellers. They formed small communes in various parts of the country and worked the land together in a communal fashion. They "set out to declare the earth a common treasury and to call for an end to all private property and buying and selling."[15] Another very loose group, the Fifth Monarchists, believed the Second Coming of Christ was imminent and that social levelling was necessary in preparation for this, but overall as a collection of individuals "possessed no coherent ideology."[16] The Society of Friends, or Quakers, believed the inner light of God was in all people. Their views contained "an inherent social radicalism."[17] They "challenged norms of social deference" and refused "to recognize titles and thus to bow or doff hats."[18] This group "grew as a protest movement concerned not only with religious issues but political and social ones as well."[19] Thomas and Rebecca are associated with the most radical group of all that became known as Ranters. Hill says the Ranters described God as Reason and suggested God was in everyone and every living thing.[20] He quotes Jacob Bauthumley as saying that God was in "man and beast, fish and fowl, and every green thing, from the highest cedar to the ivy on the wall" and that God was in "this dog, this tobacco pipe, he is me and I am him."[21] Hill adds that the only name the Ranters appeared to accept for themselves collectively was "My one flesh" and says this name together with "their salutation of 'fellow creature' were intended to emphasize unity, with mankind and with the whole creation."[22] He quotes the Ranter, Laurence Clarkson, as saying that, "There was no life after death: 'even as a stream from the ocean was distinct in itself while it was a stream, but when it returned to the ocean it was therein swallowed and became one with the ocean: so the spirit of man whilst in the body was distinct from God, but when death came it returned to God, and so became one with God, yea God itself.'"[23] And Clarkson, Hill says, "added that he would 'know nothing after this my being was dissolved.'"[24] Nigel Smith sums up the Ranters' position by saying they believed "the strict moral norms of orthodox western Christianity" were "nothing more than a cruel means of social control" and that humans were "not inherently sinful and may find their true and innocent relationship with God in a liberated present: heaven on earth."[25] Smith quotes Clarkson's poem, "A Single Eye":

> . . . look not above the Skies
> For God, or Heaven; for here your Treasure lies
> Even in these Forms,[26]

This is clearly the most challenging of the sects, willing to push what they saw as constructed and false social boundaries to the limit. Smith says, for example, and clearly we see this in *Fanny Lye Deliver'd*:

> . . . the Ranters found ways of incorporating sexual performance into their theology. In some accounts, like Clarkson's, they treated sex as prelapsarian and hence devoid of sin, and communal, escaping from the bondage that came with monogamous marriage. Holy sex beyond wedlock was as innocent as swearing in the name of the Lord.[27]

Almost four hundred years later in the twenty-first century these sorts of views remain radical in the extreme. In genre terms, the filmmakers may be creating a historical drama but it quickly turns out to be much more challenging than an audience might expect of a conventional period piece. What are being debated are the possibilities for a way of life existing at the extremes of liberty and freedom.

*Fanny Lye Deliver'd* is set in 1657. The key events at the time that open up the discussion of England's religious, political, and social future are the military victory of the Parliamentarian army over the King's forces in 1646 and the execution of the King, Charles I, in 1649. In delivering the verdict which endorsed the King's death sentence, the High Court of Justice made it clear the King's guilt lay in attempting "to overthrow the rights and liberties of the people."[28] The questions society then went on to argue about in the 1650s revolved around exactly what was meant by "rights and liberties" and who was included in the concept of "the people." The threat to those who controlled society, whether the landed upper classes or the well-to-do middle classes, was that those from the lower orders (like Thomas and Rebecca) might begin to believe concepts of "rights and liberties" should apply to them as much as anybody else. In *The World Turned Upside Down:*

*Radical Ideas During the English Revolution*, Hill suggested: "Although there was considerable popular support for Parliament in the 1640s, the long-term consequences of the Revolution were all to the advantage of the gentry and merchants, not of the lower fifty per cent of the population."[29] Ellen Meiksins Wood and Neal Wood summarize the situation by saying that in winning the Civil War, "Cromwell mobilized a popular army whose rank and file he would allow to fight but not to vote."[30] This is the reality of the eventual outcome of the upheavals of the 1640s and 1650s, but elsewhere Hill describes this period as "an intoxicating era of free discussion and free speculation."[31] This sense of a wide open horizon of possibilities is what—through the characters of Thomas, Rebecca, and Fanny—the filmmakers are exploring in this film.

## V

In this chapter we have viewed *Fanny Lye Deliver'd* as a historical drama, but the film has been linked to a series of further genres. It is certainly the case that it is a period drama offering strong attention to details of costume and place,[32] but it has elements of a thriller that constantly threatens to erupt into violence and it repeatedly employs elements of not only the western[33] but also the home-invasion horror movie.[34] It provides a strong sense of realism before it "boldly breaks away from plausibility."[35] It is playful in its postmodernist skipping between genres and in its willingness to offer itself as a broken-backed text as it abruptly moves from verisimilitude to flagrant excess, but at its heart there is a serious debate about the nature of society and the possibilities for any future society. For all its genre-hopping and its use of homage, its central drive is towards making it imperative for its audience to view the past in relation to the present, to take these ideas and to see them in relation to contemporary social contexts. In his review, David Katz recognizes the essence of this film as being "a principled sense of wanting to explore British history, at a time where its present is facing similarly grave divisions."[36] He is right; we are not only guided through a twenty-first-century exploration of ideas that were abroad in the 1650s but we are also inevitably asked to consider the nature of our current society and to reflect on possibilities for change: moving forward, what would be possible, and what would be desirable? In her review, written for the London Film Festival, Rosamund Kelby is concerned that Rebecca's voiceover creates "constant interruptions" that "remove us from the present moment."[37] But this is perhaps the point: there are two "present moments" at stake here. Kelby's interest is in the supposed "present moment" that exists within the events of the film narrative, but the filmmakers are just as interested in the "present moment" we are occupying in the twenty-first century as they are in the creation of an immersive moment from the 1650s.[38] In effect, we are urged by the voiceover to adopt a more distanced, reflective perspective than would otherwise be the case. And this is also what happens with the postmodernist aspects of the film. Both the High Sheriff and his deputy (Perry Fitzpatrick) are flat caricatures, functioning towards the end of the film as pantomime villains, arousing not the fear and dread created in watching a thriller but the laughter of the horror-film fan. This is the postmodernist aesthetic used with purpose. It remains possible simply to enjoy the cinematic ride being provided but the filmmakers are also working to jolt us out of easy escapism, asking us to reflect on the symbolic nature of Fanny's final bloodletting.[39] Kelby regrets that "powerful performances' from the actors 'are not quite enough to lift us fully from the desolate world in which we find ourselves."[40] Torn in the bind of wanting the audience to escape into an imagined world but not wanting the audience to evade a responsibility to reflect on the ideas being put forward, the filmmakers might see this as a reasonable final position in which to leave the viewer.

As has been suggested, each of the central roles has its own importance for the matrix of ideas under investigation. Ultimately, however, despite Thomas' zeal in advocating the possibilities of unrestrained anarchy, the film endorses some moderation of this position. In her defiance of his sexual advances, it is Fanny who exposes the possibility that Thomas' version of sexual freedom might merely endorse a further subjugation of women; and it is to Fanny, moving within the more moderate forum of the Society of Friends, or Quakers, that Rebecca finally transfers her allegiances. Without departing too far from her original Ranter beliefs, Rebecca says she has "since been persuaded that not all we held back then was true," and she goes on to endorse Fanny's preaching, which advocates "the right of a wife to hold property, speak equal marriage vows, and be free of her husband's whip." The debate is, perhaps, between reform and revolution: can the current system be reformed (through careful regulation) into a way of life that creates (or moves increasingly towards) equality, or is this such an impossibility that any society run for the benefit of the "propertied classes"[41] needs to be totally overturned and replaced by something entirely different? Fanny's narrative trajectory, the birth of her new liberated self with Thomas and Rebecca as attendant midwives, demonstrates this film to be a thoroughgoing attack on patriarchy.[42] It also throws open for the audience the question of what the nature of society should be and suggests that whatever the current configuration may be, this can be changed.

**Notes**

1. Christopher Hill, *The World Turned Upside Down: Radical Ideas During the English Revolution* (London: Viking Press, 1972), p. 12.
2. See George Thomason, *Catalogue of the Pamphlets, Books, Newspapers, and Manuscripts Relating to the Civil War, The Commonwealth, and Restoration, Collected by George Thomason, 1640–1661*, Vol. I, 1640–1652 (London: William Clowes, 1908), p. 431. Available at https://www.bl.uk/collection-guides/thomason-tracts (accessed 16 September 2020).
3. Ibid.
4. Nigel Wheale tells us this poem was first published in 1642 by John Taylor ("a Thames waterman" and "a quite new phenomenon: a relatively uneducated person who makes a reputation, even occasionally a living, by writing," p. 89) as "Mad Fashions, Odd Fashions, All out of Fashions, or, The Emblems of these Distracted Times." See Nigel Wheale, *Writing and Society: Literacy, Print and Politics in Britain, 1590–1660* (London and New York: Routledge, 1999), pp. 94–7.
5. The attribution of the second poem, for example, is given as, "By T.J. a well-wisher to the King, Parliament and Kingdom." See Thomason, *Catalogue of the Pamphlets, Books, Newspapers, and Manuscripts Relating to the Civil War, The Commonwealth, and Restoration*, p. 490.
6. See E. A. White, "The Diggers' Song," *Journal of the English Folk Dance and Song Society*, 4 (1), December 1940, pp. 23–30. Available at www.jstor.org/stable/4521172 (accessed 11 September 2020). The Diggers were one of several radical groups that emerged after the Civil War. Around 1650, advocating abolition of the private ownership of land, they set up communes in several parts of the country, most famously at St George's Hill in Cobham, Surrey. This song is generally attributed to Gerrard Winstanley (1609–76), their most well-known leader.
7. This was a commonly used biblical passage, and the notion of suffering clearly links in the Christian mind to the Crucifixion. However, we might note that the Society of Friends, or Quakers, published in 1665 *The Remonstrance of the Suffering People of God, called Quakers: Clearing their Innocency from the many False Aspersions, Slanders and Suggestions, which are lately come Abroad in the Nation*, in which it was stated, "Be known unto all men we are resolved . . . to bear all things, endure all things, and suffer all things for Christ's sake." See Anon, *The Remonstrance of the Suffering People of God, called Quakers: Clearing their Innocency from the many False Aspersions, Slanders and Suggestions, which are lately come Abroad in the Nation* (London, 1665), p. 15.
8. As John is expounding at length, for example, on what he is going to do to Thomas, having found him hiding in his barn, Fanny cuts in with a simple, "Let him speak, sir," that allows Thomas to explain his position.
9. After the Parliamentarian army defeated the King's forces to win the English Civil War in 1646, negotiations with the King designed to formalize the future constitution and limit the power of the monarch failed, and in January 1649 Charles I was executed. England was governed as a republic throughout the 1650s.

10. In anti-clerical pamphlets, Winstanley, among others, argued for "the right of anyone to preach, regardless of their education or status." See Wheale, *Writing and Society: Literacy, Print and Politics in Britain, 1590–1660*, p. 134.
11. A Home Office website reports the current situation in the UK is that "1 in 4 women will experience domestic abuse and 1 in 5 sexual assault during their lifetime." The Home Office estimates 3.4 million women in the country have experienced some sort of sexual assault. See Anon, "Violence against women and girls and male position," GOV.UK, Home Office, 2019. Available at homeofficemedia.blog.gov.uk/2019'03/07/violence-against-women-and-girls-and-male-position-factsheets (accessed 16 September 2020).
12. William Tyndale, who translated the Bible into English in the early 1520s to make it accessible to ordinary people, is famously reported to have said when debating with "a learned man" that "if God spare my life, ere many years I will cause a boy that driveth the plough shall know more of the scripture than thou dost." See Wheale, *Writing and Society: Literacy, print and politics in Britain, 1590–1660*, p. 41.
13. Does this word "shining" reference the Digger pamphlets *Light Shining in Buckinghamshire* (1648) and *More Light Shining in Buckinghamshire* (1649)? See George H. Sabine (ed.), *The Works of Gerrard Winstanley: With an Appendix of Documents Relating to the Digger Movement* (Ithaca, NY: Cornell University Press, 1941), pp. 611–26, 627–42.
14. Geoffrey Robertson, "Introduction," in Philip Baker (ed.), *The Putney Debates: The Levellers* (London and New York: Verso, 2018), p. x.
15. John Gurney, *Brave Community: The Digger Movement in the English Revolution* (Manchester and New York: Manchester University Press, 2007), p. viii.
16. R. J. Acheson, *Radical Puritans in England, 1550–1660* (London and New York: Routledge, 1994), p. 75.
17. Philip Baker, "Rhetoric, Reality, and Varieties of Radicalism," in John Adamson (ed.), *The English Civil War: Conflicts and Contexts, 1640–49* (London and New York: Palgrave Macmillan, 2009), p. 222.
18. Ibid.
19. Benjamin Woodford, *Perceptions of a Monarchy Without a King: Reactions to Oliver Cromwell's Power* (Montreal and London: McGill-Queen's University Press, 2013), p. 140.
20. Hill, *The World Turned Upside Down: Radical Ideas During the English Revolution*, p. 165.
21. Ibid.
22. Ibid.
23. Ibid., p. 166.
24. Ibid.
25. Nigel Smith, *A Collection of Ranter Writings: Spiritual Liberty and Sexual Freedom in the English Revolution* (London: Pluto Press, 2014/1983), p. xiv.
26. Ibid., p. 4.
27. Ibid., p. 30.
28. John Wroughton, *Seventeenth-Century Britain* (London: Macmillan, 1980), p. 59.

29. Hill, *The World Turned Upside Down: Radical Ideas During the English Revolution*, p. 11.
30. Ellen Meiksins Wood and Neal Wood, *A Trumpet of Sedition: Political Theory and the Rise of Capitalism, 1509–1688* (London: Pluto Press, 1997), p. 79.
31. Christopher Hill, *The Century of Revolution, 1603–1714* (London: Van Nostrand Reinhold, 1980), p. 153.
32. Tom Grater records "the farmhouse that serves as the single-location setting" was built "over the winter of 2015–16 in consultation with experts on construction from the period," and that recording the music "took time as the director only wanted to use instruments from the time." See Tom Grater, "The Winding Journey of Puritan Western *Fanny Lye Deliver'd*: On-set Flooding, Three Years in Post, and a Determined Director," *Deadline*, 8 October 2019. Available at https://deadline.com/2019/10/inside-story-uk-drama-fanny-lye-deliverd-flooding-three-years-post-determined-director-1202753825/ (accessed 14 September 2020).
33. For example, the way Fanny "transforms herself" (p. 56) and displays this alteration in her power dressing at the end of the film mirrors the performance of Natalie Portman in *Jane Got a Gun* (Gavin O'Connor, 2016). See John White, "Defending Home, Defending Homeland: *Jane Got a Gun* (2016)," in John White, *The Contemporary Western: An American Genre Post-9/11* (Edinburgh: Edinburgh University Press, 2019), pp. 54–70.
34. David Katz, "Review: *Fanny Lye Deliver'd*," *Cineuropa*, 14 October 2019. Available at https://cineuropa.org/en/newsdetail/379745/ (accessed 14 September 2020).
35. Ibid.
36. Ibid.
37. Rosamund Kelby, "Fanny Lye Deliver'd," *The Upcoming*, 11 October 2019. Available at https://www.theupcoming.co.uk/2019/10/11/london-film-festival-2019-fanny-lye-deliverd-review/ (accessed 14 September 2020).
38. Christopher Hill asserted: "History has to be rewritten in every generation, because although the past does not change the present does." For the same reason, films about particular historical periods have to be rewritten and reshot in every generation, and every historical drama has to be read within the socio-political and socio-economic contexts of the period in which it has been made. See Hill, *The World Turned Upside Down: Radical Ideas During the English Revolution*, p. 13.
39. There is also a thought-provoking domesticity attaching to Fanny's violence. If Fanny slaughtered the roasted pig brought into the house earlier in the film, for example, she would have been likely to have cut its throat in much the same way she dispatches the deputy.
40. Kelby, "Fanny Lye Deliver'd."
41. Ellen Meiksins Wood and Neal Wood, *A Trumpet of Sedition: Political Theory and the Rise of Capitalism, 1509–1688*, p. 72.
42. In contrast to the women, in the final attack on the homestead both men, John and Thomas, are utterly ineffectual.

CHAPTER 4

# Politics in "The Corridors of Power" Then (and Now): *The Favourite* (Yorgos Lanthimos, 2018)

## I

On the evidence of this film, the fundamentals of politics and the methods by which both foreign and domestic policy are created would seem to have changed little since the early 1700s. In simple terms, *The Favourite* presents us with an example of the way in which government strategy is determined by the machinations of political factions within "the corridors of power." The narrative centers on the relationship between the three most politically powerful women in England during the early 1700s—Queen Anne (Olivia Coleman), Sarah Churchill (Rachel Weisz), and Abigail Masham (Emma Stone). Over the course of the film the audience is shown the way in which Sarah is dislodged as the Queen's "favorite" by Abigail, but beyond this there is a wider context that presents a picture of the nature of politics in general. The potential for the monarch to intervene in decision-making may have been greater in the early eighteenth century than it is today, but the sovereign in this film, Queen Anne, is shown to be pretty much a pawn in the hands of the major political players.[1] During this period, top-ranking government ministers tended to be the products of a handful of elite English schools and universities, and to be members of families with long-standing connections to political power. Nominally, in the early eighteenth century the government of England[2] was parliamentary in form. In reality, both the monarch and Parliament were controlled by a relatively small number of titled families. The leading government minister in the film, Sidney Godolphin (James Smith), in historical reality was the brother of the provost of Eton, and both his father and grandfather were Members of Parliament. The historical figure providing the basis for the leader of the Opposition in Parliament in the film, Robert Harley (Nicholas Hoult), was educated at Eton; and, as with Godolphin, both his father and grandfather were Members of Parliament during the 1600s.

It is, however, a woman who is shown as having almost total behind-the-scenes power during the opening part of *The Favourite*. This is Sarah

Churchill, a character based on a historical figure from a wealthy landowning family in Hertfordshire. The presence of women at the heart of politics for a brief period at the start of the eighteenth century is the novel point of difference, or hook, on which the filmmakers hang their story. At a time of intense patriarchy—just as keen as that seen in *Mary Queen of Scots* or *Fanny Lye Deliver'd*—not only is there a female monarch but because of this fact, those who are appointed to the role of lady of the royal bedchamber can potentially wield tremendous power. Essentially they become an advisor and confidante to the Queen, and because they organize the affairs of the royal household they are able to control the Queen's schedule of appointments, effectively providing politicians with access to the head of state or denying such access. Even so, we should bear in mind that within the historical context of the period Sarah Churchill is just as much a part of the socio-economic elite ruling England as Godolphin and Harley. In a similar lineage to these two men, both her father, Sir Richard Jennings, and her paternal grandfather, Sir John Jennings, were MPs. Her husband, John Churchill, Duke of Marlborough (played in the film by Mark Gatiss), attended St Paul's School, an institution with a similarly elite intake to other public schools such as Eton, and he too came from a family of politicians. Harley's family were landowners in Herefordshire, Godolphin's family were leading landowners in Cornwall, while the Churchills were a major landowning family in Dorset.[3] Within the family trees of each of these "great" families, knighthoods are the norm rather than the exception. In the final analysis, despite what is portrayed in the film as their personal animosity, and leaving aside gender for the moment, the only difference between Sarah and Godolphin on the one hand and Harley on the other is their political estimation of the best strategy for the country in seeking to maximize future possibilities for those with affluence to hold onto their wealth or, even better, to access increased levels of prosperity. The political and economic reality of England in the early 1700s was that the parliamentary electorate was extremely restricted. Perhaps around 300,000 adult male Protestants were able to vote, and neither Catholics nor women had the franchise.[4] Even by the second half of the century, Kirstin Olsen says, "201 boroughs had fewer than 500 eligible voters," while the town of Bath "had just thirty-two,"[5] and each of these boroughs was responsible for returning two Members of Parliament during an election.[6]

*The Favourite* offers us a fictional interpretation of history but, in essence, what it places before the audience is a representation of a ruling elite shown to be arrogantly self-confident and totally debauched. Early within the first part of the film there is a scene demonstrating both the decadence and extravagance of the upper class. In a long-room within the palace, surrounded by tables laden with food, men in exaggeratedly showy outfits and extravagant wigs are spending their time racing ducks. Later, as he is waiting for an audience with the Queen, Godolphin has under his arm his prize duck, Horatio. On the one hand this is bizarre behaviour and begins to create a dimension of surrealism in the film, but on the other it establishes with a few quick filmic brushstrokes the film's perspective on the well-off English ruling class in this period. This is particularly so when moments later we move to a scene showing the below-stairs maids all sleeping together in the cramped space of one small room. The contrast between this very bare room and the opulence of the room with its high ceilings and sumptuous furnishings in which we have just seen the wealthy elite could not be clearer. The point is further driven home when we cut to see the same maids naked and washing together in cold water using cheap, rough soap. These two scenes showing glimpses of the experience of the female servants are shot using tight, claustrophobic camerawork in such a way as to emphasize both the restrictions on the lives of these people and the control exerted over them. And, in order to make sure we recognize the contrasting life experiences of these two classes, we next cut to see the Queen and Sarah meeting in a huge long-room with the space open to them and available for them to walk through emphasized by the use of a long shot.

The division within the state between rich and poor—the wealthy elite and the working servant class—is therefore made clear from the outset. At several points, Abigail, who is related to Sarah but has fallen in social rank and is attempting to make her way in the lower reaches of the royal household, is either threatened with being stripped and whipped or her expected easy, sexual availability to upper-class males is made clear ("Going to ride that one are we?" says Harley at one point to Abigail's future husband, Colonel Samuel Masham (Joe Alwyn)). But beyond the gulf between the excessively well-off and the lower classes, a further crucial division is also shown to exist. This is the divide within the political elite between the landowning aristocracy and the nouveau riche mercantile class. What we have on display is an upper class within which there is considerable disagreement about the political (and economic) way forward. The debating and maneuvering that is taking place is this class attempting to move towards a political position that will ensure not only that the status quo is maintained within English society but also that the future will be shaped in such a way as to bring increased opportunities for wealth creation; precisely the position, in other words, that we face within contemporary UK society. In a sense, the same sorts of personality clashes and backroom arrangements are taking place today as occurred within Queen Anne's reign. Boris Johnson won a massive parliamentary majority in 2019 and yet there are still those in the Conservative Party who are not happy with the direction "their" party is taking. This is particularly true with regard to whether the UK should be in or out of the European Union. Former Conservative prime minister John Major, for example, broke ranks to claim that, "When the nation voted on Brexit it did so on a diet of fiction and undeliverable promises."[7] Fundamentally, both in the early 1700s and today, the division on display within a group of politicians seemingly sharing the same general principles highlights an ideological schism between blocs within the country's socio-economic elite that is much more profound than any of those involved in the struggle is prepared to admit. Different factions that have come together beneath the same umbrella organization can, it seems, have quite distinct conceptions of the economic trajectory the country should pursue. As has been suggested, until the emergence of the Covid-19 pandemic these differences centered in recent times on the UK's relationship with Europe. Some members of the Conservative Party saw improved economic possibilities as likely to emerge from the UK leaving the European Union, while others believed the best prospects for the country's economic stability remained in staying within this European trading alliance. In this sense, Covid-19 makes little essential difference to the policy struggles taking place. The film demonstrates that the political debate in the early 1700s was essentially the same as it is now: what is the best strategy to pursue in order to enable those with powerful economic interests to achieve the best outcome with respect to their investments?

## II

These crucial divisions within the country between an immensely wealthy upper class and the lower orders and between warring factions within the ruling political elite (both of which are mirrored within contemporary society) operate as a backdrop to the central arena of narrative action within *The Favourite*. However, despite the way in which paring away the complexities of the politics of the period left the filmmakers with a clear set of parallels to the contemporary context of a divided UK, press and publicity for the film almost exclusively emphasized the obvious surface situation of a female–male division at the heart of the narrative: the men become peripheral and the film's focus settles on a bitter entanglement between three women that beyond the personal has a potent political dimension determining the direction a whole country will take. During the past thirty years, stories focusing on central female characters have been given increased prominence within mainstream filmmaking (as they have within media representations more generally). It has also been argued that in the last twenty years the range of female roles has become increasingly diverse, with actors proclaiming the expanding variety of characters they are being asked to portray. *The Favourite* follows this trend for a new visibility of women in film.

The film centers on dynamic, high-profile female figures from the period. Sarah Churchill was the long-standing favorite of Queen Anne who had been appointed a lady of the bedchamber twenty years earlier. In 1704 she engaged her distant cousin, Abigail, as an additional lady of the bedchamber but then found she was gradually replaced as the Queen's favorite by Abigail. Historians differ in their opinion as to how much influence Sarah and Abigail were able to exert over government policy through the sway they may have had over the Queen, but in the film Abigail's ascendancy is linked to the dismissal of Anne's chief minister, Sidney Godolphin, in 1710 and the coming to power of his rival, Robert Harley. In the film we see both Sarah and Abigail riding and shooting as competently as men. However, in reality the general position for women, even aristocratic women, in this period was not one that proffered much in the way of freedom from patriarchal control:

> The life of the female aristocrat was much more circumscribed than that of her male counterpart. Where she was confined to decorous pursuits such as walking, sketching, and painting the landscape, men were much more active.[8]

On the face of it, the sort of increased media profile for women epitomized by this film—here, taking the three leading roles in a film and being empowered in ways beyond the likely historical reality—might be seen to either promote or reflect (or maybe both promote *and* reflect) an enhanced female socio-economic presence within contemporary western society.

**Figure 4.1** Women in *The Favourite* (Yorgos Lanthimos, 2018) handle guns as competently as men: here, Abigail Masham (Emma Stone).

The viewer is shown women deploying multiple identities to their own ends in the achievement of political success and personal enhancement among the highest ranks of early eighteenth-century English society, though it might be important to question the nature of the freedom and power that seems to be on offer for women in the film. Some writers have questioned the credentials of certain elements of contemporary feminism. Jo Reger has pointed out, "a number of older feminists" have been "stepping forward to label contemporary feminism as apolitical and ineffectual."[9] More critically, Jessa Crispin has said: "To understand how surface-level contemporary feminism really is, we need only note that the most common markers of feminism's success are the same markers of success in patriarchal capitalism. Namely, money and power."[10] She suggests there is now so much focus on "lifestyle" that contemporary feminism has become "just another thing to buy."[11] Directly in relation to the concept of "power," she adds:

> Much of contemporary feminism uses the language of power. Girls need to be "empowered," women need to fight for "self-empowerment," "girl-power," etc. There is little conversation about what that power is to be used for, because that is supposed to be obvious: whatever the girl wants.[12]

It could be argued what we are given in *The Favourite* is no more than the appearance of female empowerment, individual liberty, and the freedom to make unimpeded choices in shaping one's life. It is certainly the case that, by way of contrast to *Mary Queen of Scots*, examined earlier, there is no sense of sisterly solidarity on display here, nor is such a concept even discussed. Here we are struck by the intensity of the antagonism and distrust between Sarah and Abigail, between Sarah and the Queen, and by the end of the film between the Queen and Abigail. Despite the vivid foregrounding of (historically disputed[13]) lesbian sexual relations between Sarah and the Queen, and between Abigail and the Queen, this film refuses at any point to entertain the notion of sisterhood.[14] Both Sarah and Abigail might be said to function at the level of male or, perhaps more correctly, genderless political intrigue. These women are not "powerless victims of patriarchal structures of domination."[15] They operate within the realm of male structures of domination, employing the full extent of such arrangements to their own ends, essentially proceeding as surrogate males. Sarah is directly and forcefully confrontational with Harley, who opposes her plans to continue the war with France. When he demands an audience with the Queen to state his case for suing for peace with the French, Sarah's provocative response (after she dismisses him as "a fop, a prat" who "smells like a ninety-six-year-old French whore's vajuju"[16])—effectively barring him from obtaining access to the Queen—is, "State it to *me*, I love a comedy." The power a politician is able to wield depends on whether they are "in favour" or "out of favour" with the monarch, whether they "have the ear" of the King or Queen, or not. Harley believes the unofficial political arrangement operating in England at the time is one that enables both government ministers and opposition politicians to present their positions to the sovereign. He views interventions into politics by Sarah as a lady of the bedchamber as "a disgusting distortion of the system" and believes she has "no place in this." Both Sarah here and Abigail on other occasions, when she defies men who within the realities of the period have much more power than her, provide the audience with strong images of women.[17] Men are consistently shown being thwarted by women and, in this way, *The Favourite* provides viewers with a modern, twenty-first-century feminist angle on events. Men are pushed into the margins of the text. They are portrayed as mincing pantomime dames in high heels and heavy make-up, as juveniles indulging in infantile public-school pranks, or as teenage boys way out of their depth when it comes to dealing with women who are confident sexual beings. To this extent this might be seen as a subversive text.

## III

In the relationships between the three women it is initially Sarah's dominance over the Queen that is emphasized. When these two meet as Queen Anne is on her way to attend an official engagement, Sarah is dismissive of the bizarre way in which Anne has had her make-up applied: "Do you really think you can meet the Russian delegation looking like that?" In response, the Queen is immediately downcast and submissive, replying meekly with a simple, "No." Sarah, by contrast, is assertive, confident, and quick to take control of the situation: "I will manage it. Go back to your rooms." When at the start of the second part of the film[18] the leader of the government, Godolphin, and the leader of the Opposition, Harley, are waiting to speak to the Queen, after having kept them waiting for an hour it is eventually Sarah who sweeps into the room. "I'm here," she says. And when Harley responds by saying, "Might I remind you, you're not the Queen," it is Sarah's position as quasi-regent that is asserted with simple confidence: "She has sent me to speak for her." The implication is clear: it is in fact Sarah who is making policy decisions and effectively operating as if she were the sovereign. Real political power is shown to be at stake here, with Sarah being able to persuade the Queen to continue to pursue the war with France despite considerable opposition in Parliament. Her husband, the Duke of Marlborough, has defeated the French at the Battle of Blenheim (1704) and the debate now is over whether this is a good moment to make peace or not. Harley believes the war is costing too much and this is the time to secure a peace treaty. The country is divided, he says, with the landowners having essentially paid for the war while the city merchants have enriched themselves from it. "A treaty would save money and lives: a win for all Englishmen," he says. Godolphin (aligned with Sarah), on the other hand, believes: "We go to them after one victory; they know we are scared. We bury more of them: they know we have them." This is a brutal imperialistic discussion, the nature of which can easily be missed. At its heart there is again a debate about wealth and the creation of financial profit. How is England's future prosperity best secured, through inward-looking maintenance of an essentially feudal economic landscape, or through the achievement of dominance within the structures of global trade? Old aristocratic wealth based on the ownership of land and exploitation of agricultural labour wishes to adopt a more cautious, conservative approach. New mercantile (soon to become capitalist) wealth, based on trade and industry, favors a more calculatedly global-focused entrepreneurial approach.

*The Favourite* announces to potential audiences that it is "about" a struggle for power between two women, Sarah and Abigail, each attempting to outdo the other in gaining the ear of the Queen. Both of the contenders to become the Queen's "favorite" are presented as complex, so that our sympathies waver between the two. At the outset, Abigail is portrayed as a victim, someone who has "fallen" through no fault of her own from a position of some social status and is now attempting to make her way "below stairs." In this world, in which rank counts for everything in determining your experience of life, Abigail has, as Sarah says, "fallen far." Abigail's explanation that "When I was fifteen my father lost me in a card game" is bizarre in the strangeness of the concept for a contemporary audience but also succinctly summarizes the position of women in society in England at the end of the 1600s: daughters, even those of high social rank, are there to be disposed of according to the patriarchal will. However, as the film progresses Abigail comes to be seen as much more scheming and manipulative than this initial assessment would suggest,[19] so much so that the viewer might begin to wonder if she has not contrived the whole set of circumstances that leads to her being taken into the Queen's household and then into her inner circle of confidantes. In just the second part/chapter of the film, Abigail, standing unnoticed as a servant, coughs as Queen Anne leaves the room in her wheelchair and says, "I'm sorry, your majesty, I think I caught a chill picking those herbs for your leg." The Queen had been unaware who had produced the salve that had eased her gout but through her subterfuge Abigail has gained recognition of the fact that she was responsible for this. Sarah is initially shown to be bullying of Anne and uncaring in personal relationships. However, by the end of the film we are left wondering if she, rather than Abigail, is not the one who actually has caring feelings for the Queen. At this level there are interesting discussions to be had around what we might mean by feminism, and how there are stark divisions and antagonisms that exist between feminists. Each of these three women faces a clear set of difficulties in charting their course through the patriarchal society within which they find themselves; and from what we can see, little has changed between the early eighteenth century and the early twenty-first century. Critical theory, as it has developed through the twentieth century and into the twenty-first century, has articulated the position of women in society, revealed the range and variety of stereotypes employed to maintain the oppression of women, and laid bare the full extent of sexual inequality; and yet the fundamentals of the experience of women within western society would seem to have remained unchanged in all of its essential patriarchal restraints.

## IV

Beyond this, however, it is crucial to note that although this is a film that places women and the female experience of life center stage, there remains a very particular representation of women that is given to the audience. In *The Favourite*, women are represented precisely as they are traditionally viewed from within patriarchy. We see woman as hysterical: Queen Anne is frequently, suddenly, and unexpectedly shrill and violently vocal, and her physical symptoms of illness appear as manifestations of her mental anguish. At one point, Queen Anne is being pushed in her wheelchair by Abigail when they come across a quartet with conductor performing outside on a lawn. As they watch the performance the camera shows the Queen beginning to cry, before screaming, "Make them stop … Stop … Enough … Stop. Be gone. I command it. Leave. I don't want to hear it." We also see woman as ice queen: Sarah is cold, calculating, and able to accept quite coolly that in order to achieve desired ends, "collateral damage" may be unavoidable; as she tells Abigail, "There is always a price to pay. I am prepared to pay it." We see woman as she-devil: Abigail is malicious and spiteful. And we see woman as virago: both Sarah and Abigail are domineering and potentially violent, containing a strength more usually associated with men. Sarah is shown, for example, inducting Abigail into shooting as a sport. "Let's shoot something," she says to Abigail, and then as she successfully kills a partridge thrown into the air for her to shoot she laments uncaringly, "Sad really, they're so pretty." The metaphor for the ruthlessness that it takes to operate within the male realm of politics is clear, as is Abigail's movement towards being able to successfully take her place alongside Sarah within this cut-throat business as she too manages to make "a kill." Summarizing the positions open to women under patriarchy, Lois Tyson says:

> ... patriarchal ideology suggests that there are only two identities a woman can have. If she accepts her traditional gender role and obeys the patriarchal rules she's a "good girl": if she doesn't, she's a "bad girl." These two roles,— also referred to as "madonna" and "whore" or "angel" and "bitch"—view women only in terms of how they relate to the patriarchal order.[20]

Both Sarah and Abigail are portrayed as dispassionate and always in control of their emotions; and in this way they are deliberately positioned as the complete opposite of the stereotype of the out-of-control woman given to hysteria. Within classic female stereotypes, Abigail is also the vixen in that she is spirited and vindictive. Such representations have been the stock of literature for centuries and have been identified within the media for decades. In studying TV stereotypes in the United States as long ago as the early 1980s, Diana Meehan identified, for example, among others:

- the bitch—the manipulative cheat, much like Abigail,
- the victim—the long-suffering, passive woman, much like Anne,
- the decoy—the apparently helpless woman who is actually strong, much like Abigail,
- the harpy—the aggressive, single-minded woman, much like Sarah.[21]

**Figure 4.2** Woman as hysterical: Queen Anne (Olivia Coleman) bellows for the musicians to stop playing in *The Favourite* (Yorgos Lanthimos, 2018).

We might question what has changed and to conclude note that Abigail is also seen as the minx, or the sexually provocative woman. Such stereotypes are, as with all representations, cultural constructions, but they are also the gender constructions imposed on women for generations. In watching this film they are also the subject positions offered to audience members by the text. Both Sarah and Abigail might be seen as strong, independent women and therefore as positive role models. However, it is also the case that they are defined in terms of certain patriarchal notions of feminine beauty and sexual attractiveness.

This is not to deny that the fundamental human experiences we see women exposed to in this film are ones that are central to understanding the female experience. Queen Anne has lost seventeen children. As she explains to Abigail, "Some were born as blood, some without breath, and some were with me for a very brief time . . . Each one that dies, a little bit of you goes with them." Abigail appears not only to have been married off by her father to somebody she detested but also to have subsequently suffered a series of rapes. As she explains it to the Queen, "The rapes were the hardest. They made me feel like I was at their mercy. That I was nothing." It is also the case that Sarah, in particular, remains a powerful presence, calmly self-assured even in her final defeat and exile from England. Despite the fact that she is married to the central heroic military figure of the age, the Duke of Marlborough, the film places her rather than him firmly in control of the trajectories their lives are to take. The male hero, her husband, with a string of military victories to his name is reduced to a walk-on bit part. In the final scene with his wife he is in the background while it is Sarah who takes all of the camera's attention. Each of these "feminist" elements *is* present in *The Favourite* and yet there remains something very male and very patriarchal in the final overall representation of women that is to be found in the film.

## V

Ultimately, however, it may be a significant absence that is the most important aspect of this film worth noting. This gap in the text is hinted at through the presentation in passing of a series of luxury goods, each of which operates as a status symbol: chocolate, oranges, a pineapple, an Indian servant boy. The lifestyle we see being lavishly enjoyed by the upper classes is built on the growing economic success of the slave trade during this period. Members of Parliament were absorbed not only with defending Britain's network of colonies against rival imperial powers through the pursuit of war[22] but also further expanding their empire via the intensification of trade in general, and in particular the slave trade. William Pettigrew estimates:

> From 1690 to 1714, members of Parliament debated the slave trade in sixteen parliamentary sessions, absorbing about the same amount of legislative time as discussions of its abolition decades later.[23]

Pettigrew explains that the main debate taking place was:

> Would a joint-stock monopoly company—the Royal African Company—better satisfy the colonies' demand for slave labor and better serve the British state than an open trade in which any subject was free to trade in slaves?[24]

Here the notion of "any subject" naturally applies only to entrepreneurial businessmen from the upper classes.

Generally in this period there was some movement away from the notion that single companies should be given the state-backed monopoly of trade in particular parts of the empire and towards the opening up of free trade. Entrepreneurs saw anything other than this as the curtailment of their liberty, and were seemingly unaware of the irony of debating in favor of this position in relation to the slave trade.[25] Even so, and despite losing out in the long run,[26] Pettigrew says that towards the end of Queen Anne's reign the position of the Royal African Company gained some ground when Robert Harley became the new first minister. At this point, the extent to which all of these politicians and their extended families are enmeshed in global trade in order to underpin their enormously expensive lifestyles becomes clear. Pettigrew explains:

> It is likely that Harley, an expert on the Africa trade debates, did not wish to see the company destroyed because he saw a role for it as a supplier on the African coast for his South Sea Company. In 1713 the South Sea Company preferred the Royal African Company over the separate traders as contractors to supply forty-eight hundred slaves from the coast of Africa, which represented more than 50 percent of the annual slave trade volume at that point.[27]

Another source tells us Harley's uncle, Sir Robert Harley, "had an interest in plantations in Barbados, Antigua and Surinam, as well as connections with other slave trading companies."[28]

When Abigail says she is waiting for a new novelty, a pineapple, to be brought to her by servants, she is referring to an item that has been described as "the ultimate status symbol of 18th century England"[29] [30] and was widely known as "the West Indian Pine-apple."[31] Prior to this, in terms of fruit, the aristocracy displayed their wealth through their orangeries. Explaining something of the background to the pineapple as an image of conspicuous wealth, Fran Beauman says: "Europe's first greenhouses were designed to protect orange and lemon trees—as status symbols, the forerunners to the pineapple—from frost through the coldest months of the year."[32] What we see in one scene in *The Favourite*, of course, are members of the upper class who are so amazingly rich and so clearly unburdened by the need to take on work of any sort that they can afford to use oranges as projectiles in a decadent version of a coconut shy. On a par with the pineapple, and in earlier years the orange, were "Indian servants who . . . had been brought to London by the white 'nabobs' of the East India Company and its fellow travellers."[33] These were seen as "possessions of status and fascination."[34]

In three scenes, Sarah and Abigail are shown shooting partridges together, and at these shooting matches the birds to be used for target practice are thrown into the air by an Indian servant boy. On the first occasion the violence of the activity is emphasized by Sarah's initial invitation to Abigail, "Let's shoot something," and then by her throwaway comment, "Sad really, they're so pretty," after she has blasted a bird from the sky. And at the end of the final shooting scene this savagery is underlined when Abigail shoots a bird and blood from the kill splatters across Sarah's face. This may symbolize Abigail's preparedness to engage with Sarah on her own ruthless terms and maybe the willingness of both women to partake in the violence of patriarchy. However, it should also serve as a reminder both of the involvement of English forces in constant warfare throughout this period and of the bloody nature of the trade in human livestock that is the unseen, unspoken absent presence underpinning *The Favourite*.[35] No text exists in innocent cultural isolation. In reading all texts it is necessary to make contexts manifest.

**Notes**

1. Whether this was actually the case is open to debate. In the early twentieth century, Edward Stanley Roscoe believed that, "In following the fortunes of the statesmen of the age of Anne, personal contests and Court intrigues have been too much considered. Larger causes were affecting the course of English politics: the progress of the European war, the unrecognised strength of the English party system, the powerful factor which existed in the sovereign's individual will, and the intense determination of the people never to accept a Roman Catholic sovereign" (pp. 42–3). On the other hand, the same commentator later suggests, "Lady Masham was ever by the side of the Queen, and her influence, veiled under the attractive guise of friendship, was the final factor in Harley's fall as it was in his rise to supreme power" (p. 165). See Edward Stanley Roscoe, *Robert Harley, Earl of Oxford, Prime Minister, 1710–14: A Study of Politics and Letters in the*

*Age of Anne* (London: Methuen, 1902). After acknowledging how Queen Anne "has often been portrayed as a pasteboard character, a dull, weak, irresolute woman dominated by favourites" (p. xvi), Edward Gregg arrives at a more sober assessment. He says: "Her daily consultations with ministers, her presiding role in the cabinet, her assiduous attendance in the House of Lords, and the contacts which she developed and maintained with all shades of political opinion enabled the queen to influence, if not to dominate, the political developments of her reign" (p. 403). See Edward Gregg, *Queen Anne* (New Haven, CT and London: Yale University Press, 2001/1980).

2. From 1707, when the Act of Union joined England and Scotland under one system, this became Great Britain rather than just England.
3. "This was the age of the great estate, which then formed the largest unit of political and economic power." See Gordon Mingay, *English Landed Society in the Eighteenth Century* (London and New York: Routledge, 2007/1963), p. 15.
4. Kirstin Olsen, *Daily Life in 18th Century England* (Westport, CT and London: Greenwood Press, 1999), p. 6.
5. Ibid.
6. To put this in perspective, the population of England in 1701 was estimated by Christopher Clay to be "just over 5 million." See C. G. A. Clay, *Economic Expansion and Social Change: England 1500–1700, Volume 1: People, Land and Towns* (Cambridge: Cambridge University Press, 1984), p. 3. See also E. A. Wrigley and R. S. Schofield, *The Population History of England 1541–1871: A Reconstruction* (Cambridge: Cambridge University Press, 2002/1981), p. 209.
7. John Major, "I'm a Conservative. But it is time to vote with your head as well as your heart," *The Guardian*, 6 December 2019. Available at theguardian.com/commentisfree/2019/dec/06/john-major-conservative-general-election-vote-head-heart (accessed 1 June 2020).
8. Christopher Christie, *The British Country House in the Eighteenth Century* (Manchester and New York: Manchester University Press, 2000), p. 159.
9. Jo Reger, *Everywhere and Nowhere: Contemporary Feminism in the United States* (Oxford and New York: Oxford University Press, 2012), p. 5.
10. Jessa Crispin, *Why I Am Not a Feminist: A Feminist Manifesto* (Brooklyn, NY and London: Melville House, 2017), p. 20.
11. Ibid., p. 41.
12. Ibid., p. 87.
13. Suggestions of an intimate relationship between Abigail and Queen Anne emerge in a song from the period, *A New Ballad* (1708), "probably written by the Whig hack Arthur Mainwaring, an ally of Sarah Marlborough, who very likely aided its production." One verse reads:

> Her Secretary she was not
> Because she could not write
> But had the Conduct and the Care
> Of some dark Deeds at Night.

See Patricia U. Bonomi, *The Lord Cornbury Scandal: The Politics of Reputation in British America* (Chapel Hill: University of North Carolina Press, 1998), pp. 111–12.
14. There are, however, moments of what appear to be genuine tenderness between women. Sarah, for instance, reminisces with the Queen: "Do you remember when we were young and we were not allowed out in the snow and we opened all the windows in the ballroom and sat there as the snow flurries just wafted in?"
15. Lois McNay, *Foucault and Feminism* (Cambridge: Polity Press, 1992), p. 66.
16. From his foppish behaviour, Harley would in many ways seem to be based on Mr Foppington in Sir John Vanbrugh's play *The Relapse; or Virtue in Danger* (1697).
17. Through her marriage to Colonel Masham, Abigail became a relative of the philosopher and proponent of female education Damaris Cudworth Masham, seen as an early "feminist." Damaris Masham also offered thoughts on the stupidity of men in her era, saying, for example:

> The improvements of Reason, however requisite to Ladies for their Accomplishment, as rational Creatures; and however needful to them for the well Educating of their Children, and to their being useful in their Families, yet are rarely any recommendation of them to Men; who foolishly thinking, that Money will answer to all things, do, for the most part, regard nothing else in the Woman they would Marry.

See Damaris Cudworth Masham, *Occasional Thoughts In Reference to a Vertuous or Christian Life* (1705), The Project Gutenberg. Available at https://www.gutenberg.org/cache/epub/13285/pg13285.html (accessed 30 May 2020).
18. The film is split into eight parts, or chapters, with each given a seemingly random title from the script.
19. Abigail's ascendancy is assessed in chapter 9 of James Anderson Winn's *Queen Anne: Patroness of Arts* (Oxford and New York: Oxford University Press, 2014), pp. 437–512.
20. Lois Tyson, *Critical Theory Today: A User-Friendly Guide* (New York and London: Routledge, 2006), p. 89.
21. Diana Meehan, *Ladies of the Evening: Women Characters of Prime-Time Television* (Metuchen, NJ: Scarecrow Press, 1983).
22. Principally, the War of the Spanish Succession (1701–14) in Europe—in which the British troops were led by Sarah Churchill's husband, the Duke of Marlborough—and Queen Anne's War (1702–13) fought against the French in North America.
23. William A. Pettigrew, "Free to Enslave: Politics and the Escalation of Britain's Transatlantic Slave Trade, 1688–1714," *The William and Mary Quarterly*, 64 (1), 2007, p. 3. Available at www.jstor.org/stable/4491595 (accessed 14 June 2020).
24. Ibid.
25. Madge Dresser and Andrew Hann have suggested that:

> both the merchants and the members of Britain's landed elite who were involved in the proliferation of country houses from the late 17th century (the latter to consolidate their status and the former to gain entry into that elite) increasingly utilised

notions of gentility, sensibility and cultural refinement in part to distance themselves from their actual connections to the Atlantic slave economy.

See Madge Dresser and Andrew Hann (eds.), *Slavery and the British Country House* (Swindon: English Heritage, 2013), p. 14.

26. Christopher Hill claimed ending the Royal African Company's monopoly "made possible the development of Jamaica," that is to say, increasing the numbers of slaves being taken to the island massively increased the productivity of the plantations. Christopher Hill, *The Century of Revolution, 1603–1714* (Wokingham: Van Nostrand Reinhold, 1980), p. 224.
27. Ibid., p. 28.
28. Susanne Seymour and Sheryllynne Haggerty, "Slavery Connections of Bolsover Castle (1600–1830)," Report for English Heritage, July 2010, p. 6. Available at https://historicengland.org.uk/images-books/publications/slavery-connections-bolsover-castle/slavery-connections-bolsover-castle/ (accessed 15 June 2020).
29. Anon, "Picture This # 16, Portrait of a Pineapple," Fitzwilliam Museum, 16 February 2012. Available at https://www.cam.ac.uk/research/news/picture-this-16-portrait-of-a-pineapple-fitzwilliam-museum (accessed 15 June 2020). A still-life painting of a pineapple completed in 1720 by Theodorus Netscher and held in the Fitzwilliam Museum, Cambridge.
30. "The first reliable crop of pineapples in Britain was in fact achieved by a Dutch grower, Henry Telende, gardener to Matthew Decker, at his seat in Richmond between 1714 and 1716." Johanna Lausen-Higgens, "A Taste for the Exotic: Pineapple Cultivation in Britain," n.d. Available at https://www.buildingconservation.com/articles/pineapples/pineapples.htm (accessed 15 June 2020).
31. See Charles McIntosh, *The Orchard: Including the Management of Wall and Standard Fruit Trees, and the Forcing Pit* (London: Orr, 1839), p. 276.
32. Fran Beauman, *The Pineapple: King of Fruits* (London: Vintage, 2006), p. 56.
33. Jerry White, *A Great and Monstrous Thing: London in the Eighteenth Century* (Cambridge, MA: Harvard University Press, 2013), p. 136.
34. Ibid.
35. See the website, *Legacies of British Slave-ownership*, researched by the Department of History at UCL, for an in-depth, owner-by-owner documentation of Britain's involvement in the slave trade. Available at: ucl.ac.uk/lbs/ (accessed 30 January 2021).

CHAPTER 5

# Class as the Crucial Division in UK Society: *Peterloo* (Mike Leigh, 2018)

## I

This film deals with one of the most infamous moments in British political history, when in 1819 cavalry with drawn sabers charged an open-air protest meeting in Manchester, leading to seventeen people being killed and hundreds injured. The crowd, estimated to number as many as 60,000 men, women, and children, had gathered at St. Peter's Field to demand parliamentary reform and an extension of voting rights. In his book, *Peterloo: The English Uprising*, Robert Poole says, "nearly 700 were seriously injured, more than 200 of them by sabre wounds, many of them women, some of them children."[1] A weaver from Middleton near Manchester, Samuel Bamford, a well-known local campaigner for political reform, described the situation after the attack:

> In ten minutes from the commencement of the havoc the field was an open and almost deserted space ... Several mounds of human beings still remained where they had fallen, crushed down and smothered. Some of these still groaning,—others with staring eyes, were gasping for breath, and others would never breathe more. All was silent save those low sounds, and the occasional snorting and pawing of steeds.[2]

The incident came to be known as the Peterloo Massacre, or simply Peterloo, in mock reference to the Battle of Waterloo which had taken place just four years earlier. Poole tells us there were veterans from Waterloo—the Duke of Wellington's final decisive victory over Napoleon—on both sides.[3]

In the immediate short term, this critical episode in British labour history led to increased government suppression of political dissent. Acts of Parliament were quickly passed that, for example:

- restricted attendance at political meetings to only those living within the parish where the gathering was held;

- allowed magistrates to try the cases of radical reformers that would previously have needed to be put before a judge and jury;
- increased the tax on newspapers in order that they would become too expensive for ordinary people to buy;
- permitted magistrates to search any property for literature that might be seen to advocate sedition.[4]

In the longer term, it has been argued Peterloo led to intensified pamphleteering and campaigning for reform to both the voting system and working conditions. Michael Scrivener says that although Peterloo was quickly followed by a series of repressive Acts of Parliament, "the massacre inspired the reform movement to hope for victory because of the public revulsion against the government."[5] E. P. Thompson went so far as to argue that such was the public outcry against the authorities following this incident it effectively guaranteed the right of public assembly:

> Since the moral consensus of the nation outlawed the riding down and sabreing of an unarmed crowd, the corollary followed—that the right of the public meeting had been gained.[6]

Because *Peterloo* centers on an actual historical incident, it does inevitably to some extent document events, but the director, Mike Leigh, is clear this film is not a documentary. Instead he describes it as "a dramatic distillation" of what happened leading up to and during the massacre.[7] The characters John Bagguley (Nico Mirallegro) and Samuel Drummond (Danny Kirrane), for example, take the names of people chiefly remembered for being involved in the "March of the Blanketeers" that set out two years earlier to march from Manchester to London to petition the Prince Regent.[8] Leigh conflates them into the story of Peterloo as a means of providing the audience with a stronger sense of the debate between competing ideas that was occurring in the period. The spy Oliver (Stephen Wight) is chiefly documented as a suspected agent provocateur in the Pentrich rising in Derbyshire of 1817.[9] Around that time, although not necessarily at the time of Peterloo, historians have suggested he was operating in exactly the way we see in the film:

> Throughout the spring of 1817 the spy, Oliver, was going to and fro in the industrial districts, posing as a delegate from the London "Physical Force Party." Wherever he went he assured the local Radicals that the rest of the country was ready for a general insurrection, and only that particular place was lagging behind.[10]

He is, therefore, seen carrying out the role for which he is known in the historical record but not in relation to the particular moment of heightened working-class discontent with which he is usually associated. Again, the Habeas Corpus Act (1679) was actually suspended in 1817 in order that suspects could be imprisoned without trial, but in the film it appears to occur much closer to the time of Peterloo.

## II

The relationship of the film to history can therefore be mapped quite clearly. But the question remains as to why the filmmakers may have chosen to retell the story of Peterloo at this particular juncture in British history. Obviously, in closely coinciding the making of the film with the two hundredth anniversary of Peterloo it is likely the project may have been easier to "sell" to potential financial backers and producers: the timing would provide a certain marketability. However, over and above such practical considerations, what relevance could this event be said to have to the contemporary period? Just as importantly, if the filmmakers are incorporating into their "dramatic distillation" characters and activities from slightly earlier in the historical period, why have they done this? What is it about the ideas that are consequently highlighted that might be seen as relevant to the early twenty-first century?

The single fact about the society under scrutiny in *Peterloo* which comes through most strongly is the way in which the rich and powerful live their lives within an entirely different sphere of existence to that experienced by the poor. The reality of this situation in early nineteenth-century Britain is presented with such vigor that it takes on the force of a general statement of ideological conviction in relation to capitalism as a whole. The film switches back and forth between the distinct worlds of workers in Manchester cotton mills and the provincial ruling classes, and between the workers and the aristocratic landowners who run the country. The daily experiences of life for these social groups are juxtaposed in such a way as to highlight the gulf between both workers and local magistrates/industrialists, and between workers and the aristocratic upper classes. *Peterloo* takes us into a society riven by social and political divisions and presents us with a moment of crisis for British capital. Both landowners and factory-owners are already immensely prosperous, and rampant capitalism offers the potential for this society as a whole to attain an unprecedented historical high point of wealth accumulation for the few. However, at the same time, discontent among the working class means this possibility is under severe threat.

In historical terms, the urban labouring class working in factories has grown quickly in the years preceding Peterloo; as industrial towns and cities have expanded, production has increased, and profits have soared. However, small-time handloom-weavers working from home have seen their livelihoods threatened by the advent of industrialization, with machine looms being set up across vast factory floors. Particularly around 1811–12 but again in 1816, weavers have responded by entering factories mob-handed and destroying the machines they have found there. These groups become known as Luddites, signing their warning letters to industrialists with the fictitious name, Ned Ludd. At the same time, although the expanding industrialized workforce in factories are the source of new wealth, they are also seen as a further potential threat to the factory-owners, as they push forward demands for improved wages and work conditions.[11][12] Alongside all of this industrial unrest, provincial factory-owners and magistrates, the government, and the landed aristocracy are all intensely aware of what is from their perspective the terrifying example of the French Revolution that has taken place thirty years earlier. Calling for the suspension of the Habeas Corpus Act in the film, Lord Sidmouth (Karl Johnson) says: "The malignant spirit born of the odious French Revolution is even now plainly persuading our people that alone by open violence can their grievances be redressed." Referring to the monarch at the time, George III, and the Prince Regent (Tim McInnerny), one of the more revolutionary radicals, John Johnston (Johnny Byrom), states: "Our French brethren have showed us the way. We must punish our mad king and his gluttonous offspring by taking off their heads."

Leigh is clear not only that he had all of these socio-political contexts in mind during the creation of the film but also that he was conscious of the way in which these contexts not only mirrored current social realities for the United Kingdom but also how they reflected contemporary global realities. He has spoken of "the ever-increasing contemporary relevance of the story" of Peterloo,[13] adding that:

> Despite the spread of universal suffrage across larger parts of the globe, poverty, inequality, suppression of press freedom, indiscriminate surveillance, and attacks on legitimate protest by brutal regimes are all on the rise.[14]

Through engaging with the issues of a particular historical moment, Leigh sees *Peterloo* as contributing to discussions relevant to today both within the UK and globally. The gap between rich and poor that he identifies as the central socio-political reality for England during the early 1800s is reflected in contemporary society.

It is, then, the intense antagonisms between the emerging proletariat and the factory-owners, and between the laboring poor in general and the aristocracy, that are at the heart of *Peterloo*; but there are also a series of further divisions within this society—between men and women, between women of different classes, between London and the provinces (or "the North"), and between different religious beliefs—that are brought to the fore. This is an intensely divided society, and it may be that many of these elements of social tension and dislocation should be seen as interlinked. Still, it is clear that for Leigh the key factor with which he wishes to confront his audience is the gross inequality to be found between the wealth of the few and the poverty of the many.

## III

In the film, the relative degrees of wealth and poverty marking out magistrates, factory owners, tradespeople, and ordinary workers in Manchester, and delineating between the Royal Family, Members of Parliament, government officials, Army officers, and ordinary people in the country at large, are made clear through the mise-en-scène employed in a range of settings. For example, near the beginning of the film, after viewing Joseph (David Moorst), a bugler with the British Army, and other foot-soldiers trekking miles to make their own way home after Waterloo, we cut to a scene showing the Prime Minister, Lord Liverpool (Robert Wilfort), in the House of Commons proposing in upper-class tones that the Duke of Wellington should be granted "the sum of £750,000" in recognition of his having defeated Napoleon. The disparity between the two groups could not be shown with any greater clarity. Joseph, suffering what would now be recognized as post-traumatic stress, is throughout the film the ever-present, mute, psychologically maimed reminder of the depths to which frontline troops pay the price for a government's foreign policy. By opening their film with the brutal reality and confusion of the Battle at Waterloo, the filmmakers not only link this event to Peterloo but emphasize a connection between the working class being used as cannon fodder in battles abroad and as factory fodder in workplaces at home. In reality the battle took place four years before Peterloo, but Leigh's "dramatic distillation" of events again enables him to condense the timescale and make the imagined and metaphorical link between the two "battles" with greater clarity. Wellington himself on more than one occasion referred to the ordinary British soldiers as "the scum of the earth."[15] In the film, this word is echoed by a factory owner when he finds his mill is empty as a result of the workers having gone to join the meeting at St. Peter's Field that is to turn into the Peterloo Massacre: "Scum, that's what they are: scum. I put food on their table and this is how they repay me." The gulf between officers and men in the Army, and the gulf between factory owners and workers, is made clear; but at the same time these two institutional disparities of class, wealth and power—one within the military and the other within the context of work—are linked and shown as part of the same socio-economic climate.

This cutting between classes in order to juxtapose the experience of one group with that of the other continues throughout the film. For example, in order to further emphasize the comparison between the classes, from the scene showing the Prime Minister in Parliament mentioned above we cut back to Joseph walking along a rocky shoreline with vast mudflats and the sea beyond, before cutting to a man dressed like Joseph in a British Army red military uniform but with an experience of life that is in total contrast to that enjoyed by Joseph. It is immediately clear to us, as it would have been to anyone living in the early 1800s, that the second man we see here in an Army uniform, rather than being an ordinary soldier is from the officer class. His uniform is in pristine condition and exists in stark contrast to the dirty and tattered uniform worn by Joseph. Each uniform—Joseph's and this officer's—operates as a bitter, satirical comment on the other. We next see a butler taking the smartly dressed officer, identified as General Sir John Byng (Alastair MacKenzie), upstairs to the office of the Home Secretary, Lord Sidmouth (Karl Johnson). Extensive pleasantries follow between the two men before a maid enters to offer them tea. Throughout these opening sections of the film the audience is, therefore, introduced to characters and given important information for the story that is to follow. However, more importantly, the stark contrasts achieved in juxtaposing scenes in Parliament and in Sidmouth's offices with scenes showing Joseph hobbling his way home highlight the film's central theme of the gulf between classes.

Pressing home the point, the chasm between rich and poor is further emphasized in the following scenes, in which we are introduced to Joseph's family. It is the hands of the mother, Nellie (Maxine Peake), that are first shown to us, and the hands are at work. Nellie is shaping the pastry bases to pies we will later see her attempting to sell. Only after showing the hands does the camera tilt up to show us Nellie's face and her concentration. In a direct and deliberate parallel, the father, Joshua (Pearce Quigley), is introduced in the same way. First of all we see his hands checking a working loom, and it is only after this that we tilt up to see his body and face. Nellie may be in the home while her husband is in a factory but they are connected through the concept of work. Their common experience of life is work. The unrelenting nature of this work is given through the series of pastry bases Nellie is producing and the series of looms Joshua is shown overseeing. In a further connection, everything we see in these scenes is in motion. And so, in the currency of narrative storytelling we are introduced to two new characters but simultaneously in thematic terms we are introduced to these people's experience of life. Importantly, at the same time in effect we are introduced to the experience of a whole class. When we cut from inside the factory to outside we are shown the black smoke from a nearby works' chimney. Back inside we see not only men and women but also children at work.[16] However, the dominant, overwhelming sense is of the noise of the constant repetitive motion of the looms set out in a series of close-packed rows filling every available inch of the factory floor.

In establishing a working-class context and perspective for the film, while all the time allowing us to view this reality against the contrasting experience of a life of well-provided-for ease being enjoyed by others, Leigh to a large extent allows setting, costume, props, and performance to speak for themselves. The editing that takes us easily and simply between scenes involving members of different classes allows the build-up of juxtapositions to create their own impact.[17] However, there are also moments within the script that subtly and economically reveal crucial contexts for the audience. When Nellie manages to persuade a street-seller to give her extra eggs with the promise of paying for them later, a moment that can seem innocuous reminds us the family is "on the breadline" and that in harsh practical terms Joseph's return from the Army simply means there is another mouth to feed. This reality is unspoken in direct terms, but as with the other realities of the social

**Figure 5.1** When we are introduced to Nellie (Maxine Peake) in *Peterloo* (Mike Leigh, 2018), it is her hands we see first.

condition of England being revealed in the opening sections of the film, it is there for us to "discover." In the same way, when Joseph is shown trudging through Manchester in the rain trying unsuccessfully to find work, not only is the individual situation of his family needing to feed an extra mouth reinforced but the general situation for a whole class facing a recession and the accompanying possibility of unemployment is highlighted.

## IV

Crucially, at various points the filmmakers show this ordinary working-class family (and therefore by extension the labouring classes as a whole) as capable of discussing their social conditions in abstract political terms. This clearly reflects a reality from the period in which labour was beginning to organize itself and the discussion of social conditions and reform was rife in pamphlets, periodicals, and newspapers, to say nothing of more literary poetry and prose.[18] Conversations within Nellie and Joshua's extended family involving their son Robert (Tom Meredith), their daughter Mary (Rachel Finnegan), and Robert's wife Esther (Simona Bitmate) not only revolve around unemployment, wage cuts, and the bread tax, but also who is responsible for these things and who is gaining from the current situation. The audience is given important information about the period, particularly relating to the Corn Laws,[19] but at the same time ordinary people are shown as taking themselves away from a situation of victimhood and into a realm of political debate. Furthermore, Nellie in particular is shown to have a clear historical grasp of the ways in which current social conditions have come about. She states, for example, that the landowners have been "getting fat on land they stole from us in the first place." What she is referring to is the enclosure of common land for private agricultural use. This was a process adopted by landowners from Tudor times but which developed particularly quickly during the eighteenth century. In *The Making of the English Landscape*, W. G. Hoskins says practically the whole of the "vast transformation" of the landscape through enclosure took place "between 1750 and 1850."[20] In the English countryside before this, he says, the situation was that "beyond the arable fields and meadows lay great tracts of common pasture, much of it covered by gorse and furze."[21][22]

Set against this ability to discuss the social condition of England in rational terms, we have set-piece scenes in which local magistrates are seen sentencing three poor people in a high-handed fashion. In the first of these scenes, an older woman is mocked by the magistrate, Reverend Ethelston (Vincent Franklin),[23] as he sentences her to be whipped and then to spend fourteen days in gaol for stealing two bottles of wine. In the second, a man is sent to a higher court by Reverend Hay (Jeff Rawle)[24] with a recommendation he should be transported to Australia for fourteen years for stealing a pocket watch, a crime he denies. And in the third, another man is also sent to a higher court, this time with a recommendation he should be hanged for the theft of a coat. This defendant claims he is a "reformer" and what he has done should not be seen as stealing but as "sharing." Episodes such as this, and indeed episodes such as those in which we see Nellie at home with her family, do not move the narrative forward but they do reinforce an understanding of the power dynamic in this society. The audience is being referred to wider truths about the nature of this society, for example, the reality of transportation as a punishment: convicts were sent to work on plantations in America before the colonies there gained their independence in 1783, and then from 1788 the courts began sending people to Botany Bay in Australia. Until 1868, executions in England were carried out in public and in the early 1800s this was not an uncommon practice: following Luddite attacks on machinery in 1812, seventeen people were hanged in York.[25]

When Nellie and her family are discussing the idea of extending the vote to all men, her attitude is, "They'll never give us owt." She expresses this in such a way as to make it seem she believes protest meetings will not bring about changes to the political system, and we are able to view what she has to say against the backdrop of the actions of the magistrates we have just witnessed.[26] When pushed by her son who says she has given up hope, she responds that she will never give up hope because hope is "all we've got." It is, however, definitely the case that Nellie is always urging caution: "You've got to start small; as they say, from little acorns mighty oak trees grow." The political reality is this is a period in British history during which only a very few people were able to vote. According to the National Archives, a survey conducted in 1780 revealed that:

> ... the electorate in England and Wales consisted of just 214,000 people—less than 3% of the total population of approximately 8 million. In Scotland the electorate was even smaller: in 1831 a mere 4,500 men, out of a population of more than 2.6 million people, were entitled to vote in parliamentary elections. Large industrial cities like Leeds, Birmingham and Manchester did not have a single MP between them, whereas "rotten boroughs" such as Dunwich in Suffolk (which had a population of 32 in 1831) were still sending two MPs to Westminster.[27]

In two further set-piece scenes that additionally highlight the gulf between those in authority in this society and the "lower orders," magistrates read extracts from letters they are preparing to send to Sidmouth reporting on the local situation. The first magistrate says he has never before witnessed "the scale and size of these people's ambition" and goes on to raise the specter of the French Revolution, claiming the workers are "ripe for insurrection" and "will never give up their course until they have established a republican court." The second magistrate rages about "the greed of a labouring class" and claims "they speak not of reform but of destruction." Stylistically, Leigh uses the material in a form reminiscent of Brechtian theatre. These sorts of set-piece scenes leave narrative to one side and demand that the audience engage with the ideas being put forward. In a somewhat similar vein, on a couple of occasions Leigh uses the device of a female weaver singing songs from the period. The first song has the refrain "for the sun it will shine on the weavers again"[28] and, in stark contrast to the despondency on her face as she delivers the line, contains the idea of hope for the future that recurs throughout the script. The second sums up the situation of the working classes through, for example, the repeated line "twixt hunger and cold."

The antagonism between the classes is further reinforced when we are shown the proceedings of two meetings calling for radical reform of the political system. Two sentiments are repeated, firstly, "what good is a Parliament if it does not represent its people," and secondly, the idea that "we have it within our power to begin the world again."[29] At the same time, at these meetings there is a clear split between those calling for reform and those who would like to see more radical changes to society. As some of the speeches become increasingly revolutionary in tone, reformers such as John Knight (Philip Jackson) and John Thacker Saxton (John Paul Hurley)[30] are shown through their performance to become increasingly uncomfortable. And this division between those who believe the system can be changed through parliamentary action and those who believe the system itself has to be fundamentally altered remains potent today. The more revolutionary voices heard in the film, such as those of Samuel Drummond (Danny Kirrane) and John Johnston (Johnny Byrom), suggest the people have the right to imprison the King and his family if no notice is taken of the petition they present. However, trying to control the meeting, Knight thanks these speakers for their "impassioned rhetoric" but says he cannot "concur that the imprisonment of the King would advance the cause." He believes "the distress of the people is too great to be removed by any power other than that of Parliament." The debate underpinning this is one that always faces those wishing to change society—whether it is possible to bring about change through piecemeal adjustments to the in-place system, or whether meaningful change can only occur when a whole system is thrown out and replaced by something else. When Henry Hunt (Rory Kinnear), a famous radical from the period, addresses a rally in St. Peter's Field demanding parliamentary reform, he is clear his message will be solely about the idea of universal male suffrage. In itself this might be seen as radical enough when so few people in England have the vote at this point in history, but Richard

Carlile (Joseph Kloska), who Hunt is careful to prevent from speaking at the meeting, wants to go further, saying it is vital people should appreciate that "reform is not merely a matter of achieving universal suffrage but of freedom from the tyranny of the Church and of the destruction of monarchy."[31]

## V

In addition to the poverty and inequality he sees as common factors linking the historical moment of Peterloo and the contemporary period, Leigh also suggests the suppression of press freedom, indiscriminate surveillance, and attacks on legitimate protest can be seen occurring in both eras. As the magistrate orders the prisoner to be taken away in the final set-piece court scene, mentioned above, an unknown character enters the courtroom and walks forward to whisper in the ear of the magistrate. Only when the audience sees him again at a local reform meeting does it become clear he is a spy, or informant. Earlier we have heard the Home Secretary, Sidmouth, giving General Byng "full access to all files concerning seditious activity in the North." Later we see Oliver offering Sidmouth his services as a spy. What becomes clear is that both the local magistrates in and around Manchester and the central government are operating spy rings, and extensive files are being kept on all potential "enemies of the state." Whenever there is a scene showing a meeting addressed by reformers, the audience is made aware of the presence of an informant or spy listening to proceedings. Generally, Deputy Chief Constable Nadin (Victor McGuire), a dark, bulky, brooding presence, is also shown to be in the background.[32][33] The concept of surveillance and the use of spies, informants, and agent provocateurs as an arm of government is central to the ideational framework of *Peterloo*, and this feeds into not only the film's concern with the importance of the freedom to protest, but also the emphasis that is placed on the role of the press during the period in getting the story of Peterloo out to the public.

Continuing the theme of surveillance, we are never shown a scene in the government building where Sidmouth has his office without seeing clerks at work reading intercepted mail and deciding what needs to be passed to the Home Secretary. The parallel to the heightened level of government surveillance of digital communications in place today is clear. Discussing recent approaches to surveillance in the UK, Rhodri Jeffreys-Jones says:

> The campaign within the United Kingdom for more effective surveillance extended beyond the traditional intelligence agencies. In July 2014 the director of the National Crime Agency, a kind of fledgling British FBI, demanded more access to communications data. More controversially, covert policing

was a factor in public debate—there were 1,200 undercover police officers in the United Kingdom ... Undercover policemen penetrated protest and political action groups that had nothing to do with terrorism. *They posed as radicals in order to gain credence* [my italics], and sometimes engaged in intimate relations with group members.[34]

In many ways, in the film Manchester—a new town with its wealth built on industry rather than agriculture—is seen as rather distant from and different to London, but at the same time shots of the mail coach highlight the increasing speed of transport and communication during the period. Reformers travel from Manchester to London to hear Hunt speak, and (in addition to reporters coming from northern cities such as Leeds and Liverpool) a reporter, John Tyas of *The Times*, comes from London to attend the mass meeting in St. Peter's Field. The historical record shows reports of the events at St. Peter's Field appeared quickly in papers and periodicals over the next few days.[35]

Interestingly, at the same time as showing us the workings of a surveillance society in which interconnectedness is reaching new levels, *Peterloo* also highlights the manner in which London and Manchester are dislocated from one another. Although it is true that this is an era in which industrial development is demanding communications should become faster and Royal Mail coaches are facilitating this advance,[36] there remains a strong sense of geographical distance between London and Manchester, which is to say, between the capital and the provinces in general. In is clear that those in power in London are rather dismissive towards those who are living outside of the capital. In fact, in one of the final scenes it is suggested Manchester is such a new entity within the country that the Prince Regent is not really aware of its position as a significant place within his realm. This might be seen to echo the contemporary gulf often seen to exist between London (or the South-east) and "the North." One of the reasons frequently given for working-class people voting to leave the European Union in the 2016 referendum and for a raft of traditional Labour voters choosing to vote Conservative in the 2019 election was a feeling that Labour's London-based hierarchy was out of touch with ordinary working people outside of the capital. Contemporary social inequality is often seen to be between those who are "doing well" in London and those in the regions, especially "the North," who have been "left behind."[37] According to Philip McCann,

> ... by 2008 the typical gap in personal disposable household income per head between London and the large industrial regions of the midlands and north of England was now over 40 per cent of the UK average household disposable income per head.[38]

McCann goes on to say that in recent years this wealth gap has continued to grow, with the downturn in London after the 2008 global economic crisis being "less severe and shorter than in other regions."[39]

## VI

The sympathies expressed throughout *Peterloo* are clearly with working people. Before a scene in which the magistrates are shown gathered in a dark room full of shadows discussing what should be done about the planned protest meeting, we are given a tableau shot of three generations of working-class women sitting in bright sunlight peeling vegetables. As we go on to hear the magistrates discussing the working class as "polluting our streets" and as "ignorant souls" who "know not what they want," and as the magistrates put forward views suggesting what is required is "a show of military might" and "the iron hand of the law," all of this exists in our minds against the backcloth of the opening image of these generations of the working class. The shot of the women is unnecessary in terms of moving the plot forward, and for emphasis is held longer than necessary. It is deliberately chosen in order to contribute towards shaping our understanding of, and response to, the magistrates and their attitudes. Consistently, scenes showing Nellie and her family are well-lit and scenes showing the Manchester magistrates are dark and oppressive. The magistrates are permitted to express a range of views on the working class but all of them are condescending: they only understand force, they are too ignorant to know what they want, they just need to be kept well-fed and they will forget anything about "improving" society.

At the same time there are clear differences within the ranks of those who are in favour of reform. Hunt is seen as vain and self-important. He is, for example, reluctant to talk to Bamford (Neil Bell) and Joseph Healy (Ian Mercer) when they have traveled from Manchester to London to hear him speak. He is a landowner and from a different class to any of the other reformers we see in Manchester. It is also the case that the founders of the *Manchester Observer* seem to believe themselves to be slightly above ordinary working people. Furthermore, when we are shown a meeting of the Manchester Female Reform Society the differences between the middle-class and the working-class women in the room are apparent from their clothes, from what they have to say, and from the antagonism between them. And when we see working-class women marching to St. Peter's Field on the day of the demonstration, the filmmakers ensure we see and hear fellow working-class women heckling them and calling for them to "Get back to your husbands."

Leigh creates a drama in which we identify with the central working-class family, but it is not a drama with a single central hero. We begin with the

**Figure 5.2** A carefully placed and constructed shot of three generations of working-class women in *Peterloo* (Mike Leigh, 2018).

confusion of Joseph on the battlefield at Waterloo and we end seeing his burial after being run through at Peterloo; but Joseph is a completely ineffectual central protagonist in terms of his actions, and is reduced to the margins of the narrative almost immediately after the opening scenes. Yet in that position he is also a continual presence/absence against which we are asked to measure the events we see taking place. Similarly, in the same way in which there is no single "hero" in *Peterloo*, there is also no single antagonist. Instead, during the central scenes in the film we are shown a range of characters covering the full class spectrum from the gaudy pavilioned splendor enjoyed by the Prince Regent to the poverty of Nellie and Joshua's home; and since we see so many different characters we are never allowed to identify with any one character. We are deliberately denied this possibility. Instead, the structure of the scenes demands we should engage with the ideas that are at stake in each scene and attempt to conceptualize the socio-political structure of the whole society. This is an approach to filmmaking which adopts a particular ideas-driven, Brechtian theatrical style.[40] We are denied the escape of a plot-driven, action-centered narrative in the same way in which we are denied the possibility of character identification.

We are forced to consider the way in which everything about the society we see hinges on social inequality and status. Class distinctions determine your housing conditions, your working conditions, the clothes you wear, the food you eat, the language you use, your treatment before the law, etc.

Each scene makes clear to us the historical research that has been undertaken; but the interpretation of that history is as always a matter of political perspective. As we have said, Leigh begins the film by showing us a scared young man on a battlefield in the process of being traumatized by all he has seen, and he ends the film with the parents of this young man burying their son. Leigh has a message and an agenda. He has identified something about a moment in the past that he sees as relevant to the present and worth presenting to his audience: he works to demonstrate that the struggle of the poor in the early 1800s is in many ways the struggle of the poor today, and that the world inhabited by these characters is not so different to the world today. Both the opening scene and the final scene show us that it is the poor who pay the price for the decisions of those who are in power. Downturns in the economy in the early 1800s meant unemployment, poorer terms and conditions of work, lower pay, hunger, and debt for the poor; and, as zero hours contracts, food banks, and homelessness demonstrate, they mean the same today.

*Peterloo* presents the audience with a determined restatement of history and endorsement of the importance of history, and in particular the linearity of history. Postmodernism may suggest the search for a systematic explanation of relationships within human society is futile, but this film asserts the primacy of causality, of events existing in relation to each other and being linked to each other. The emphasis is on the concrete reality of the social conditions of existence found within a given society. The filmmakers play out the ongoing (historical and contemporary) crisis of the working class, and parallel to that the (similarly atemporal) exploitation of the majority by an influential minority. The difficulty is *Peterloo* seems unable to envisage any alternative to defeat for the working class and for socialism. When her son Robert says he does not blame her for giving up hope, as we have said, Nellie replies: "I haven't lost hope, son. I'll never lose hope. Times is too hard to lose hope. Hope is all we've got." That is as may be, but standing around your son's grave in the rain while reciting "Forgive us our trespasses as we forgive those who trespass against us" would not seem to leave the central working-class family in our film with that much hope. Nellie should perhaps be seen as a realist, believing she and her class must expect defeat after defeat, must not expect anything to be given to them, and yet must not give up hope. How bleak is that? The reformers and the radicals we are shown experience utter defeat; their attempt to take action and to change the world is comprehensively defeated by the forces of the state and the forces of capitalism. None of the characters responsible for the oppression of the working class—from the Prince Regent and Sidmouth, through Ethelston and the other magistrates to Nadin and Oliver—are punished. *Peterloo* necessarily leaves the audience envisaging that these characters continue into the future performing in the same way they have throughout the film. The film shows very clearly the oppression of the working classes by the middle and upper classes; and although there is some sense of community and fellow-feeling between those who are oppressed, it is fragile and constantly under threat. Nellie, who becomes the most prominent character and is made to perform the stereotypical role of the matriarch holding the family together, is conservative in her outlook. If she believes in anything it is the family, that most conservative of social institutions. In the end, all that is on offer is stoical acceptance of the way the world is ordered. A socialist film such as *Pride* (Matthew Warchus, 2014) turned the defeat of the Miners' Strike into a kind of feel-good victory but *Peterloo* only emphasizes the defeat. The danger with a feel-good movie is, of course, that it potentially leaves the audience with an entirely false sense of reality. This may also be the danger with an interpretation of the historical events of Peterloo such as that offered by E. P. Thompson when he suggested the outcry against the incident practically guaranteed the British the right of public protest. Leigh refuses these sorts of get-out clauses: he confronts the audience with the reality of defeat and (having clearly indicated his own assessment of the rights and wrongs through the presentation of his characters) leaves them to decide their response.

## Notes

1. Robert Poole, *The English Uprising: Peterloo* (Oxford: Oxford University Press, 2019), p. 1.
2. Samuel Bamford, *Passages in the Life of a Radical and Early Days: Volume II* (London: T. Fisher Unwin, 1905), p. 157.
3. Poole, *The English Uprising: Peterloo*, p. 1. According to Poole: "There were enough Waterloo veterans to keep up an annual dinner into the 1860s" (p. 233).
4. This legislation, which became known as the Six Acts, along with a "spate of press prosecutions—96 in 1819," according to Robert Goldstein, "succeeded in crushing the radical press and movement for a decade." See Robert J. Goldstein, *Political Repression in 19th Century Europe* (London and New York: Routledge, 1983/2010), p. 116.
5. Michael Scrivener, *Poetry and Reform: Periodical Verse from the English Democratic Press 1792–1824* (Detroit, MI: Wayne State University Press, 1992), p. 219.
6. E. P. Thompson, *The Making of the English Working Class* (Harmondsworth: Penguin, 1980), p. 780.
7. Jacqueline Riding, *Peterloo: The Story of the Manchester Massacre* (London: Head of Zeus, 2018), p. xii.
8. Samuel Bamford describes the marchers assembling in St. Peter's Field and the magistrates arriving and reading the Riot Act before "the meeting was soon afterwards dispersed by the military and special constables, and twenty-nine

persons were apprehended, amongst who were two young men, named Bagguley and Drummond, who had recently come into notice as speakers, and who being in favour of extreme measures, were much listened to and applauded." See Samuel Bamford, *Passages in the Life of a Radical and Early Days: Volume II*, p. 33. Bamford later names Bagguley and Drummond, along with "John Johnstone, of Manchester," as among an array of reformers held in prisons across the country (ibid., p. 112).

9. The uprising in Derbyshire led to three people being hanged and fourteen transported to Australia for life, but Oliver was exposed "in a series of sensational articles in the *Leeds Mercury*." See Kirsten McKenzie, *A Swindler's Progress: Nobles and Convicts in the Age of Liberty* (Cambridge, MA: Harvard University Press, 2010), p. 185. Referencing a George Cruickshank satirical print from the period showing three government spies, in a later book McKenzie says, "Oliver was by no means the only government agent exposed in this period." See Kirsten McKenzie, *Imperial Underworld: An Escaped Convict and the Transformation of the British Colonial Order* (Cambridge: Cambridge University Press, 2016), p. 89.

10. G. D. H. Cole and Raymond Postgate, *The Common People, 1746–1946* (London: Methuen, 1938/1961), p. 223.

11. At a reconstructed meeting of the Manchester Female Reform Society shown in the film, we hear how the workers came out on strike for seven weeks last year but were "beaten" back to work and ended with "nothing to show for it."

12. Donald Read says "by July 18th it was estimated that some twenty thousand spinning operatives were idle in the Manchester area" and that the weavers also struck at the end of August, but that in the end neither the spinners nor the weavers "gained anything." See Donald Read, *Peterloo: The "Massacre" and Its Background* (Manchester: Manchester University Press, 1958), pp. 103–4.

13. Riding, *Peterloo: The Story of the Manchester Massacre*, p. xi.

14. Ibid.

15. In a full appraisal of the use of this phrase, Edward J. Coss suggests Wellington's "attitude toward the lower social orders—which included the soldiers, who were primarily drawn from the labouring class—may reflect some of the prejudices of the affluent and powerful societal groups in Georgian England. Rural and urban laborers were often viewed as threats, lying in wait to upset the societal order, abscond with stolen goods, and overthrow those who held power." See Edward J. Coss, *All for the King's Shilling: The British Soldier Under Wellington, 1808–1814* (Norman: University of Oklahoma Press, 2010), pp. 37–8.

16. The Cotton Mills Act of 1819 prevented children under nine (!) working and reduced the hours of those under sixteen to seventy-two (!) per week.

17. The privileged position of a film viewer permits us to move between classes within a society where this would be impossible in the face of rigid class demarcations.

18. Percy Bysshe Shelley's poem "The Mask of Anarchy ('Written on the Occasion of the Massacre at Manchester')," completed in September 1819 but not published until 1832, is the most famous single piece of writing on Peterloo.

19. Discussing the Corn Law of 1815, Eric J. Evans explains: "This restricted the import of foreign corn into Britain; its primary purpose was to keep domestic prices high in the interests of farmers and landowners. It was denounced as 'class' legislation . . ." See Eric J. Evans, *The Great Reform Act of 1832* (London and New York: Routledge, 1983/2000), p. 30.
20. W. G. Hoskins, *The Making of the English Landscape* (Toller Fratrum: Little Toller Books, 1955/2013), p. 171.
21. Ibid., p. 164.
22. As an indicator of the way things were heading, under strengthening of the Game Laws in 1816 anyone found with a net for snaring rabbits was liable to a seven-year prison sentence whether they were actually caught poaching or not.
23. In *Ballads and Songs of Peterloo*, Alison Morgan cites a satirical poem attacking Reverend Charles Wicksted Ethelstone and entitled "Saint Ethelstone's Day," which appeared in the *Theological and Political Comet* in late 1819. See Alison Morgan, *Ballads and Songs of Peterloo* (Manchester: Manchester University Press, 2018), p. 180.
24. Samuel Bamford's poem "Ode to a Plotting Parson" was an attack on Reverend William Robert Hay. See Scrivener, *Poetry and Reform: Periodical Verse from the English Democratic Press 1792–1824*, pp. 274–6.
25. Morgan, *Ballads and Songs of Peterloo*, p. 3.
26. Even so, her words may be taken as ambiguous—the implication could be that political change has to be forced in some way because it will not be "given."
27. Anon., "The struggle for democracy: Getting the vote," National Archives, n.d. Available at http://www.nationalarchives.gov.uk/pathways/citizenship/struggle_democracy/getting_vote.htm (accessed 6 March 2020).
28. "'A New Song in Praise of the Weavers' by S. Wood, a Manchester shoemaker." See John Kirk, Andrew Noble, and Michael Brown (eds.), *United Islands? The Languages of Resistance* (London and New York: Routledge, 2016), p. 192.
29. See how this picks up themes from *Fanny Lye Deliver'd* (Chapter 3).
30. The historical figures of Knight and Saxton were two of those responsible for founding the *Manchester Observer* at the beginning of 1818. These two, along with Joseph Johnson who also worked on the paper, were arrested with Henry "Orator" Hunt as they stood on the speakers' platform in St. Peter's Field. See Morgan, *Ballads and Songs of Peterloo*, p. 26.
31. Carlile is a historical figure who was the publisher of *Sherwin's Weekly Political Register* (renamed *The Republican* later in 1819). He was tried for blasphemy and seditious libel in October 1819 and given a six-year gaol sentence. See Morgan, *Ballads and Songs of Peterloo*, p. 25.
32. As with so many others in this film, Joseph Nadin is a genuine figure from the time. He was referred to in songs from the period and was present at the arrest of radicals such as Samuel Bamford. He was central to the arrest of Hunt and others on the day of the massacre. See Morgan, *Ballads and Songs of Peterloo*, pp. 210–11 and p. 203.

33. "Joseph Nadin was deputy-constable of Manchester for more than twenty years. He resigned in March 1821." See John Harland, *Ballads and Songs of Lancashire, Ancient and Modern* (London: George Routledge, 1875), p. 195.
34. Rhodri Jeffreys-Jones, *We Know All About You: The Story of Surveillance in Britain and America* (Oxford: Oxford University Press, 2017), p. 238.
35. The account from Tyas was published in *The Times* on 19 August. See Morgan, *Ballads and Songs of Peterloo*, p. 10.
36. "In 1770 there was only one stagecoach to London and one to Liverpool, and these ran only twice a week, but by 1816 there were seventy distinct coaches; fifty-four set out every day and sixteen others three times a week." See John J. Parkinson-Bailey, *Manchester: An Architectural History* (Manchester and New York: Manchester University Press, 2000), p. 8.
37. This is not to ignore the fact that there are plenty of socio-economic groups within the South-east who could also be described as "left behind."
38. Philip McCann, *The UK Regional–National Economic Problem: Geography, Globalisation and Governance* (London and New York: Routledge, 2016), pp. 59–60.
39. Ibid., p. 63.
40. There are ways Leigh's film might remind us, stylistically and thematically, of *Serjeant Musgrave's Dance* (John Arden, 1959), directed by Lindsay Anderson when first performed at the Royal Court in London.

# Part II

# Rehearsing Twentieth-century British History

The following chapters consider some "classic" British film genres: the "upstairs-downstairs" drama, the war film, and films set within the context of the British Empire. Our interest is in how these genres have been utilized in recent films and what aspects of the past have been seen as applicable to the current state of the nation. A key focus will be on the role of cinema in consolidating national identity. This might equally be seen in other works from the period, such as *They Shall Not Grow Old* (Peter Jackson, 2018) and *1917* (Sam Mendes, 2019), which memorialize certain versions of the First World War. Some of the major issues emerging here will be to do with class and corresponding divisions of wealth and power; British social values, norms, and expectations; and concepts of nation and nationhood.

CHAPTER 6

# One-nation Conservatism 1920s/2020s: *Downton Abbey* (Michael Engler, 2019)

## I

The quick series of shots presented to the audience at the beginning of *Downton Abbey* (Michael Engler, 2019) operate in combination to create a familiar romantic vision of an England of idealized industrial power, dreamscape rural scenery, and solid imposing buildings that are seen not only to embody history but also to convey a sense of permanence. We see a steam train that turns out to be the overnight mail train, a small village with stone cottages and an ancient church, a sequence of images linked to the Royal Mail including a village post office, a quiet country road, and then, the culmination of all this, a country house set within an expansive landscape. Just as the train we see creates an impact not only in and of itself but also through the way in which it references the famous documentary short *Night Mail* (Harry Watt and Basil Wright, 1936), with words by W. H. Auden and music by Benjamin Britten, so the country house prompts the viewer to recall films and TV series that have employed the backdrop of a stately home, including *Brideshead Revisited* (ITV, 1981), *The Remains of the Day* (James Ivory, 1993), and *Gosford Park* (Robert Altman, 2001), and the TV series of *Downton Abbey* (ITV, 2010–15) that has preceded this film. However, what this stylized opening prefigures in the film is not something that can be easily dismissed as mere nostalgic yearning for a lost idyll; the political ideology at the heart of *Downton Abbey* is something much more fully formed than a vague desire for former glories. What may at first sight appear to be no more than that nebulous wistful longing repeatedly associated with heritage films is in fact a carefully woven advocacy of one-nation Conservatism.

*Downton Abbey* projects a clear political perspective from the outset. It engages with that concern within British politics generally seen to originate with the politician and novelist Benjamin Disraeli (1804–81), whereby the country is viewed as so divided that it is in effect "two nations." Disraeli's

**Figure 6.1** The country house as the culminating representation in a series of images of idealized England in the opening to *Downton Abbey* (Michael Engler, 2019).

novel *Sybil, or the Two Nations* (1845) contains the following celebrated statement of this position:

> "... say what you like, our Queen reigns over the greatest nation that ever existed." "Which nation?" asked the younger stranger, "for she reigns over two... Two nations; between whom there is no intercourse and no sympathy; who are as ignorant of each other's habits, thoughts, and feelings, as if they were dwellers in different zones, or inhabitants of different planets;"[1]

Andrew Vincent sums up the stance of this brand of conservatism that emerged from the observation of the divided state of the nation as being founded on the repudiation of three features of Victorian society: "wealth-making for its own sake, liberal individualism and class divisions."[2] "Disraelian conservatism," according to Vincent, attempts to achieve "improved industrial and social conditions" alongside "a renewed reverence for the Crown and the ancient constitution."[3] "In sum," he says, "its aim is 'one nation.'"[4] Michael Lind explains further that, as it has continued to develop, "one-nation Conservatism" is a political philosophy "that sees the purpose of the political elite as reconciling the interests of all classes, labor as well as management, instead of identifying the good of society with the business class."[5] "The Conservative Right," according to Kevin Hickson, opposes this form of conservatism, and would want to distinguish itself from this "moderate, or One Nation" wing of the Party, "which it would see as essentially liberal in character."[6]

Highlighting, first of all, the notion of "a renewed reverence for the Crown," we should notice how the opening sequence of images examined above works to link Buckingham Palace with the country as a whole: via a range of workers including servants, the Crown is connected to all parts of the kingdom. Although they may not realize it, each person we see has a role to play, a function within the interconnected network of the realm. When we begin to hear characters speaking, it immediately becomes clear there will be no suppression of opinion within the magical "one nation" world being constructed for us. Tom Branson (Allen Leech), who sits as an equal at the table with members of the aristocratic Grantham family, is straight-away identified as an Irish republican, and the assistant cook, Daisy (Sophie McShera), openly admits to sharing such sentiments. The enticing vision of a united country we are about to be given not only spectacularly ignores the socio-economic chasm between the aristocracy and their servants but at the same time demonstrates itself as being prepared to frankly present and accept diversity of thought.

The imagined world within which we find ourselves is both alluring and mesmerizing. In retirement the former butler at Downton Abbey, Carson (Jim Carter), is portrayed living a comfortable life in a pleasant house with a bountiful cottage garden. And yet, if we break out from the enchanting bubble constructed for us by the film we find reports from the early twentieth century, such as that by Violet Butler, *Domestic Service: Inquiry by the Women's Industrial Council*, recording that in point of fact the workhouse was the destination for many who left domestic service as soon as they became too old to continue in employment.[7] The reality of life as a servant in the first half of the twentieth century was much more one of class exploitation and the firm maintenance of social division between servants and employers than this film would seem to suggest. In her book *Feminism and the Servant Problem: Class and Domestic Labour in the Women's Suffrage Movement*, Laura Schwartz says servants faced problems with "low wages, terrible working conditions and authoritarian employers."[8] She quotes a letter from the *Glasgow Herald* in which a servant described her life in the following terms:

> This is my life—getting up at 6 o'clock, toiling on until 11 p.m. often later; liberty—a few hours at the end of the month... For the sake of supporting an elderly mother and myself I am in truth a slave, like many others, to idle gadabouts whose entertainment at afternoon tea consists of talking of our ignorance and dissecting our character.[9]

## II

The narrative of our focus film here revolves around the idea of a royal visit to Downton Abbey. The King and Queen, George V (Simon Jones) and Mary (Geraldine James), are to stay as part of their tour around Yorkshire and will be joined by their daughter, the Princess Mary (Kate Phillips). Carson is in awe at this prospect, not only because royalty will be visiting Downton Abbey but also because the Royal Household, that is to say, the King and Queen's servants, will be accompanying them. These are, as he says, people "who will have visited the greatest houses in the land: Blenheim, Chatsworth, Arundel." However, alongside this the film itself presents a series of questioning perspectives on the value, purpose, and usefulness of the monarchy. The above-stairs character Tom and the below-stairs character Daisy have both already self-identified as republican in their views, and at the dinner table, Isobel, or more formally, Lady Merton (Penelope Wilton), suggests the visit "seems rather a waste of money." In the servants' quarters, Daisy is querying the fuss that is being made "for a man and woman we don't even know," and even the head of the family, Robert Crawley, 7th Earl of Grantham (Hugh Bonneville) is making jokes about members of the royal family—"A shy Royal: is that an oxymoron?" Most importantly for the underlying political perspective of one-nation Conservatism, Isobel asserts: "Kind hearts are more than coronets, / And simple faith more than Norman blood." As everyone at the table knows, Isobel is quoting from a poem by Alfred Tennyson, "Lady Clara Vere de Vere,"[10][11] in which the poet asserts people's character is to be judged according to the goodness they display in the conduct of their life, and true nobility is not something that accrues simply by virtue of aristocratic birth. This is critical to the moral code advocated by the film: whichever station of life people may be born into, each person has an equal opportunity to display mental strength of character, independence of thought, and to choose to perform deeds that demonstrate compassionate fellow-feeling and a caring attitude. When he is talking to the Princess Mary, Tom explains why he is able to "love" the aristocratic Crawley family while at the same time often disagreeing with them politically. His explanation is that they are "decent at the core." Concepts such as "goodness" and "decency" may be difficult to define but they are not only the values emphasized by the film as being of paramount importance but also the principles advocated by one-nation Conservatism.

Employing the narrative device of the royal visit is crucial to the ideology of the film because from the political perspective being endorsed, the institution of the Crown sits at the top of a carefully structured and ordered way of life. Discussing the idea of Royalty with Tom, Princess Mary confidently asserts, "the Crawleys would die for the Crown if they had to." Significantly, she does not say the members of this upper-class family would die for the King, or for George V, but for the Crown. The Crown is the symbol of monarchy and here refers to the notion of a limited, constitutional monarchy that has slowly evolved over the course of hundreds of years of English history. It is the institution that symbolically guarantees the existence of an ordered society. Tom, the character with Irish roots who professes republican sympathies, is the one who prevents the assassination of the King. The would-be assassin, Major Chetwode (Stephen Campbell Moore), believed Tom's sympathies "lay with Ireland and the republic." However, although this may still be the case, Tom considers gaining the outcome of a united Ireland should not be "at any cost" and adds that he is now "a law and order man." Underpinning the script, again, is the notion of order: change may occur but it should take place as part of a gradual, evolutionary rather than revolutionary, process. The film proposes an English tradition of solidity and permanence, a history of change within continuity that creates social unity. In discussing film, Sarah Street, among others, recognizes history to be "an interpretative construct."[12] This is certainly what is on display here; and as such, in common with all other "interpretations" of history, it has the potential to shape and control our understanding of the past and, as a result, our relationship with the present. Street quotes Jeffery Klenotic's description of "the power of discourses about the past to alter reality and change history for the present."[13] Andrew Higson spoke of the way in which heritage films from the 1980s nostalgically reconstructed "an imperialist and upper class Britain" and promoted "'Englishness' as an ancient and natural inheritance."[14] And, as if to further emphasize the importance of monarchy to "Englishness," at the heart of *Downton Abbey* the filmmakers place a royal parade that culminates in the playing of the National Anthem.

## III

However, of course, this film is entitled *Downton Abbey* and as important as the monarchy (or the Crown) is to the ideology embodied here, the organization of the country house is even more significant. At various points through the film the audience is presented with long shots of Downton Abbey, a massive, imposing building rising out of the landscape, exuding a sense of solidity and permanence. The institution of the country house, here represented by Downton Abbey, functions as a microcosm of the nation and in its operation as fantasy manages to exclude any disturbing aspects of socio-economic conditions within the country. Under a certain "interpretative construct" of history, the country house could function as the definitive representation of the existence of two nations within England (or Britain), one rich and one poor, and yet, within the version of history presented here, it actually operates to create a sense of national unity in defiance of the clear and obvious presence of class divisions. The fiction with which the audience is presented smoothes the surface of potential dislocation and disunity. Even when the attempted assassination of the King threatens a catastrophic rupture of the social fabric, events are quickly brought under control and the solidity of the body politic maintained.

Despite the fact that, as Pamela Cox expresses it, each country house in reality depended on "a small army of servants working 17-hour days, all year round, with no modern technology,"[15] and the fact that there was a massive social gap between those living upstairs and those living downstairs, signified as Lucy Lethbridge suggests in the "proliferation of small passages" that "separated the kitchen, pantries and scullery regions from the main rooms of the English house,"[16] in *Downton Abbey* the servants feel they "own" the house as much as the Crawleys. They are intimately invested in an account of the social structure of the nation that is dependent on the continued existence of heavily staffed and well-maintained country houses. When the Royal Household descends on Downton Abbey and begins to take over the domestic running of the house, Daisy objects in the following terms: "I think it's rubbish: they impose, they demand, and now we're to be made nothing *in our own house*" (my italics). When Elsie Hughes (Phyllis Logan), the head housekeeper, is charged by a member of the Royal Household with meddling, her response is immediate: "Meddle, I don't believe I'm meddling *in my own house*, thank you" (my italics).

In her book *Servants: A Downstairs History of Britain from the Nineteenth Century to Modern Times*, Lethbridge says "employers and domestic advice manuals" from the period "stressed the 'innate' nature of the 'good' servant, the spiritual communion between hard domestic labour and Christian virtue."[17] This film takes the concept of the "good" servant to the point of perfection. When the new butler, Barrow (Robert James-Collier), finds that because he is felt to be out of his depth he is to be replaced for the duration of the royal visit by the former butler, Carson, he speaks back to the Earl of Grantham in a defiant manner. However, rather than being upset by this and sacking him, the Earl professes to being quite impressed, saying he had never thought of the butler as "a man of principle" before. Typically, the relationship between the family and servants is relaxed and comfortable, and this culminates in the putting out of the chairs for the royal parade. There is no real narrative requirement for this scene to be in the film, it does not move the story on, it does not provide any crucial development of character, but it does give concrete expression to one-nation Conservatism. It is late at night, it is raining heavily, and the chairs have not been set out ready for the royal visit due the next day. You might think the point to having servants is that at moments such as this you can simply send them out to get the job done, but that is not what happens. Instead, members of the family and servants work together to achieve a common goal. One relationship crystallizes what it is essential for the audience to appreciate: her maid, Anna Bates (Joanne Froggatt), realizes Lady Mary (Michelle Dockery) intends going outside to organize the layout of the chairs, and so she too insists on helping. The short scene ends with Lady Mary exclaiming, "You're a good *friend* to me, Anna," and her maid responding with, "I hope we're good *friends* to each other, m'lady" (my italics). On their own the words fail to convey the warmth of the exchange given via the acting, cinematography, and lighting, but as with the subsequent action of the family and the servants working in unison in the rain to get the job done, what is clear is that this is a comfortable coming together of the upper and lower classes. At the same time, this scene also prepares the way for a later exchange between Lady Mary and Anna in which Lady Mary wonders whether it is time to sell Downton Abbey and give up this way of life. She muses aloud to Anna:

> Isn't it time to chuck in the towel? Lots of people have. We could sell it for a school, or an old people's home or something, and buy a manor house with a modest estate and live a normal life . . . I want everything to stop being such a struggle . . . When I was putting up the chairs in the rain I kept thinking, "What am I doing?"

Leaving aside for now Lady Mary's belief that buying "a manor house with a modest estate" would equate to living "a normal life," Anna's response is critical to our understanding of the film as a whole. She responds:

> I'll tell you what you're doing m'lady, you're making a centre for the people who work here, for this village, for the county. Downton Abbey is the beating heart of this community and you're keeping it beating.

Anna puts into words the keynote of *Downton Abbey*: the indispensable importance of the country house and the way of life that exists around it to England and to the English way of life. As such, *Downton Abbey* is a celebration of division and inequality; both the characters and the audience are not only expected to be content in the face of a society displaying massive social inequality but to celebrate the fact of such inequality and understand it to be the essence of who they are and what they would want to be. The film works to define the nation and to define Britishness (or more correctly, England and Englishness), viewing it as being built on the foundation of class difference. This is seen not as a weakness but as the strength of the country. Within this vision, unity and cohesion is achieved through each member of society accepting their role within the fabric of the nation, and the film rejoices in the resulting version of Britishness. It is the layering of society as rich and poor, master and servant, that gives Britain its form, structure, and greatness, and it is because of their acceptance of this order that the different levels of society are able to work together at times of crisis. There is an expectation on the part of the lower orders that the upper echelons should display their rank and status. Those in domestic service celebrate the wealth and splendour of upper-class life as much as, if not more than, the upper classes; and the upper classes perform their wealth and splendor in such a way as to satisfy a requirement in the lower orders to be able to take pride in the whole aristocratic-cum-royal-cum-imperial edifice. Each class is fulfilling its role within a unique expression of nationhood, and this political perspective is embodied in the totality of what we are shown as being "Downton Abbey." Higson quotes the observation of Alun Howkins that a ruralist response to modernity depended on "ideas of continuity, of community or harmony, and above all a kind of classlessness" establishing the sense of "an organic and natural society of ranks, and inequality in an economic and social sense, but one based on trust, obligation and even love."[18]

## IV

However, it is crucial to note that within the rigorously structured society with which we are presented, each character, whether they are within the upper or

**Figure 6.2** The upper class and the servant class, Lady Mary (Michelle Dockery) and Anna Bates (Joanne Froggatt), working together to lay out the chairs for the royal visit in *Downton Abbey*.

lower classes, is provided with the possibility of taking up a strong degree of independence of thought and action. Alongside the necessary subservience required to be shown by servants to the acknowledged elite of society, each character in the film that shows a willingness to accept their role within the overall structure is given their own sense of agency. The implication is that whatever level of society you may have been born into, you are able to "grow" as a person and demonstrate the "best" qualities open to human beings to exhibit. Social mobility does exist; individuals are able to "advance" themselves, but in the film this is seen to be on the basis of individual worth and strength of character.[19] In this Arcadian representation of society in England between the wars, which through engaging the audience in a process of nostalgic longing is carried through into the twenty-first century, social advancement is seen not in economic terms but in terms of personal development. Life "in service" in the great country houses of England is about playing your role in working together to achieve social cohesion, not through equality but through unity of purpose. Each character we see is judged by their contribution towards this end; each action that takes place is understood in terms of the extent to which it works towards, or detracts from, the achievement of this end.

As we have seen, whether they are a member of the family or a servant, each character who is judged as "good" by the film feels Downton Abbey (that is to say, England) belongs to them. There is a sense of ownership but also of personal belonging[20] and, even more importantly, a sense of stewardship of the house and associated way of life. In order to illustrate this still further, we are shown members of the Royal Household who arrive in Downton Abbey being taught the lesson that rank within society has to be earned, that you cannot arrogantly attempt to impose yourself on others or it will result in rebellion. They need to learn that status in the eyes of others is to be measured in terms of true nobility, that is to say in terms of your inner worth and humanity, which is not necessarily related to birth or social rank. The examination taking place in the film as a whole is into which characters will display true nobility. Given the circumstances of life into which characters have been born and over which they have had no control, each is able to display decency, and also good (common) sense, without regard to the level of society they may currently occupy.

The values that emerge from all of this are seen as a national heritage that needs to be passed on to future generations. And this way of life has one further important aspect to it: integral to it is not only an acceptance of change but an embrace of liberal-nuanced social evolution which is seen both as welcome and inevitable. Even the most passionate upholder of traditional values, the elderly Violet Crawley, the Dowager Countess of Grantham

(Maggie Smith), is aware things will not (cannot) stay the same across historical time. "Our ancestors lived different lives from us and our descendants will live differently again, but Downton Abbey will be part of them," she says. Of course, it is the values for which Downton Abbey stands that she is talking about more than the building itself.

Following on from this, a series of incidents in the film indicate that at all levels of society women will have increased independence and rights in the future, and that men will take more interest in their children and their wives' pregnancies. The assistant cook, Daisy, is assertive in telling the footman, Andy Parker (Michael C. Fox): "We'll get wed when we're good and ready and not before." Among the upper classes, the film repeatedly implies criticism of the patriarchal attitudes of Henry, Viscount Lascelles (Andrew Havill), who haughtily dominates his wife and children. At the same time, the expectations of ordinary people are seen to be increasing. Daisy and Tony Sellick (James Cartwright), a plumber, agree not only that they expect more from life than previous generations but also that they are determined to have more. What *Downton Abbey* points out, however, is that these are people who are prepared to work to improve their lot: the plumber says he doesn't mind long hours because he intends to build his own business, "and you can't do that working nine to five." By way of contrast, the film presents the audience with the case of Miss Lawton (Susan Lynch), who has a different solution to the relative poverty of her life: she steals small items from each of the houses she works in. By way of explanation, she says to Anna: "Doesn't it ever worry you that on each table in this house there's an ornament you couldn't buy with a year's wages?" As with the Irish republican, Major Chetwode, who attempts to assassinate the King,[21] Miss Lawton is constructed as an isolated figure within the film. She is portrayed as a cold, self-centered individual who has no sense of belonging to a wider community. And yet, although we can see how she illustrates an incorrect way to conduct yourself within one-nation Conservatism, because of the truth inherent in her comment quoted above, she (like Major Chetwode, who highlights the intractability of what has commonly been described as "the Irish question") threatens to rupture the smooth surface of the political perspective promoted by the film.

## V

*Downton Abbey* is set just one year after the General Strike, in which the Trades Union Congress called out more than one and a half million workers in support of the country's one million coal miners, who were facing substantial pay cuts.[22] The strike continued for nine days during May before being called off by the TUC. In the film, the King references this by commenting, "Things seem calmer in the north." To which Cora Crawley, Countess of Grantham (Elizabeth McGovern), replies: "You mean after the strikes, sir? Yes, if calmer means more resigned." Commenting on the General Strike, Keith Laybourn maintains, "No event has ever divided the nation so sharply along class lines or produced so much bitterness."[23] Yet in watching this film there is no sense of this being a divided nation, quite the reverse; nor is there much indication the servant class is simply grudgingly "resigned" to their lot in life. Issues such as the position of women in society and the persecution of homosexuals are given a strong presence within individual storylines in such a way as to point reassuringly towards the achievement of more liberal contemporary values and attitudes. The struggle for Irish independence features within one of the main narrative strands, but in such a way as to allow it to be safely contained, defeated, and brought under control. Most interesting of all, however, is the way in which Miss Lawton's awareness of the gulf between rich and poor is given very little narrative traction. Her question, "Doesn't it ever worry you that on each table in this house there's an ornament you couldn't buy with a year's wages?" comes from nowhere and goes nowhere. It intrudes into the script and sits there, worryingly, naggingly. Andrew Higson has identified the way in which heritage films invite "a nostalgic gaze that resists the ironies and social critiques so often suggested narratively by these films."[24]

In the opening to her TV series *Servants: The True Story of Life Below Stairs*, Pamela Cox says, "A century ago, one and a half million of us worked as servants; astonishingly, that's more than worked in industries, or on the land . . . I want to dispel the nostalgia and fantasies we have around domestic service."[25] Cox reminds us just how much work went on in country houses. As mentioned above, Cox tells us servants worked "17-hour days, all year round, with no modern technology."[26] And despite the fact that the labour movement was beginning to organize itself in the early twentieth century and "was transforming life in Britain's shops and factories, fighting for everything from safety laws and the inspection of conditions to strict limits on working hours,"[27] the conditions and hours of work for domestic servants remained largely unchallenged. Perhaps the most interesting thing about *Downton Abbey* is that none of the servants ever seems to be doing any work. The men may serve at table, the women may have their hands in a bowl on a table in the kitchen, but there is no sense of the hours of drudgery and sheer hard graft that was required. Cox concludes her series of programmes by saying country houses that have survived into the twenty-first century and are open to the public are "a vital part of our heritage industry" and are visited by thousands of people every year.[28] She acknowledges that these houses "give us a window into the world of service" but adds that for her it is a window that is only "partially open" and concludes that the view we get through this window "is pretty rose-tinted," while "the memories of most who experienced service were anything but rose-tinted."²⁹ Cox's overall verdict is that:

> Often the fantasy of service presented in these houses is tinged with a sentimental nostalgia: old-fashioned cooking implements, retro household wares, and beautifully recreated foodstuffs from cheeses to game, are all carefully arranged in the pristinely clean, elegantly painted servants' quarters.³⁰

Her words are equally applicable to *Downton Abbey*.

Certainly Margaret Powell, writing in the late 1960s about her time in service in the 1920s, painted anything but a rosy picture of life "below stairs." Talking about employers, she says:

> They didn't worry about the long hours you put in, the lack of freedom and the poor wages, so long as you worked hard and knew that God was in Heaven and that He'd arranged for it that you lived down below and laboured, and that they lived upstairs in comfort and luxury . . .³¹

She says when you went into service "you'd say goodbye to all personal freedom."³² Servants were "not real people with minds and feelings," she adds, but rather "possessions."³³ Her verdict on all of this is that ". . . there were two nations when I was fifteen, and now I'm sixty-one I still think that there are two nations in this country . . . Just give us a period of high unemployment and you'll see what I mean."³⁴

What we might begin to recognize is that when the plumber in the film volunteers the information that he is not afraid to work long hours, this is something that is entirely relevant to the period in which the film is set (but also to today). The struggle being taken on by the labor movement in the period was as much to do with terms and conditions of employment, essentially the number of hours to be worked, as it was wages. In coal mining, local agreements across the country meant the hours worked by miners varied, but in the early 1920s in Durham those working at the coalface "worked days of between six and six and three-quarter hours."³⁵ After the General Strike the government introduced a bill "allowing mine-owners to extend by one hour the length of the working day."³⁶ Prior to this, the Sankey Commission set up in 1919 to consider the future of the coal-mining industry, including hours to be worked, had been unable to agree and had produced three different reports. The miners' union supported one of these reports, which recommended a seven-hour day to be cut to six hours in 1921, "if economically possible."³⁷ What we find is that during the early twentieth century the pressure for reduced working days was mounting across Europe (and in the United States). Summarizing the situation, Peter Scott and Anna Spadavecchia say:

> ... some form of eight-hour legislation had been adopted by most western European countries by autumn 1919, and by most other industrial nations over the next two years. Meanwhile Britain, Italy and the US had moved to a 48-hour standard by collective agreements rather than legislation.[38]

In Britain, in the mining industry "The Seven Hours Act of 1919 reduced working hours for all miners to seven per shift"[39] and in the iron and steel industry "a national eight-hour day" was agreed with employers in the same year.[40] This was a big issue in the period, and for anyone with the necessary historical knowledge the plumber's comment about "9 to5" (as with Miss Lawton's brief mention of the gap between rich and poor) threatens to breach the film's cosy surface nostalgia.

At the same time, the "work" entailed in domestic service was a difficult subject both for the labor movement and for any theoretical discussion of capitalism. Not only was this mostly women's work[41] but it also took place in the home rather than in factories or offices. Work conducted in the domestic sphere is not directly "productive" labor; it does not produce any immediately obvious goods that can be sold within the marketplace to create profit and so poses problems for a classical Marxist interpretation of capitalism.[42] Schwartz highlights a wide disinclination in society "to define domestic labour as *real* work," which has ensured "it was, and still is, undervalued and underpaid."[43] Socialist feminists in the 1970s and 1980s argued capitalism depended on domestic labor in order both to maintain the current workforce and to raise succeeding generations of workers.[44] Schwartz highlights the work of Leonore Davidoff, who "maintained that industrial capitalism was founded upon the unwaged and low paid labour of housewives and domestic servants in the family home" and asserted that servants were not unproductive "but, to the contrary, performed the crucial ideological and material labour of class formation."[45]

In line with what is being suggested here, Lucy Delap highlights the way in which in the late twentieth and early twenty-first centuries "domestic service became a site of nostalgia or fantasy," but goes on to link this to the way in which at the same time there has also been "a resurgence of paid domestic work."[46] She says, "British audiences are commonly invited to perceive domestic service as an institution of the past rather than as a feature of contemporary society."[47] And yet, at the same time,

> From an early-twenty-first-century perspective, there is nothing inevitable about the demise of servant-keeping; it no longer looks like a "feudal",

anachronistic institution that is obsolete in a modern, individualistic, secular democratic society, as many argued in the 1970s.[48]

Lethbridge says, "Some estimates suggest there were as many domestics in London in 2011 as there were in the nineteenth century."[49] She adds:

> The privilege of employing a domestic in the developed West reflects the economic hardship of the country from which the domestic originates. Few women would choose to enter domestic service as a cleaner: it entails long hours and low wages.[50]

To which we should only add the question of what it might say about Britain if the "domestic" originated (i.e. was born) not abroad but in the UK? The danger of both *Downton Abbey* and the heritage industry in general is that there is the potential for audiences to be duped into failing to see not only the past but also the present with any genuine historical clarity. Scott Magelssen discusses "living history museums" in terms of the way in which they "do not merely represent the past; they make historical 'truth' for the visitor."[51] These museums, he says, are "historiographic operations, that is, they produce history, as does any textbook, history film, or classroom lecture."[52] Janet Staiger clears a starting point for us when approaching films such as this (or indeed any other aspects of the heritage industry) when she reminds us different interpretations of the past are not random but have their origins in "social, political, and economic conditions" and are related to "constructed identities such as gender, sexual preference, race, ethnicity, class and nationality."[53] Schwartz takes us back to these sorts of starting points when she tells us "the number of domestic workers globally grew by almost 20 million between 1995 and 2010," and that in the UK "around 448,400 people worked as cleaners across the industry in 2010, employed by as many as one in ten British households, and 37 per cent of those in England were migrant workers."[54] Global inequality, she concludes, has been crucial "to delivering cheap labour back into British homes."[55] *Downton Abbey* should be viewed not only in relation to the stark social divisions to be found during the period within which the film is set but also against the backdrop of the (in many ways) similar social divisions existing during the period of the film's production.

### Notes

1. Benjamin Disraeli, *Sybil, or the Two Nations* (Ware: Wordsworth Editions, 1995/1845), p. 58.
2. Andrew Vincent, *Modern Political Ideologies* (Oxford and Malden, MA: Wiley-Blackwell, 2010/1992), p. 65.

3. Ibid.
4. Ibid.
5. Michael Lind, *Up From Conservatism* (New York and London: Simon & Schuster, 1997), p. 45.
6. Kevin Hickson, *Britain's Conservative Right since 1945: Traditional Toryism in a Cold Climate* (London: Palgrave Macmillan, 2019), p. 4.
7. C. Violet Butler, *Domestic Service: Inquiry by the Women's Industrial Council* (London: G. Bell, 1916), pp. 68–70.
8. Laura Schwartz, *Feminism and the Servant Problem: Class and Domestic Labour in the Women's Suffrage Movement* (Cambridge: Cambridge University Press, 2019), p. 3.
9. *Glasgow Herald*, 23 September 1913, p. 3, quoted in Schwartz, *Feminism and the Servant Problem: Class and Domestic Labour in the Women's Suffrage Movement*, p. 4.
10. Alfred Tennyson, *Poems, Volume I* (Boston: William D. Ticknor, 1842), pp. 155–8.
11. There might be further complications with employing Tennyson as a key literary reference. Tom Paulin characterizes Tennyson as "imperialist, racist, reactionary, sexist" (see Tom Paulin, *Thomas Hardy: The Poetry of Perception* (London: Macmillan, 1975/1986), p. 5). Nationalism is the very essence of his poem, "The Defence of Lucknow" (1879)—"Handful of men as we were, we were English in heart and limb, / Strong with the strength of race to command, to obey, to endure."
12. Sarah Street, *British Cinema in Documents* (London and New York: Routledge, 2000), p. 1.
13. Jeffery Klenotic, "The Place of Rhetoric in 'New' Film Historiography: The Discourse of Corrective Revisionism," in *Film History* 6 (1), 1994, p. 57, quoted in Street, *British Cinema in Documents*, p. 2.
14. Andrew Higson, "Re-presenting the National Past: Nostalgia and Pastiche in the Heritage Film," in Lester Friedman (ed.), *British Cinema and Thatcherism* (London: UCL Press, 1996), p. 110.
15. Pamela Cox, *Servants: The True Story of Life Below Stairs, Part 1: Knowing Your Place*, 5 April 2017, BBC4.
16. Lucy Lethbridge, *Servants: A Downstairs History of Britain from the Nineteenth Century to Modern Times* (New York and London: W. W. Norton, 2013), p. 19.
17. Ibid., p. xi.
18. Alun Howkins, "The Discovery of Rural England," in Robert Colls and Philip Dodd (eds.), *Englishness: Politics and Culture, 1880–1920* (Croom Helm: London, 1986), pp. 75 and 80, quoted in Andrew Higson, *Waving the Flag: Constructing a National Cinema in Britain* (Oxford: Oxford University Press, 1995), p. 42.
19. Tom and Lucy Smith (Tuppence Middleton) would be the obvious characters to consider in this regard.
20. Tom, who has risen from chauffeur to a member of the Crawley family, is aware of the need to "belong," saying of his daughter that she "belongs here now," i.e. at Downton Abbey. "I spent so much of my life not belonging anywhere, that's important to me," he adds.

21. When he mentions his hope for "a free Ireland," Lady Mary challenges Chetwode, "Isn't it free now?" and through repetition of the word "free" that forces reflection on what is meant by the term, she creates a momentary threat to the persuasiveness of the heritage idyll. She also draws attention to the strained nature of Tom's personal position on the matter.
22. Keith Laybourn, *The General Strike of 1926* (Manchester and New York: Manchester University Press, 1993), pp. 1–2.
23. Ibid., p. 1.
24. Andrew Higson, "Re-presenting the National Past: Nostalgia and Pastiche in the Heritage Film," in Lester Friedman (ed.), *British Cinema and Thatcherism* (London: UCL Press, 1996), p. 109.
25. Pamela Cox, *Servants: The True Story of Life Below Stairs, Part 1: Knowing Your Place*, 5 April 2017, BBC4.
26. Ibid.
27. Pamela Cox, *Servants: The True Story of Life Below Stairs, Part 2: Class War*, 12 April 2017, BBC4.
28. Pamela Cox, *Servants: The True Story of Life Below Stairs, Part 3: No Going Back*, 19 April 2017, BBC4.
29. Ibid.
30. Ibid.
31. Margaret Powell, *Below Stairs: The Bestselling Memoirs of a 1920s Kitchen Maid* (London: Pan Books, 2011/1968), p. 76.
32. Margaret Powell, *Climbing the Stairs: Further Tales of a 1920s Kitchen Maid* (London: Pan Books, 2011/1969), p. 2.
33. Ibid.
34. Ibid., p. 3.
35. Hester Barron, *The 1926 Miners' Lockout: Meanings of Community in the Durham Coalfield* (Oxford: Oxford University Press, 2010), p. 67.
36. Ibid., p. 28.
37. Anne Perkins, *A Very British Strike: 3 May–12 May 1926* (London: Macmillan, 2006), p. 13.
38. Peter Scott and Anna Spadavecchia, "Did the 48-hour week damage Britain's industrial competitiveness?" *Economic History Review*, 64 (4), 2011, p. 1271.
39. Ibid., p. 1276.
40. Ibid., p. 1285.
41. Domestic service was "the most common of all entry-level jobs available to young women until World War Two." See Lucy Delap, "Housework, Housewives, and Domestic Workers: Twentieth-Century Dilemmas of Domesticity," *Home Cultures*, 8 (2), July 2011, p. 190.
42. Leonore Davidoff says, "... through the mid-twentieth century domestic servants were a taken-for-granted part of the social landscape, of less than passing interest to mainstream and Marxist economists alike. They regarded service as unproductive labour because it added nothing defined as of economic value and was carried on outside a recognized workplace." See Leonore Davidoff, *Worlds*

*Between: Historical Perspectives on Gender and Class* (Cambridge: Polity Press, 1995), p. 3.
43. Schwartz, *Feminism and the Servant Problem: Class and Domestic Labour in the Women's Suffrage Movement*, p. 21.
44. Laura Schwartz, "Karl Marx and Domestic Servants: A historical overview of Marx's and Marxist thinking on domestic workers, reproductive labour and class struggle," 2019, p. 7. Available at https://www.academia.edu/42641042/Karl_Marx_and_Domestic_Servants_A_historical_overview_of_Marxs_and_Marxist_thinking_on_domestic_workers_reproductive_labour_and_class_struggle> (accessed 13 October 2020).
45. Ibid., p. 10.
46. Lucy Delap, *Knowing Their Place: Domestic Service in Twentieth-Century Britain* (Oxford: Oxford University Press, 2011), p. 4.
47. Ibid., p. 22.
48. Ibid., p. 3.
49. Lethbridge, *Servants: A Downstairs History of Britain from the Nineteenth Century to Modern Times*, p. 324.
50. Ibid.
51. Scott Magelssen, *Living History Museums: Undoing History Through Performance* (Lanham, MD: Scarecrow Press, 2007), p. xii.
52. Ibid.
53. Janet Staiger, *Interpreting Films: Studies in the Historical Reception of American Cinema* (Princeton, NJ: Princeton University Press, 1992), p. xi.
54. Schwartz, "Karl Marx and Domestic Servants: A historical overview of Marx's and Marxist thinking on domestic workers, reproductive labour and class struggle," pp. 8–9.
55. Ibid.

CHAPTER 7

# Defending this "Island Nation": *Darkest Hour* (Joe Wright, 2017) and *Churchill* (Jonathan Teplitzky, 2017)

I

Three films about wartime Britain with overlapping material were released in 2017. *Darkest Hour* (Joe Wright, 2017) reached the cinema alongside the much-heralded *Dunkirk* (Christopher Nolan, 2017) and the much lower-budget production *Churchill* (Jonathan Teplitzky, 2017). *Darkest Hour* provides a fictional account of events occurring around the key pivotal moment in Winston Churchill's career when he became Prime Minister in 1940 and immediately faced the potentially catastrophic defeat of British forces in France. In a lightning attack in early May, Germany had invaded Holland and Belgium, and crossed the border into France. Before the end of the month, British and French forces were hemmed in around Dunkirk and it looked likely the whole British Expeditionary Force would be captured. Both *Darkest Hour* and *Dunkirk* concentrate on these events. *Darkest Hour* covers the behind-the-scenes political machinations in London during this time, and *Dunkirk* considers the evacuation process from the perspectives of a range of fictional characters involved in the operation on the ground. *Darkest Hour* follows Churchill throughout the period as debates in the War Cabinet intensify over whether it is possible to continue to fight, or whether military defeat is inevitable and peace negotiations need to begin. Although we are given some information about plans to rescue the troops from Dunkirk—we see a massive flotilla of small boats setting out on the rescue mission on 28 May against a backdrop of the White Cliffs of Dover, and an on-screen caption at the end tells us, "Almost all of the 300,000 troops at Dunkirk were carried home by Winston's civilian fleet"—the evacuation is not the main substance of this film in the way that it is for *Dunkirk*. The third film, *Churchill*, shifts attention from the early phase of the war to the end of the war, focusing on Churchill's supposed uncertainty over the planned D-Day landings in Normandy in 1944.[1]

Coming together like this, these three films highlight a common feature of British culture since 1945, which has been the way in which it has consistently resorted to speaking about, and thereby attempting to understand, the present in terms relating to the Second World War. Certainly in the manner in which they were reviewed, these films were immediately seen in relation to this paradigm. Referring to all three films, Ian Jack suggested:

> The origins of these films, as far as one can tell, had nothing to do with Europhobia or the nationalism that was gathering in provincial England... Nonetheless, the films have come to be seen as a reflection and endorsement of the Brexit mood... According to reports, Churchill's "fight them on the beaches" speech that closes *Darkest Hour* has brought cinema audiences to their feet; and in *Dunkirk* there has been applause when an officer, asked why he will stick it out on the bomb-strafed pier, replies with the word "Hope." These reactions suggest an England congratulating itself on its past—an idealised past, shorn of inconvenient fact.[2]

Writing near the cinema release of the films, Steve Rose was sure about the way in which events of the Second World War were being culturally appropriated:

> It's not just Dunkirk: the second world war as a whole has been co-opted as a myth of English exceptionalism and isolationism. Churchill is the Brexiters' patron saint. They are always banging on about him... More than ever, nostalgia has become a major component of British cinema, and very little of it seriously challenges or questions our ossified English self-image.[3]

In the same vein, the editors of *New Perspectives on the War Film* claim *Dunkirk* "reflects contemporary British concerns around issues such as Brexit, the rising anti-immigration sentiment, and the current political moments of seemingly endless war via terrorism and a world in general crisis."[4] Meanwhile, Rudolph Adam, without directly referencing these films, highlights the thematic links that might ally Second World War films to a particular side in the Brexit referendum:

> Leave... had connotations of resolve, power, daring, unflappable courage, relief, and liberation... Remaining in the EU was made to appear as the risk... that would wipe out all Britishness and, even more important, all Englishness... Remain implied encroaching terror, tsunamis of immigrants, and a long march into the European superstate under German hegemony... Leave, on the other hand, presented the nostalgically embellished return to a rural, bucolic village life, to imperial greatness and to those plucky virtues that had made the English the toughest race on earth.[5]

During the debacle-cum-miracle of Dunkirk in which the British Expeditionary Force was pushed back by German forces into a small enclave on the French coast, and then, through a combination of luck and improvisation, managed a last-minute evacuation, British troops, commanders, and politicians did have to show "resolve," "daring," and "courage." At this time, Churchill and those who were backing him, such as Clement Attlee, the leader of the Labour Party, were attempting to rouse an energetic sense of patriotism integral to concepts of "Britishness" and "Englishness." Clearly, in line with Adam's analysis of the Brexit vote, what they were fighting against was Germany taking over the whole of Europe, and just as clearly what they were attempting to tap into was a sense of Britain's "imperial greatness," in other words, a sense of nationalism that had long been inculcated in generations of Britons. Adam's analysis of Brexit suggests political campaigners and cultural commentators are able to take advantage of these assumed national traits at the point of more contemporary historical junctures that are seen to parallel the by now mythical Dunkirk moment.

## II

Seen within these wider cultural contexts, the conscious intentions of the filmmakers responsible for *Darkest Hour* are not really important since the film exists, not in relation to what they believe they are attempting to "say" through their work, but in relation to its position within the socio-historical contexts of the time in which it is viewed. However, so prominent is the central character of Churchill that views about the film depend almost entirely on each audience member's understanding of this man who was Britain's Prime Minister during almost the whole of the Second World War but was then decisively thrown out of office in elections just before the end of the war. Churchill is commonly seen as among the most eminent of British heroes, and yet he is also a controversial figure in British history. In a BBC poll conducted in 2002 he was voted the greatest Briton of all time, but during the Black Lives Matter protests of early June 2020 his statue in Parliament Square was daubed with the words, "was a racist." *Darkest Hour* is essentially a biographical reading of a short period of time often seen as critical for an understanding of Churchill.

In the film, as an aide is about to lead him to a chauffeur-driven car that is to take him to see George VI (Ben Mendelsohn), who is to ask him to become Prime Minister, Churchill (Gary Oldman) announces, "Lead on, Macduff." The words are misquoted from Act 5 Scene 8 of *Macbeth*:

> I will not yield . . . Before my body
> I throw my warlike shield. *Lay on, Macduff,* [my italics]
> And damn'd be him that first cries, "Hold, enough!"

And, in reflecting on the way the film sets out to view Churchill, the question as to whether these words are a deliberate misquotation from Shakespeare or not, may (or may not) be crucial. The lines are spoken by Macbeth, the central character in the play, who is an anti-hero rather than hero, in that he is associated with evil and over-reaching ambition, as he is refusing to surrender. The person he is addressing, Macduff, is the hero of the moment, who is about to kill Macbeth and save his country from tyranny. So, where does this position Churchill in our film? If he is the hero, he should be Macduff about to defeat evil. If he is Macbeth, he becomes an Aguirre-like figure[6] more akin to Hitler than a saviour of the western world. What are the filmmakers implying about Churchill? That he uses quotations in an apparently knowledgeable fashion but does not actually understand the contexts of the phrases he co-opts to his own use? That the role generally ascribed to him as a hero is questionable? That he is full of overblown ambition?

The position of the filmmakers in relation to this moment from history may (or may not) be made somewhat clearer through the use of two props: one is a painting entitled "Whistlejacket" by George Stubbs, which is first seen when in 1940 the King is told by the current Prime Minister, Neville Chamberlain (Ronald Pickup), that he needs to appoint Churchill as the new PM, and the second is a painting, "Horse Attacked by a Lion" by the same artist, seen as the King actually invites Churchill to form a new government. The horse, Whistlejacket, was viewed as temperamental and difficult to handle. It had a strong pedigree but its racing career never really matched up to this, and at the time it was painted by Stubbs it had been put out to stud for about ten years. The painting has been described by Jonathan Jones as "a romantic study in solitude and liberty."[7] Since the painting has no background—the horse is set against a plain green backdrop—and this is extremely unusual for the period, it has been speculated it is unfinished and both the rider and the context have yet to be completed. Intriguingly, there are a series of paintings by Jacques-Louis David completed in the early 1800s that show a horse in a similar stance being ridden by Napoleon.[8] There might be seen to be a range of parallels between this horse, this painting, and Churchill's position in 1940. The second painting, "Horse Attacked by a Lion," might be seen as being humorous, since the King admits later in the film to being scared of Churchill. However, more seriously, Britain is at this moment in 1940 in the process of being savaged by an altogether more powerful enemy. Furthermore, reversing the roles, Churchill is about to embody in his oratory the lion, which has long been employed as a heraldic symbol embodying English nationalism. In painting this subject Stubbs was, at one level, demonstrating his interest in the concept of the sublime. As Edmund Burke explained this idea, while straightforward beauty is calming, the sublime is terrifying and disturbing. That is to say, this is a form of excitement that depends upon and is increased by terror. According to Burke, the sublime "comes upon us in the gloomy forest, and in the howling wilderness, in the form of the lion, the tiger, the panther, or the rhinoceros."[9] All of this seems as if it may be appropriate for Britain's position in 1940. Going further, we might note these paintings are dated to 1762 and 1763 respectively. In other words, Stubbs is painting these images at the end of the Seven Years War (1756–63), in which after a catastrophic start to hostilities for Great Britain, William Pitt the Elder, had been put in charge of the war and totally turned things around. Like Churchill, Pitt came from a highly privileged background—Eton and Trinity College, Oxford, rather than Churchill's Harrow and Sandhurst. Like Churchill, Pitt was considered a powerful orator and, like Churchill, he spoke strongly against foreign policy decisions that attempted to secure peace at any cost.[10]

Both the reference to *Macbeth* and the use of the two paintings by Stubbs raise intriguing possibilities for our understanding of the character of Churchill in this film and our interpretation of Churchill the historical figure. Is the film confused about Churchill, or is it suggesting Churchill is a complex and, therefore, potentially confusing character? Whatever the conscious intentions of the filmmakers may be, to a large extent the viewer's reading of these sorts of allusions will depend on their own ideological perspective.

## III

A strong direction to our reading of the film is given by the title, which is a powerful statement of the position of Britain in early 1940. Prospects for the country are bleak. The phrase "imminent invasion" is repeated at least three times in the script. Viscount Halifax (Stephen Dillane), the chief advocate of peace talks and therefore the main antagonist to Churchill in the narrative, tells Churchill: "We are facing certain defeat on land, the annihilation of our army, and imminent invasion." Later, against a backdrop of filmed documentary images of German soldiers and guns, emphasizing the magnitude, regimented order, and relentlessness of the threat, a military officer pronounces the verdict, "We must prepare for the imminent invasion of our island." Finally, the King urges Churchill to tell "the people" the truth: "If invasion is imminent, if our troops in France are lost, they must be prepared." On top of this, Churchill is repeatedly framed in such a way as to suggest he is trapped by events. After the first mention of "imminent invasion" he is shown small within the frame, boxed and surrounded by blackness. A little later, Halifax closes a door on him and we view him boxed within the centre of the shot, framed within a small central window on the door that has been shut on him. However, despite the increasing sense of Churchill's entrapment, the phrase "darkest hour," of course, comes from the saying, "The darkest hour is just before dawn."[11] The implication is that things often seem at their worst immediately before they get better. Thus, with this title and despite the mounting sense of doom and gloom, not only hope but an implied triumphant outcome for the film is given from the outset.

Even so, the picture created is one of a country under intense threat. Invasion is a real possibility; the borders of what is repeatedly referred to as "our island" or "this island" are menaced. Churchill asserts the importance of the Channel; "it's our moat, our battlement," he says, conjuring the image of a castle defending itself from the threat from without. The documentary images of German forces, mentioned above as being used in the middle of the film to suggest the remorseless onward march of the enemy, are first used at the beginning of the film. The camera pans across ranks of German troops filing across the screen, over rows of large-scale guns being manufactured for ships, and along a procession of tanks being built on an industrial production line. The only recourse left open to Britain is to retreat behind the country's natural sea defences, in order to, as Churchill puts it when addressing Parliament, "defend our island home." This is a film that sets up a particular relationship between Britain and continental Europe[12] (indeed, between Britain and the dangers posed by the entire world beyond the borders of the United Kingdom). The Channel is a boundary between contesting ways of seeing the world, a defensive line keeping out what Churchill calls "the menace of tyranny."

**Figure 7.1** In early scenes from *Darkest Hour* (Joe Wright, 2017), Churchill (Gary Oldman) is repeatedly framed in such a way as to suggest he is trapped.

Wendy Webster asserts:

> Right-wing nationalist propaganda ... often uses images from the Second World War to evoke pride in past national greatness. It identifies membership of the European Union and immigration as two key developments that have brought national decline since 1945. The British National Party's policy is to stop all immigration—"mass immigration and artificially promoted miscegenation is destroying Britain and the British." This narrative places the history of the Second World War—a symbol of British greatness in the past—in opposition to subsequent immigration, which destroys the nation.[13]

Themes and images conveying a story focused on retreating within an island fortress in order to defend a country, a nation, and a people against the threat of invasion posed by alien hordes massing on the European coast undeniably play into a narrative that is not only nationalistic but also racist. The reality of the wartime period, according to Webster, was that "between 1939 and 1945, the population of Britain became more diverse by nationality and ethnicity than it had ever been before."[14] Movements of "migrants, refugees and troops" to the UK during the Second World War took place on "an unprecedented scale."[15] White Britons, she says, "became increasingly familiar with meeting black servicemen, servicewomen and war workers as the war progressed."[16] But then, when the war ended awareness of just how diverse the wartime population had been was lost, and subsequently "has played little part in public memories of the war."[17] The charge is that the ethnic diversity of those involved in various ways in the war effort has been erased from the popular historical record. However, this is perhaps not an accusation that can be levelled at *Darkest Hour*, since the film gives a crucial role to a young black man, Marcus Peters (Adé Haastrup), who meets Churchill on the London Underground.

This is the part of the film that has been criticized perhaps more than any other. Churchill is under pressure to enter into peace negotiations with Hitler but baulks at the idea. The King has suggested, if he is in doubt, he should, "Go to the people: let them instruct you." And so, in the film, Churchill almost instinctively hops out of his chauffeur-driven car, takes the Tube with ordinary Londoners, and asks their opinion as to what he should do. Thematically, this elevates "the people" to a critical status in society and, more importantly, suggests both King George and Churchill concur in the elevation of "the people" to the level of an oracle able to deliver the advice of the gods. In *The Guardian*, Jack felt this not only pushed the bounds of historical possibility but took the character of Churchill into an emotional and empathetic region he was never likely to have inhabited. He asked:

> Did Winston Churchill in the summer of 1940, or any other time, ever take a tube? Did he on that tube talk in a friendly way to his fellow passengers, whose mouths hung open when they saw him? Did he ask for their names and opinions on whether Britain should fight, or sue for peace? Did he quote aloud from Thomas Macaulay's *Lays of Ancient Rome*, to have the verse completed by a young black man, whose hand Churchill amicably touched? And then did he return to Westminster to announce his renewed resolve in a speech to parliamentarians that quoted the names and opinions of the Londoners he had met on the train . . . No, he did none of these things.[18]

Webster points out that:

> In May and June [1940], many British people lumped all foreigners in Britain together as potential spies and fifth columnists . . . Both Mass Observation and Home Intelligence reported that many people wanted internment for all aliens, not just those of enemy nationality—as many as 55 per cent of those surveyed in four areas of London in June by Mass Observation.[19]

She adds that in the middle of 1940, "Britain was not a good place to be non-British, for those not wearing uniforms."[20] And yet, Marcus Peters seems completely comfortable on the Tube, accepted by his fellow passengers and able to take a more relaxed response to Churchill's presence on the Underground than any of his co-passengers. This is the racial Other fully integrated into the British way of life: racism does not exist. It has been erased from the historical record in the structuring of the narrative. Webster draws attention to the fact that military uniform was crucial. After the war, she says, most West Indians who had served in Britain were demobbed back home, but then what happened was that "those who returned were no longer in uniform, but in civvies, no longer 'allies,' but 'immigrants.'"[21]

## IV

If Churchill were to have ventured onto the Tube in 1940 there was some small chance he may have bumped into a black man. Ian Spencer tells us, in 1939 the permanent Asian and black population of the whole of the United Kingdom was officially estimated at about 7,000 people.[22] Spencer counsels we should be careful not to think of the United Kingdom as multicultural until comparatively recently. "Without denying in any way the presence in Britain of small, isolated Asian and black communities of very long standing," he says, "care must be taken not to place the inception of multi-racial Britain too far back in time."[23] In the early 1950s, he says, half of the British population had never met a black person.[24] People who derive from the Indian subcontinent, Africa and the Caribbean were, until very recent times, a tiny fragment of the permanent settled population of Britain—a fraction of 1 percent of the whole until the changes in migration and settlement patterns in the 1950s.[25] However, there were concentrations of Asian and black communities to be found in the multi-ethnic dockland areas of seaports such as London, Liverpool, Cardiff, South Shields, and Glasgow.[26] Furthermore, there was a small community of black intellectuals living in and around Camden in London in the inter-war period.[27] In his book *Black London: The Imperial Metropolis and Decolonization in the Twentieth Century*, Marc Matera documents especially strongly the work of black activists in this period such as George Padmore and C. L. R. James.

In *Darkest Hour* the fictional black character, Marcus Peters, completes Churchill's quotation from Thomas Babington Macaulay's *Horatius*. This poem formed part of Macaulay's *Lays of Ancient Rome* (1842), written while he was a member of the Governor General of India's Supreme Council in the 1830s—in other words, when he was one of the white rulers of part of the British Empire. Churchill addresses those around him on the Tube as "you, the British people," thereby explicitly including Peters, and recites to them the words of Horatius in Macaulay's poem: "To every man upon this earth death comes soon or late, and how can man die better than facing fearful odds . . ." At which point, Peters intervenes to complete the quotation with, ". . . for the ashes of his father and the temple of his god," inspiring Churchill to reach across with tears in his eyes to gently touch his hand.[28] As viewers, we witness in this moment the creation of a further strand to the myth of Churchill. This is a drama. It is a fictionalized account of events. It is a requirement of the form that we should be presented with a creative response to actuality. However, we are also dealing with the dramatization of a crucial figure in British history and the representation of a critical moment in that history. Do we have a representation of Churchill that is faithful to the historical reality? And does it matter whether we do, or do not? Is this a reinterpretation of history in the coinage of a liberal, educated, middle-class, twenty-first-century audience? Does this use of the socially integrated black member of a comfortably multicultural society tell us more about the contemporary period than wartime Britain?

Macaulay's poem recounts the story of Publius Horatius Cocles, who in the sixth century BC, along with other Roman soldiers, held the narrow end of the Pons Sublicius, a bridge into Rome, against Etruscan troops.

**Figure 7.2** Marcus Peters (Adé Haastrup) with Churchill (Gary Oldman) on the London Underground in *Darkest Hour*.

They achieved a sufficient delay for their compatriots to be able to destroy the bridge behind them and prevent the Etruscans invading Rome. The parallels to Dunkirk that make this appropriate to this moment in 1940 are clear. However, the use of Macaulay is even more interesting in relation to the issue of Churchill's attitude towards other ethnicities, and perhaps in relation to the approach to history being taken in this film. Macaulay gave his name to Macaulayism, which was the introduction of English education to the colonies, and because of this he remains a controversial figure. His aim in relation to the Indian subcontinent was explained as being "to form a class who may be interpreters between us and the millions whom we govern; a class of persons, Indian in blood and colour, but English in taste, in opinions, in morals, and in intellect."[29] In trying to obtain a sense of the man we might also consider Macaulay's best-known work, *The History of England from the Accession of James the Second* (1848), which explores the destructive power of mob rule, shows how progress is achieved through efforts of great men, and demonstrates his belief in European cultural superiority. Doug Underwood has spoken of "Macaulay's tendency to see figures of the past in heroes-versus-villains terms, and his hagiographic view of history as always involving sweep, drama, and the genius of leadership."[30] Each of these terms, and possibly critically the mention of a "hagiographic view of history"— hagiographies are biographies that flatter their subject and are often about saints—might seem particularly appropriate for this film. Michael Makovsky says Churchill

> saw the world in grand, often romantic, terms and himself in the tradition of great leaders like Napoleon, Castlereagh, Marlborough, Disraeli, and Gladstone. The ultimate issue for Churchill was the advance of "civilization," by which he meant the British and Western way of life—its liberal values, laws, culture, industry, and science. He saw Britain and its empire as propagators of civilization, imbuing his nationalism and imperialism with a moral imperative.[31]

Running alongside all of this, it is undeniably true that Churchill held strongly racist views. Max Hastings says, "Most reputable historians acknowledge Churchill as a racist," and adds that "his conduct towards black and Asian peoples as prime minister injured his reputation."[32] Debating the issue of Palestine and the Palestinians, Churchill (in)famously stated:

> I do not admit, for instance, that a great wrong has been done to the Red Indians of America, or the black people of Australia. I do not admit that a great wrong has been done to those people by the fact that a stronger race, a higher grade race, or, at any rate, a more worldly-wise race, to put it that way, has come in and taken their place.[33]

He saw the British Empire as an essentially altruistic enterprise. According to Richard Toye, he believed that, "The subject peoples of the Empire were to rely for their welfare ... on the elevated moral qualities of their conquerors."[34][35] As a fictional character, who was also a historical figure, to what extent should his attitude towards Marcus Peters on the London Underground take account of these aspects of the man?

In a contemporary context, race has come to be seen as a defining issue not only in relation to Churchill but also in relation to war films that position Britain as having to desperately defend itself against an external (continental) threat. Zachary Michael Powell has suggested, "the lack of Indians, and non-white bodies in *Dunkirk* speaks to a larger anxiety about white power in the world, its vulnerability, and its destructive defiance in the face of the Other."[36] Aside from the presence of Marcus Peters on the Tube in *Darkest Hour*, neither this film nor *Churchill* presents the audience with anything other than white characters.[37] Anna Blackwell suggests, "*Dunkirk*'s questionable racial politics opens it up to the symbolic significance that Brexiteers like Farage wish to affix to the historical event: a strategic retreat that isolates Britain from Europe, leaving it safer, prouder and more determined than ever."[38] In various ways *Darkest Hour*, in particular, might similarly be said to lend itself to a Brexiteer's agenda. Given that historical dramas are only nominally about the past while actually being about the contemporary period, including a well-integrated black man in the portrayal of the general public would seem to be positive. However, we do need to question the nature of the voice given to this black character. Through his knowledge of Macaulay's verse, Peters reinforces the notion of beneficial colonialism. Potentially, because he has become "English in taste, in opinions, in morals, and in intellect"[39] he is able to fulfill the role allocated him under Macaulayism, to function as an intermediary between the English rulers and the natives.

## V

The same sorts of issues around the approach that is to be taken to the interpretation of history and historical figures are to be found in *Churchill*. This is in many ways a more literary or theatrical piece than *Darkest Hour*. The Churchill portrayed here by Brian Cox is an old man haunted by his past demons. In the opening scene on a beach he is presented as a single figure in long shot with the sea behind him. He is small and trapped by the sea. This is going to be a film about wartime landings on beaches: the D-Day landings in Normandy in 1944 are fast approaching and the closer we get to that event the more the Gallipoli landings of the First World War (during which horrific losses were suffered by British, Australian, New Zealand, and French troops) haunt Churchill. As First Lord of the Admiralty in 1915, he had been one of the main voices arguing for a landing in Turkey in the Dardanelles Straits around Gallipoli.

There are then specific reasons for Churchill to be shown as hearing the screaming voices of dying men and feeling that the sea has turned blood red, in that he is recalling the debacle of those attempted landings during the First World War. However, he also becomes at this point something of an everyman figure, experiencing the individual's anguish before the human condition rather like a character in an absurdist drama. And so, in this scene he is like a character from a Samuel Beckett play; but at the same time he is also somewhat like Lear in Shakespeare's play *King Lear*, an older man forced to face the reality of the failures and the personality failings of his earlier self. "So many young men, so much waste," Churchill mutters to himself, "I mustn't let it happen again." The Lear-like qualities become even clearer when we see him later in the film, in his impotent rage calling on God and the elements of wind and rain to prevent the D-Day landings:

> Let the heavens open and a deluge burst forth . . . let lightning flash, let thunder crash and roll and bellow. Let winds tear up the beaches and spin the sand

> into storms. Let the sea churn into peaks and troughs, and tidal waves call spirits from the vast deep.[40][41]

Churchill virtually turns into an anti-war campaigner. We are presented with the irony of our acclaimed greatest wartime leader, forever associated with bulldog tenacity and a never-say-die fighting mentality, portrayed as someone protesting against the stupidity of war. He fumes:

> Still the commanders have not learnt for they do not care to learn. They keep away from the battlefields and do not see the cost. Eyes shot out by snipers' bullets, legs blown off by mines, blood on the sea-foam: that's what the men see. That's what they face.

All of this creates a thoroughly interesting film, especially when the dynamic of a faltering marriage between Churchill and his wife, Clementine (Miranda Richardson), is added to the mix. However, how does this position the film in relation to history, and how does the film position the viewer in relation to history? Andrew Roberts, author of *Churchill: Walking with Destiny*, claims in historical terms this film "gets absolutely everything wrong" and amounts to "a totally untrue account." He says, "although Churchill did indeed oppose an over-hasty return of Allied forces to north-west France in 1942 and 1943, by the time of D-Day in 1944 he was completely committed to the operation."[42][43]

Both *Churchill* and *Darkest Hour* contain "love scenes" between Churchill and George VI.[44] In *Churchill* it is a slightly more formal meeting but as in *Darkest Hour* the King turns up unannounced when Churchill is at his lowest ebb and shines a light on the way forward for the hero. The King says it is his job as sovereign "to unite, to bring hope" and reminds Churchill that this is his duty too. He ends by telling Churchill: "Britain will thank you for it, Winston. I believe all of us will: forever." In *Darkest Hour*, when the King turns up unexpectedly to see Churchill, the two characters are positioned in a room with a large space between them. In the scene, George VI strides decisively across the room to sit next to Churchill. He tells him: "We shall work together: you shall have my support at any hour." And when Churchill forlornly announces, "I have very few people to whom I can talk frankly," the King responds, clinching the love scene, "Perhaps now we have each other." In this film in particular it is Churchill and the King who have to evaluate between them the way forward for the nation. In both films, Churchill is a man of liberal values and attitudes, a man of compassion with a love of common people. In both films he is (practically) alone in shouldering the responsibility for taking care of Britain's future. This is a very particular form of history that is being sold to the audience.

## VI

By emphasizing the role of Churchill, both *Darkest Hour* and *Churchill* in particular, add to the popular myth of the man and help to reinforce an understanding of history as revolving around the exploits of "great men." By focusing on British heroism, *Dunkirk* and *Darkest Hour* in particular, reinforce nationalist sentiment and an anti-European stance at a specific contemporary Leave/Remain moment in British history. By failing to accurately address questions of ethnicity and racism, both *Darkest Hour* and *Dunkirk* in particular, open the door to racist readings. As a group these films work to renegotiate British identity within the contemporary world, but seem most easily to reinforce nationalism and anti-European sentiment. They conspicuously expand and develop the already highly developed myth of Churchill as a heroic wartime leader, and they demonstrate how cinema (and the media more widely) play a crucial role in asserting particular versions of history that assist the consolidation of a popular (and populist) national identity. Columba Achilleos-Sarll and Benjamin Martill suggested the Brexit vote demonstrated "a latent nostalgia for the British Empire and the power and control it afforded the colonisers."[45] These films as a whole demonstrate essentially the same yearning. We might also note (ironically) that in the preface to his *Lays of Ancient Rome*, Macaulay noted: "a wise man will look with great suspicion on the legend that has come down to us."[46]

### Notes

1. See Chapter 20, "A Rare Miss: Churchill Misperceives the Chances of D-Day Success," in James C. Humes, *Churchill: The Prophetic Statesman* (Washington, DC: Regnery, 2012), pp. 151–60, for a brief account of Churchill's position.
2. Ian Jack, "*Dunkirk* and *Darkest Hour* fuel Brexit fantasies—even if they weren't meant to," *The Guardian*, 27 January 2018. Available athttps://www.theguardian.com/commentisfree/2018/jan/27/brexit-britain-myths-wartime-darkest-hour-dunkirk-nationalist-fantasies (accessed 16 June 2020).
3. Steve Rose, "The Dunkirk spirit: how cinema is shaping Britain's identity in the Brexit era," *The Guardian*, 20 July 2017. Available athttps://www.theguardian.com/film/2017/jul/20/dunkirk-spirit-british-film-brexit-national-identity-christopher-nolan (accessed 16 June 2020).
4. Clementine Tholas, Janis L. Goldie, and Karen A. Ritzenhoff (eds.), *New Perspectives on the War Film* (London: Palgrave Macmillan, 2019), p. 13.
5. Rudolf G. Adam, *Brexit: Causes and Consequences* (Berlin: Springer, 2020), p. 72.
6. Werner Herzog's *Aguirre, Wrath of God* (1972) focuses on a man who takes despotic control of a conquistador expedition in South America.

7. Jonathan Jones, "Whistlejacket, George Stubbs (1762)," *The Guardian*, 22 April 2000. Available at theguardian.com/culture/2000/apr/22/art1 (accessed 16 June 2020).
8. These paintings, completed between 1801 and 1805, are variously titled around the theme of "Napoleon Crossing the Alps."
9. Edmund Burke, *A Philosophical Inquiry into the Origin of Our Ideas of the Sublime and Beautiful* (New York: Harper, 1860), p. 83.
10. Churchill opposed Chamberlain's efforts to secure peace agreements with Hitler, and Pitt consistently resisted Robert Walpole's attempts to prevent Britain engaging in wars with other European powers.
11. It may be this saying originates from the seventeenth century. Thomas Fuller suggests, "Thus, as it is always darkest just before the day dawneth, so God useth to visit His servants with greatest afflictions when he intendeth their speedy advancement." See Thomas Fuller, *A Pisgah-sight of Palestine and the Confines thereof, with the Historie of the Old and New Testament acted thereon* (London: Tegg, 1869/1650), p. 206.
12. We might note in *The Favourite* the political debate also revolves around whether Britain should sue for peace with its continental enemy or not. The enemy in this case threatening invasion is France, who Sarah Churchill (Rachel Weisz) suggests threatens to "sodomize" men's wives and plant the fields of England with garlic! See Chapter 4.
13. Wendy Webster, *Mixing It: Diversity in World War Two in Britain* (Oxford: Oxford University Press, 2018), p. 2.
14. Ibid., p. 3.
15. Ibid.
16. Ibid., p. 14.
17. Ibid., pp. 11–12.
18. Jack, "*Dunkirk* and *Darkest Hour* fuel Brexit fantasies—even if they weren't meant to."
19. Webster, *Mixing It: Diversity in World War Two in Britain*, pp. 43–4.
20. Ibid., p. 61.
21. Ibid., p. 19.
22. Ian R. G. Spencer, *British Immigration Policy Since 1939: The Making of Multi-Racial Britain* (London and New York: Routledge, 1997), p. 3.
23. Ibid., p. 4.
24. Ibid.
25. Ibid.
26. Ibid., p. 3.
27. Marc Matera, *Black London: The Imperial Metropolis and Decolonization in the Twentieth Century* (Oakland: University of California Press, 2015), p. 7.
28. Although he would have left London for the United States by 1940, it is true to say at least one black man living in London in the 1930s would have been likely to have been able to complete this verse. C. L. R. James speaks of reading books by Macaulay as a young man at Queen's Royal College, in Port of Spain,

Trinidad. He has recorded how he had access to the teachers' common room and "would go in and take out a Macaulay, or take out a Saintsbury, or take out a Matthew Arnold and start to read and that's what I did all the time." Ken Ramchand, "Interviews with C. L. R. James," September 1980, p. 35. Available at http://www.clrjames.uk/wp-content/uploads/2015/10/Interviews-with-C.L.R.-James-by-Ken-Ramchand.pdf (accessed 17 June 2020).
29. Quoted by T. V. Sathyamurthy, "Victorians, socialisation and imperialism: consequences for post-imperial India," in J. A. Managan (ed.), *Making Imperial Mentalities: Socialisation and British Imperialism* (London and New York: Routledge, 2012/1990), p. 110.
30. Doug Underwood, *Literary Journalism in British and American Prose: An Historical Overview* (Jefferson, NC: McFarland, 2019), p. 52.
31. Michael Makovsky, "Being Winston Churchill," *The New Republic*, 8 December 2010. Available at https://newrepublic.com/article/79718/winston-churchill-life-battle-britain (accessed 17 June 2020).
32. Max Hastings, "Churchill was a racist, but he still deserves respect," *The Sunday Times*, 14 June 2020, p. 21. Hastings goes on to say, "It nonetheless seems grotesque to suppose that if this fault is weighed in the balance against his vast services to Britain, and to mankind, it can justify defacing his image in public, or toppling him from the pantheon of national heroes."
33. Martin Gilbert, *Winston Churchill: Companion Documents*, 5 (3) (London: Heinemann, 1982), p. 616.
34. Richard Toye, *Churchill's Empire: The World That Made Him and the World He Made* (London: Macmillan, 2010), p. 27. Toye also states, for Churchill "the British capacity for racial tolerance was a fundamental part of British racial superiority" (p. 18).
35. Similarly, we might question the fictional Churchill's position in relation to the working class. He does, of course, acknowledge his experience of privilege and implicitly his attitude towards any members of the working class who take part in strike action. He tells his chauffeur:

> Do you know I've never ridden a bus? . . . I've never queued for a train . . . I believe I could boil an egg but only because I've seen it done . . . The only time I tried riding the Underground was during the General Strike.

Chris Wrigley points out that "Churchill's democratic principles had firm class limitations." And Paul Addison sums up the situation by saying:

> Churchill was, of course, an aristocrat in his conviction that he was born to rule. But he saw it as the duty of his class, and hence of the state, to protect the weak and the poor. The strong and rebellious were an altogether different matter.

His view of Hitler, given in the film, would seem to be based on class prejudice. The list of words he uses to bitterly describe Hitler may contain "tyrant," "monster," "butcher," and "savage," but it begins with "the corporal" and ends with "house painter."

36. Zachary Michael Powell, "The Form of the White Ethno-State: *Dunkirk* (2017) Omits Indian Soldiers for White Vulnerable Bodies," in Clementine Tholas, Janis L. Goldie, and Karen A. Ritzenhoff (eds.), *New Perspectives on the War Film* (London: Palgrave Macmillan, 2019), p. 282.
37. There are two scenes in *Darkest Hour* in which one or two black or Asian faces are shown as Churchill looks out from his chauffeur-driven car in London at the passing street scene.
38. Anna Blackwell, *Shakespearean Celebrity in the Digital Age: Fan Cultures and Remediation* (London: Palgrave Macmillan, 2018), p. 176.
39. See section IV above.
40. 
> Blow, winds, and crack your cheeks! Rage, blow!
> You cataracts and hurricanoes, spout
> Till you have drenched our steeples, drowned the cocks!
> You sulfurous and thought-executing fires,
> Vaunt-couriers of oak-cleaving thunderbolts,
> Singe my white head! And thou, all-shaking thunder,
> Smite flat the thick rotundity o' th' world,
> 
> *King Lear*, Act 3 Scene 2

41. Churchill's Shakespearean depths emerge again just after this when he talks of the thousands who died at Gallipoli and proclaims, "Their blood soaks my hands." In *Macbeth*, Act 2 Scene 2, Macbeth says:

> Will all great Neptune's ocean wash this blood
> Clean from my hand? No, this my hand will rather
> The multitudinous seas incarnadine,
> Making the green one red.

42. In his biography of Churchill, Roberts quotes the First Sea Lord, Sir Andrew Cunningham, saying of Churchill on the day before the landings: "He really is an incorrigible optimist. I always thought I was unduly so but he easily outstrips me." Andrew Roberts, *Churchill: Walking with Destiny* (London: Penguin, 2019), p. 822.
43. Andrew Roberts, "Fake History in *Churchill*, starring Brian Cox," 1 May 2017, The Churchill Project, Hillsdale College. Available at https://winstonchurchill.hillsdale.edu/fake-history-in-churchill-starring-brian-cox/ (accessed 25 June 2020).
44. See Roberts pp. 528–9 for an account of how moved Churchill was by the death of the King in 1952.
45. Columba Achilleos-Sarll and Benjamin Martill, "Toxic Masculinity: Militarism, Deal-Making and the Performance of Brexit," in Moira Dustin, Nuno Ferreira, and Susan Millns (eds.), *Gender and Queer Perspectives on Brexit* (London: Palgrave Macmillan, 2019), p. 32.
46. Thomas Babington Macaulay, *Lays of Ancient Rome with Ivry and the Armada* (London: Longmans/Green, 1882), p. 3.

CHAPTER 8

# Identity Politics: *Where Hands Touch* (Amma Asante, 2018) and *A United Kingdom* (Asante, 2016)

## I

Is personal identity innate, or is it acquired? If it is acquired, how is it acquired? From where do your individual values and beliefs originate? How much control can a person exert over who they are and who they will become? To what extent can the self be shaped and performed through the exercising of personal will, and to what extent is it determined by social, cultural, political, and economic factors beyond any individual's control? What would it be like to have been born black in Germany as the Nazis were coming to power in 1933 and during the ensuing period of Hitler's Third Reich; to have grown up in this particular place at this particular time and to be attempting as a young person to form your sense of self? How would you have been viewed by others? How would you have regarded yourself? These are some of the questions raised by *Where Hands Touch* (Amma Asante, 2018), a film in which both central characters are teenagers emerging into adulthood (and, as part of that process, searching for a secure sense of self) in Germany in the last years of the Second World War. One, Lenya (Amandla Stenberg), is the daughter of a white Aryan mother, Kerstin (Abbie Cornish), and a Senegalese soldier who met after the First World War when he was stationed with the French occupation force in Germany. The other, Lutz (George MacKay), is the son of a German SS (Schultzstaffel) officer, Heinz (Christopher Eccleston), and is a member of the Hitler Youth (Hitlerjugend). When Lenya and Lutz enter into a sexual relationship, they defy the most basic tenet of the xenophobic Third Reich. From 1935, both marriage and extramarital sex between "Aryans" and either Roma, or blacks, or their respective racial "hybrids" (Mischlinge) was banned.[1]

Asante's determination to bring explorations of the black experience of racism to the screen sits at the heart not only of this film but also her earlier movie, *A United Kingdom* (2016), in which a black African prince, Seretse Khama (David Oyelowo), marries a British working-class, white woman,

Ruth Williams (Rosamund Pike). This film examines just how permeated British society was with racism in the period immediately after the Second World War. At the time, black people comprised "less than 0.02 per cent of the population."[2] Officially, there was no "colour bar" in operation, and yet the reality of everyday lived experience was that black people "were routinely refused employment and accommodation."[3] As with *Where Hands Touch*, in which there are controversial images of Lenya and Lutz kissing in front of a German flag, so too in *A United Kingdom* a crucial part of Asante's approach involves presenting the audience with images of miscegenation. Although there is a range of potential audience responses to such scenes covering a spectrum of liberal to illiberal positions, the effort on the part of the film-makers is to present images offering the strongest possible defiance to white supremacist views. In each film the respective couples are shown lying full-length next to each other in such a way as to emphasize the union of black and white bodies. It is these moments of intimacy that offer the clearest, in-your-face evidence of the transgression of socio-politically imposed boundaries between people—a visual representation of the refusal of the characters and the film to accept the supposed natural divisions between people that racism wishes to insist on.

In both films the issue of race, or ethnic identity, is constantly pushed to the forefront of the narrative. In *Where Hands Touch* this is powerfully linked to notions of national identity. As a "coming-of-age" film, Lenya and Lutz are moving towards establishing their own sexual and gender identities against the background of their respective mother–daughter and father–son generational tensions; but these more universal familial frictions attaching to

**Figure 8.1** Miscegenation: black and white bodies next to each other in *Where Hands Touch* (Amma Asante, 2018).

the emergence into adulthood are positioned within very specific contexts of racism and nationalism. *A United Kingdom*, on the other hand, links the issue of race more strongly to colonialism. Outlining the post-war colonial context, A. Susan Williams says,

> Britain after the war was directly responsible for fourteen African states, with a total population of 56 million. For African students in London, at the political heart of the Empire, the idea that it was now time for change was reinforced by the election of the Labour Party in July 1945.[4]

The beginnings of any sizeable immigration to Britain from the colonies is often traced to June 1948, when the *Empire Windrush* docked in Southampton from Jamaica, bringing about 450 people looking for work. However, Williams suggests any optimism there might have been regarding Labour's position on race was quickly undermined when "within two days" of that ship arriving, "a group of eleven Labour MPs wrote to the Prime Minister calling for controls on black immigration."[5]

Whether we are dealing with Germany under Nazism, post-war Britain, or the contemporary situation of the UK in the early twenty-first century, issues of racism, nationalism, and colonialism remain interlinked.[6,7] Each of these societies, set within their own time, place, and historical context, exhibits a contestation of norms, values, and beliefs, and within each a dominant culture has emerged offering "a shared system of meaning" that people use "to make sense of the world"—a "set of values, beliefs, and ways of behaving."[8] In each of these societies this dominant culture is providing "a country with its identity."[9] However, although cultures are inclusive in the way in which they draw people together to provide meaning for their lives,[10] they are also, of course, exclusive in the way in which they reject those who are seen as "Other." What we are shown in both *Where Hands Touch* and *A United Kingdom* are societies in which it is the divisions between people that offer the very definition of those societies. This is also what we see in contemporary Britain—a society defined by its divisions. As Howard J. Wiarda suggests, a country "may have its own dominant culture and identity or there may be disagreement over the culture and, hence, over the future direction of the country."[11] In the same way we are proposing the UK is divided, Wiarda says you could theorize that the United States "is really two countries, two cultures, and two identities" and that "the gaps and differences are so wide that they are unlikely to be bridged anytime soon."[12] In other words, the socio-political dynamics we see at work within *Where Hands Touch* and *A United Kingdom* contain a similar basis within cultural theory, and in this sense both films bear a direct relationship to contemporary UK (and US) society.

## II

As a black German, Lenya in *Where Hands Touch* is part of a small ethnic minority in Germany at the time;[13] and, as a child born during the foreign occupation of her homeland immediately after the First World War, she is viewed as belonging to an even smaller ethnic group that became known as "Rhineland bastards." This group operated as a visual reminder not only of the country's defeat in the First World War but also of what was seen as the victimization of the country under the Treaty of Versailles.[14] Clarence Lusane illustrates the level of hatred felt towards this small group of black Germans:

> Hitler's minister of agriculture Richard-Walther Darre, made the case that for the future of the German nation, the Rhineland children had to be taken care of. In the harshest possible terms, he wrote: "It is essential to exterminate the leftovers from the black Shame on the Rhine. These mulatto children were created either through rape or by white mothers who were whores ... as a Rhinelander I demand: sterilization of all mulattoes with whom we were saddled by the black Shame of the Rhine. This measure has to be carried out in the next two years."[15]

And yet, in general, the historical record seems to show black Germans in the 1930s continued to feel "German." Hans J. Massaquoi, for example, says: "There I was, a kinky-haired, brown-skinned eight-year-old boy amid a sea of blond and blue-eyed kids, filled with childlike patriotism, still shielded by blissful ignorance."[16][17] In the film, Lenya tells her mother: "I'm German, even if you want to pretend you're not, even if you want me to pretend I'm not." Lusane says that,

> ... despite a vicious and unyielding determination to create an Aryan-only society, and an ongoing rhetoric of Negrophobia and antiblack racism, the Nazis did not deport or (initially) exterminate Afro-Germans and Africans, or remove them completely from German social life. In fact, in many cases, they were allowed to attend schools and work while Jews and Gypsies were not.[18][19]

Iris Wigger recounts the way in which the presence of black African soldiers in the Rhineland in the period after 1918 "provoked massive protests in Germany, Europe and the United States."[20] She tells us: "Despite provably committing fewer crimes than other divisions of Allied troops, they were frequently represented as violent beasts, against which one needed to protect the German people, the white race and culture."[21] The protests, we should note, were not confined to Germany; a reflection of the fact that particularly in

Britain and the United States but also in other European countries racism was a socially accepted cultural norm. Larry A. Greene points out the reality was that all the nations involved in fighting the Second World War, including the United States, were "colonial powers" and were "not interested in extending 'self-determination' to their colonized subject peoples."[22] Greene also highlights "the similarity of American and Nazi sterilization policies"[23] and the fact that concepts of "racial superiority" and "black inferiority" required the separation of "supposed superior and inferior races" in order to maintain "racial purity."[24][25]

Wigger asserts that even before the start of the war the Nazis were moving forward with a programme of sterilization. "In Spring 1937," she says, "the Special Commission 3, founded in the residence of the Gestapo in Berlin ... got the task to procure in a move to be kept strictly confidential the forced sterilisation (Zwangssterilisierung) of all 'Rhineland bastards.'"[26] However, Lusane reminds us that the concept of sterilization was not something peculiar to Germany or to Nazi policy but was "informed by the global eugenics movement."[27] Tina Campt identifies the way in which "a scientific discourse of race as a biologically immutable category of human difference," along with "the significant (according to geneticists and eugenicists) genetic consequences of racial mixture," plus a "colonial discourse" regarding "racial mixture" and "mixed marriage," came together with "a discourse of German victimhood" to create the sense of fear and uncertainty experienced by "Rhineland bastards" during the 1930s and early 1940s.[28] However, once again, not only was the concept of sterilization not unique to Germany but racism itself was neither unique to Germany nor unique to the National Socialist Party within Germany. Robert Kesting points out not only that "The Weimar press preceded that of the Nazis in inflaming racism against mulatto children and their German mothers,"[29][30] but also that "British occupation authorities" endorsed this position because they were "concerned that images of black troops ordering whites about at gunpoint might find their way into its own overseas territories, calling into question the 'naturalness' of European rule."[31] It appears the concept of racial inferiority was so powerfully ingrained within the dominant culture in Germany that massacres of black French troops took place as the Germans swept into France in 1940. In his book, *Hitler's African Victims: The German Army Massacres of Black French Soldiers in 1940*, Raffael Scheck concludes that the German Wehrmacht (i.e. not the paramilitary Schutzstaffel (or SS) that was in charge of concentration and death camps but the regular military) conducted "a race war against black Africans in the Western campaign of 1940."[32] The simple fact is racism was embedded within Germany well before the Second World War and possibly before the emergence of Nazism. Robert Proctor suggests:

> The Nazi medical experiments and even the program for the destruction of "lives not worth living" represent only the tip of a much larger iceberg. In fact, the ideological structure we associate with National Socialism was deeply embedded in the philosophy and institutional structure of German biomedical science long before the beginning of the euthanasia program in 1939—and to a certain extent, even before 1933. The published record of the German medical profession makes it clear that many intellectuals cooperated fully in Nazi racial programs, and that many of the social and intellectual foundations for these programs were laid long before the rise of Hitler to power.[33]

## III

The threat to black Germans explored in *Where Hands Touch* therefore emerges as a result of a lengthy process within German history. More than this, the threat to black Germans we witness in watching this film emerges as a result of a lengthy process within global history. *Where Hands Touch* cannot explore this background because of the necessarily concise nature of film narratives. However, it is clear the filmmakers wish the audience to view the incidents that take place within a specific time and place in their story as having a much wider resonance since the film opens with a quotation from James Baldwin, the US author and race activist, a prominent figure in the 1950s and '60s: "There are days when you wonder what your role is in this country and what your future is in it." This immediately suggests the events the audience is about to observe should be seen as relevant to all minority ethnic groups marginalized within the country of their birth. Taking in a little more of the interview from which this quotation is extracted, we find this is what Baldwin had to say:

> There are days—this is one of them—when you wonder what your role is in this country and what your future is in it. How, precisely, you are going to reconcile yourself to your situation here and how you are going to communicate to the vast, heedless, unthinking, cruel white majority that you are here... I'm terrified at the moral apathy, the death of the heart, which is happening in my country. These people have deluded themselves for so long that they really don't think I'm human. And I base this on their conduct, not on what they say. And this means that they have become in themselves moral monsters.[34]

The relevance of this to the situation in Germany in the 1930s and early '40s is immediately clear. However, we are also instantly struck by the fact that these words are actually being spoken about the United States, one of the main countries responsible for the defeat of Germany in 1945. In *Where Hands Touch*, Lutz's father, the SS officer, is a secret fan of black blues and jazz,[35] and as they are discussing this fact Lutz tells Lenya, "They hang people like you in America." The violent abuse of minority groups within societies is presented by the film as a social reality that cannot easily be dismissed as the product of the mind of a single dictator like Hitler, or symptomatic only of Nazism rather than any other political system. In *A United Kingdom*, while living in Britain, Seretse is not only attacked by a group of white working-class thugs who immediately label him as "Other," calling him "coon," "black bastard," and "savage," but he is also abused in a university boxing match in which in a clinch his opponent calls him a "monkey."[36] Racism, in other words, is to be found at all levels of British society. It is also made clear the events we witness in *A United Kingdom* are directly related to the system of apartheid being formally introduced at the time in South Africa. In other words, although Jews in Germany in the 1940s were singled out for uniquely horrific levels of brutality, Asante consistently points us towards the uncomfortable reality that the scapegoating and abuse of ethnic minorities was (and is) a widespread reality within western societies as a whole.

Looking at the history behind *A United Kingdom*, Williams summarizes the situation by saying under British colonial control Seretse's homeland of Bechuanaland (to become Botswana on independence in 1966) was managed "on a shoestring," so that "little was provided in the way of formal education or health care."[37] The few services that did exist, she says, "were segregated along racial lines, with hugely preferential facilities for whites,"[38] and she concludes:

> Many of the children and adults in Bechuanaland were malnourished and suffered preventable diseases: malaria and yellow fever were endemic and diphtheria widespread. Throughout the period of British administration, at least a third of all children did not live to the age of 5.[39]

Williams highlights the method used to exploit the labour of men from Bechuanaland:

> All over British colonial Africa, people had to pay a hut tax; in Bechuanaland, the hut tax had been introduced in 1899 for every man of 18 years or more. Since traditionally most families' wealth lay in cattle and grain, which would not pay taxes, men were forced into wage labour. Most of the able-bodied men of the Protectorate went to South Africa to find work ... most worked in the gold mines of Johannesburg and the diamond mines of Kimberley. The working conditions of miners in South Africa were brutal.[40]

Williams explains how conditions in these camps were brought to light in the 1940s by the American photo-journalist Margaret Bourke-White, who worked for *Life* magazine.[41] Bourke-White herself describes how these workers "would sleep in concrete barracks, without windows, rolled up like sausages on the floor, forty to a room, crowded into compounds surrounded with barbed wire."[42] And, clearly, this image of barracks surrounded by barbed wire resonates within any discussion of *Where Hands Touch*.

Recognizing this global context for racism, James Whitman identifies the way in which the United States offered a model for Hitler's race laws. He says that "in *Mein Kampf* Hitler praised America as nothing less than 'the one state' that had made progress toward the creation of a healthy racist order of the kind the Nuremberg Laws were intended to establish."[43][44] Whitman asserts that in the inter-war period the United States was "a global leader in 'scientific' eugenics" and "promoted the sterilization of the mentally defective and the exclusion of immigrants who were supposedly genetically inferior."[45] Furthermore, he suggests, not only that in the early twentieth century the United States put into place a raft of legislation that barred immigration to America from certain areas of the world and favored immigration from other areas such as north-west Europe,[46] but also that in Germany "Nazi expansion eastward was accompanied by invocations of the American conquest of the West, with its accompanying wars on Native Americans."[47] Going further, he insists, the United States was not alone in introducing the sorts of measures and type of legislation mentioned here, declaring that,

> . . . as the Nazis were very much aware, America was part of a broader historically British world. British imperialism deposited a network of "free white men's democracies" around the globe, displaying a common commitment to maintaining what Columbia professor, J. W. Burgess influentially praised in 1890 as "ethnically homogeneous" states.[48]

Furthermore, Whitman claims that since the election of 2016,

> American racism has climbed back up out of the gutter and into national politics. Liberal values, and our basic institutions of justice, have come under steady assault. The same aspects that appealed to Nazis seventy-five years ago are with us again . . . The relevant questions are no different today from what they were in the early 1930s.[49]

In considering contemporary British films, the question becomes whether this might not also be relevant to the current situation in the UK. In the 1930s, racism was not something that only applied to Germany but instead was something that could be found throughout the rest of Europe and North America. *Where Hands Touch* considers the interracial transgression of miscegenation within Germany in 1944 (and via its backstory, within Germany immediately after the First World War), but the questions it raises very much fit the context of the contemporary period of Black Lives Matter. *A United Kingdom* considers the racist attitudes to be found at all levels of British society in the post-war period, but the issues with which it confronts its audience remain directly relevant to the UK in the early decades of the twenty-first century.

## IV

As was suggested in the opening to this chapter, *Where Hands Touch* hinges on issues of personal identity. As young people, both Lenya and Lutz are absorbed by considerations of how they are going to present themselves to others, and driven in their attempts to choose who they are going to become. However, what the film makes clear is that your identity is only a matter of personal choice up to a point. Our identities are constrained by social norms and values, and by the historical realities of the moment into which we are born. In fact, *Where Hands Touch* emphasizes exactly how important the socio-cultural and socio-political parameters of the individual experience are to the determination of identity. As Lenya and her mother, Kerstin, leave the factory where they are working as conscripted labor, Lenya, who is keen to see Lutz, lingers and urges her mother to go on ahead. Her mother's pointed response is, "It's your *choice*, Lenya" (my italics). We then see Lenya and Lutz kissing but positioned in such a way as to be tightly boxed into a doorway, before planes fly overhead symbolizing the intervention of the war into their lives. There is then, some sense of choice taking place, but the two protagonists are also trapped within the inescapable context of the time and place in which they find themselves. Later, Kerstin tells her daughter that in her relationship with the black Senegalese soldier she too was "chasing the same impossibility" Lenya is chasing, with the suggestion that it is not feasible to go beyond the norms and values of the society into which you are born, or at least that if you choose to do so there will be consequences. In *A United Kingdom*, Ruth's father tells her: "You marry a black, you make it impossible for us, for your mother . . . You may choose a life of insults and shame but what about us?" Again, the concept of being able to choose your future and who you are to become is contained within the script, but also once again the context of the norms and values of the society into which you are born is emphasized. In *Where Hands Touch*, strongly aware of the dominant values of the society in which he finds himself, Kerstin's brother-in-law rebukes her because she has compromised his family by coming to his house to ask for help. However, the brother-in-law then secretly supplies Kerstin with the official papers she needs, making it clear that despite what he may say (that is, despite appearances) he is actually continuing to make choices as to how he is going to define himself, position himself, and see himself within the context of the (repressive) society in which he finds himself. George MacKay, who plays the character of Lutz in *Where Hands Touch*, offers an accurate assessment of the situation faced by the central protagonists in this film in relation to identity: "This story is so compelling but it's not necessarily active choices being made all the time by the central characters . . . They are being moved by the world that is bigger than them and all the forces that dictate who they are and who they are to be."[50]

Within their own storylines and, by extension, within the contemporary period in which these films are being made and viewed, both *Where Hands Touch* and *A United Kingdom* express the complexity of identity. Both films employ the simple, well-used narrative scenario of love between a couple that struggles against the odds to find expression in order to highlight racial oppression. The main character in each film is a black person facing persecution at the hands of whites. In this sense, each of these films engages with identity politics,[51] the crucial defining feature of which is that: "Rather than accepting the negative scripts offered by a dominant culture about one's own inferiority, one transforms one's own sense of self and community."[52] According to Wiarda, identity politics aims to raise the self-awareness of various groups and "provide them with political power as a force to be reckoned with in the political arena."[53] However, Campt reminds us that the terms

**Figure 8.2** Boxed in a tight space, Lenya (Amandla Stenberg) and Lutz (George MacKay) look up as planes fly overhead in *Where Hands Touch*.

"Afro-German" and "Black German" have only come into use in more recent times:

> Afro-German (Afro-deutsch) is a term of identification that emerged in the mid-1980s among Germans of African descent to describe their mixed ethnic and racial heritages. As the Afro-German movement has evolved and come to include individuals of more diverse cultural backgrounds (individuals of Indian, Arab, and Asian heritage, for example), the term Black German (Schwarze Deutsche) has also come to be a widely accepted term of identification among members of this community.[54]

In assessing the political contexts of these films, we need at least to be aware that history is a version of the past shaped in the cultural currency of the present. In performing representations of black history we approach the past carrying the attitudes towards race we have accumulated in more recent periods. In both the US and the UK, filmmakers might therefore "naturally" tend to use a combination of the post-war emergence of African-American black consciousness and twenty-first-century woke attitudes as a lens through which to consider racial attitudes under Nazism. This is despite the fact that the testimonies of black Germans who lived through the period suggest there was at the time no essential blackness or black experience but instead only a range of multifaceted individual black experiences.

## V

Both films considered here focus on divisions within society created on the basis of race, and these types of division can be seen to be strengthening within contemporary Britain.[55] However, some people have questioned whether identity politics might not create more difficulties than it solves. Michael Ignatieff, for example, says,

> There is no essential identity called black or white, any more than there is a binary meaning to gender. Identity is a lie that binds when we allow it to imprison us but equally it remains a lie when we suppose we're free to choose our identities at will.[56]

Emphasizing the concept of identity that co-joins us—as white (or black), for example—in a single united group solely by virtue of one aspect of who we are can be seen to foster nationalism. Reviewing Kwame Anthony Appiah's book *The Lies That Bind: Rethinking Identity*,[57] Ignatieff writes:

> Nationalists, like religious fundamentalists, insist that there is some essence of nationhood that marks you, like a dye, with national characteristics. In reality,

national identity is a continual contest about who belongs to the national "we." In 2016, Boris Johnson said Brexit was "about the right of the people of this country to settle their own destiny." Which people, Appiah wants to know, was the former UK foreign secretary talking about? Not the Scots, not the Northern Irish, not Londoners who voted overwhelmingly to remain. Brexit has laid bare all the fissures—of region, interest, income, history and education—that any "essentialist" British nationalism wants to tarmac over.

German nationalism in the run-up to the Second World War was, of course, intent on "tarmacing over" exactly the same sorts of "fissures," or simple differences: all those elements of national totality that might from another perspective be celebrated as the multifaceted mix of community. Eric Hobsbawm suggested identity problems only arose when people were "prevented from having the multiple, combined, identities which are natural to most of us."[58] His position was that people "cannot be described, even for bureaucratic purposes, except by a combination of many characteristics," but that identity politics assumed "that one among the many identities we all have is the one that determines, or at least dominates our politics."[59] He felt people usually had "no problem about combining identities" and that this was "the basis of general politics as distinct from sectional identity politics."[60] Hobsbawm warned against identity groups that were "about themselves, for themselves, and nobody else," and that were not "held together by a single common set of aims or values."[61] His concerns with identity politics are among those identified by Wiarda, who discusses the way in which critics have seen such an approach as detracting from "more fundamental issues of society such as class conflict and capitalist oppression" and ultimately amounting to no more than "expressions of narrow, bourgeois values."[62] "Identities" have also been criticized as "social constructions rather than natural" and as "indelibly marked by the oppressive conditions that created them."[63] However, Linda Martin Alcoff, Michael Hames-Garcia, Satya P. Mohanty, and Paula M. L. Moya offer something of a counter to this perspective in *Identity Politics Reconsidered*. They suggest:

> Our identities are not just imposed on us by society. Often we create positive and meaningful identities that enable us to better understand and negotiate the social world . . . They also make it possible for us to change the world and ourselves in valuable ways. This is what democratic and progressive social movements, such as the struggles for civil rights or the equality of women, show very clearly.[64]

Both *Where Hands Touch* and *A United Kingdom* are serious interventions into a contemporary political context of widening social divisions. The representations of race found within these films alert us to the political parameters of not only the period to which they refer but also the period in which they have been made. Identity politics is a relatively recent social construct that has become a major dynamic within the contemporary political arena. However, the role of choice and free will in the creation of the self has been a perennial philosophical debate.

## Notes

1. Sybil H. Milton, "'Gypsies' as Social Outsiders in Nazi Germany," in Robert Gellately and Nathan Stoltzfus (eds.), *Social Outsiders in Nazi Germany* (Princeton, NJ and Oxford: Princeton University Press, 2001), p. 231.
2. A. Susan Williams, *Colour Bar: The Triumph of Seretse Khama and His Nation* (London: Allen Lane, 2006), p. 6.
3. Ibid.
4. Ibid., p. 12.
5. Ibid., p. 22.
6. One reason given for blacks being able to survive Nazism more easily than Jews is that "the regime fostered hopes of recovering a colonial empire" within which these people may have been useful. See Robbie Aitken and Eve Rosenhaft, *Black Germany: The Making and Unmaking of a Diaspora Community, 1884–1960* (Cambridge: Cambridge University Press, 2013), p. 20. See also the notion of Macaulayism dealt with in the previous chapter on *Darkest Hour*.
7. "Some historians have suggested German treatment of Blacks was not more brutal because Blacks were neither numerous nor perceived as powerful . . . and that German political strategy as it related to expanded interests in sub-Saharan Africa required a less confrontational approach." See Stephen Kaufman, "Blacks in Germany During the Third Reich: Star of David Not Required," in Kevin Reilly, Stephen Kaufman, and Angela Bodino (eds.), *Racism: A Global Reader* (New York and London: M. E. Sharpe, 2003), p. 272.
8. Howard J. Wiarda, *Political Culture, Political Science, and Identity Politics: An Uneasy Alliance* (London and New York: Routledge, 2016), p. 151.
9. Ibid.
10. Ibid., pp. 151–2.
11. Ibid., p. 152.
12. Ibid., p. 153. Wiarda is specifically looking at the split between Republicans and Democrats, or conservatives and liberal progressives.
13. "In the Nazi era, from 1933 to 1945, African-Germans numbered in their thousands. There was no uniform experience, but over time, they were banned from having relationships with white people, excluded from education and types of employment, and some were sterilised, while others were taken to concentration camps." See Damian Zane, "Being black in Nazi Germany," *BBC News*,

22 May 2019. Available at https://www.bbc.co.uk/news/world-africa-48273570 (accessed 22 August 2020).
14. In the fervour of anti-Semitism, Hitler linked the arrival of blacks in Germany to the scheming of Jews: "It was and it is Jews who bring the Negroes into the Rhineland, always with the same secret thought and clear aim of ruining the hated white race by the necessarily resulting bastardization, throwing it down from its cultural and political height, and himself rising to be its master." See Adolf Hitler, *Mein Kampf* (New York: Houghton Mifflin, 1943), p. 325.
15. Clarence Lusane, *Hitler's Black Victims: The Historical Experiences of Afro-Germans, European Blacks, Africans, and African Americans in the Nazi Era* (London and New York: Routledge, 2003), p. 138.
16. Hans J. Massaquoi, *Destined to Witness: Growing Up Black in Nazi Germany* (New York: Perennial, 2001), p. 2.
17. In her "Translator's Preface" to Theodor Michael's *Black German: An Afro-German Life in the Twentieth Century* (Liverpool: Liverpool University Press, 2017), Eve Rosenhaft describes how "as a certified 'racial alien,'" Michael was "excluded from educational, work and training opportunities and even from the possibility of military service." She says: "What weighed on him most was 'fear, nothing but fear,' the need to keep his head down and not be noticed. He was oppressed not only by his own circumstances but also by the knowledge that worse things were happening to other members of the black community: forced sterilization, the break-up of families, death in prisons and concentration camps—all driven by the regime's determination that Mischlinge —people of 'mixed blood'—like him should not exist" (p. 4).
18. Lusane, *Hitler's Black Victims: The Historical Experiences of Afro-Germans, European Blacks, Africans, and African Americans in the Nazi Era*, p. 6.
19. "Because German conceptions of Black Germans in this period were so profoundly shaped by one very specific, though much publicized, segment of this population—the six to eight hundred children of the Rhineland occupation—other individuals who did not belong to this group could to some extent escape Nazi scrutiny." See Tina M. Campt, *Other Germans: Black Germans and the Politics of Race, Gender, and Memory in the Third Reich* (Ann Arbor: University of Michigan Press, 2004), p. 21.
20. Iris Wigger, *The "Black Horror on the Rhine": Intersections of Race, Nation, Gender and Class in 1920s Germany* (London: Palgrave Macmillan, 2017), p. 1.
21. Ibid.
22. Larry A. Greene, "Race in the Reich: The African American Press on Nazi Germany," in Larry A. Greene and Anke Ortlepp (eds.), *Germans and African Americans: Two Centuries of Exchange* (Jackson: University Press of Mississippi, 2011), p. 71.
23. Ibid., p. 73.
24. Ibid., p. 74.
25. Greene says, "The black press, most notably the *Pittsburgh Courier*, continually characterized Herman Goering and Governor Eugene Talmadge of Georgia as

two racists cut from the same cloth, as were Mississippi's racist U.S. senator, Theodore G. Bilbo, and Germany's Joseph Goebbels." Ibid., p. 72.
26. Wigger, *The "Black Horror on the Rhine": Intersections of Race, Nation, Gender and Class in 1920s Germany*, p. 182.
27. Lusane, *Hitler's Black Victims: The Historical Experiences of Afro-Germans, European Blacks, Africans, and African Americans in the Nazi Era*, p. 16.
28. Campt, *Other Germans: Black Germans and the Politics of Race, Gender, and Memory in the Third Reich*, p. 26.
29. Robert Kesting, "The Black Experience during the Holocaust," in Michael Berenbaum and Abraham J. Peck (eds.), *The Holocaust and History: The Known, the Unknown, the Disputed and the Re-examined* (Bloomington and Indianapolis: Indiana University Press, 2002), p. 359.
30. "The image of the 'Rhineland Bastard' ... came to embody the children these soldiers left behind as a complex representation of the manifold tensions of the occupation." See Campt, *Other Germans: Black Germans and the Politics of Race, Gender, and Memory in the Third Reich*, p. 25.
31. Ibid.
32. Raffael Scheck, *Hitler's African Victims: The German Army Massacres of Black French Soldiers in 1940* (Cambridge and New York: Cambridge University Press, 2006), p. 9.
33. Robert N. Proctor, *Racial Hygiene: Medicine under the Nazis* (Cambridge, MA and London: Harvard University Press, 2002/1988), p. 6.
34. Kenneth B. Clark, "A Conversation with James Baldwin," 24 May 1963, WGBH-TV, transcript available in Fred L. Standley and Louis H. Pratt (eds.), *Conversations with James Baldwin* (Jackson and London: University Press of Mississippi, 1989), pp. 38–45.
35. "In Nazi Germany, jazz remained popular and the efforts at banning the music merely sent it underground rather than destroying it. More broadly, even among Nazis themselves, jazz was often condoned and even encouraged with the result that a number of concentration camps had jazz bands." See Lusane, *Hitler's Black Victims: The Historical Experiences of Afro-Germans, European Blacks, Africans, and African Americans in the Nazi Era*, p. 17.
36. The same word, "monkey," is used by a group of Hitler Youth in *Where Hands Touch*, who suggest Lenya should be marching to the death camps with a group of Jews passing by under armed guard.
37. Williams, *Colour Bar: The Triumph of Seretse Khama and His Nation*, p. 37.
38. Ibid.
39. Ibid.
40. Ibid., p. 32.
41. Ibid.
42. Margaret Bourke-White, *Portrait of Myself* (Simon & Schuster, 1963), p. 316.
43. James Q. Whitman, *Hitler's American Model: The United States and the Making of Nazi Race Law* (Princeton, NJ and Oxford: Princeton University Press, 2018), p. 2.

44. The Nuremberg laws were anti-Jewish legislation introduced by the Nazis in 1935 disenfranchising German Jews and prohibiting marriage or extramarital relationships between Aryans and Jews.
45. Whitman, *Hitler's American Model: The United States and the Making of Nazi Race Law*, p. 8.
46. Ibid., p. 35.
47. Ibid., p. 9.
48. Ibid., p. 36.
49. Ibid., p. 11.
50. "Where Hands Touch Featurette," *Where Hands Touch* (Amma Asante, 2017), DVD.
51. Identity politics came to the fore as a term in the second half of the twentieth century on the back of the emergence of a series of large-scale political movements such as second wave feminism, black Civil Rights in the United States, and gay liberation, each "based in claims about injustices done to particular social groups." See Cressida Heyes, "Identity Politics," *The Stanford Encyclopedia of Philosophy*, Fall 2020, Edward N. Zalta (ed.). Available at https://plato.stanford.edu/archives/fall2020/entries/identity-politics/ (accessed 24 August 2020).
52. Ibid.
53. Wiarda, *Political Culture, Political Science, and Identity Politics: An Uneasy Alliance*, p. 150.
54. Campt, *Other Germans: Black Germans and the Politics of Race, Gender, and Memory in the Third Reich*, p. 9.
55. Magne Flemmen and Mike Savage say "racism and more particularly anti-immigrant sentiment" was "a key feature of the Brexit referendum vote" (p. 2). But they dispute the view that it is mainly the white working class who are attracted to racist politics, saying "significant amounts of racism" in the form of "imperial nationalism" is associated with "advantaged groups" ("The politics of nationalism and white racism in the UK." See Magne Flemmen and Mike Savage, *The British Journal of Sociology*, 68 (1), 2017. Available at: http://eprints.lse.ac.uk/87229/1 (accessed 31 August 2020), p. 30.) Kalwant Bhopal says in recent years in the UK "black identities have become associated with notions of danger and hostility." See Kalwant Bhopal, *White Privilege: The Myth of a Post-Racial Society* (Bristol: Policy Press, 2018), pp. 10–11.
56. Michael Ignatieff, "Is identity politics ruining democracy?" *Financial Times*, 5 September 2018. Available at https://www.ft.com/content/09c2c1e4-ad05-11e8-8253-48106866cd8a (accessed 22 August 2020).
57. Kwame Anthony Appiah, *The Lies That Bind: Rethinking Identity* (London: Profile Books, 2018).
58. Eric Hobsbawm, "Identity Politics and the Left," Barry Amiel & Norman Melburn Trust Lecture, Institute of Education, London, 2 May 1996. Available at http://banmarchive.org.uk/articles/1996%20annual%20lecture.htm (accessed 31 August 2020).
59. Ibid.

60. Ibid.
61. Ibid.
62. Wiarda, *Political Culture, Political Science, and Identity Politics: An Uneasy Alliance*, p. 151.
63. Linda Martin Alcoff, Michael Hames-Garcia, Satya P. Mohanty, and Paula M. L. Moya (eds.), *Identity Politics Reconsidered* (New York and London: Palgrave Macmillan, 2006), p. 3.
64. Ibid., p. 6.

CHAPTER 9

# Colonialism and the Reshaping of History: *Viceroy's House* (Gurinder Chadha, 2017)

I

*Viceroy's House* (Gurinder Chadha, 2017)—shown in India as *Partition: 1947*—offers a fictional account of the behind-the-scenes political maneuverings that occurred as British rule in the region came to an end and the Indian subcontinent was divided into two countries, India and Pakistan. The film follows Lord Louis ("Dickie") Mountbatten (Hugh Bonneville) as he travels from England to Delhi early in 1947, tasked with overseeing the end of British rule in India. The very British and populist "upstairs-downstairs" narrative form allows the viewer not only to follow the politicians as they attempt to negotiate their way towards Indian independence but also to see how the transition from British rule plays out in the lives of relatively ordinary people. The below-stairs love story between Jeet Kumar (Manish Dayal), who is Hindu, and Aalia Noor (Huma Qureshi), a Muslim, offers an entry point for the spectator to access the history of the period, which is seen as centering on the antagonism morphing into hatred expressed between these two religious groups.

During the Second World War, despite the fact that more than 1.5 million Indian troops were involved in the Allied war effort, political agitation for independence intensified; and by the end of the war it seemed clear Britain no longer had the power nor political will to retain control over a region previously seen as the "jewel in the crown" of the British Empire.[1] In the film, a servant working in the Viceroy's House, Duleep Singh (Jaz Deol), says: "England is all slums and bomb-sites. You know why the English go? This war has exhausted them; they can't afford to keep us." Shortly after this, echoing a common colonial sentiment, the Scottish administrator of the Viceroy's household, Ewart (David Hayman), asks: "Do you think you Indians are ready to run your own civil service, courts of law, your own armed forces?" The violent chaos we see occurring as India moves towards independence, and the

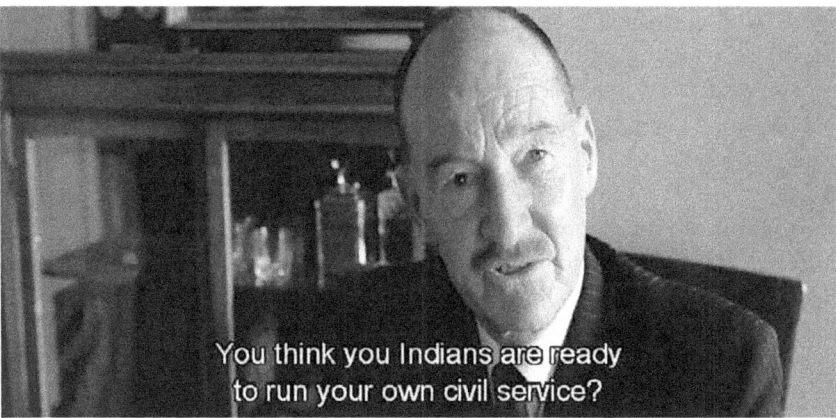

**Figure 9.1** The administrator of the Viceroy's household, Ewart (David Hayman), expresses the colonial attitude towards Indian independence within the opening minutes of *Viceroy's House* (Gurinder Chadha, 2017).

disarray we see among Indian politicians, seems to suggest the "natives" are most definitely not ready to take over.

*Viceroy's House* shows Indian politicians at loggerheads from the outset. The Muslim League led by Muhammad Ali Jinnah (Denzil Smith) is demanding India should be divided into two countries after independence in order to create a separate country for Muslims. The Congress Party led by Jawaharlal Nehru (Tanveer Ghani) and Mahatma Gandhi (Neeraj Kabi) wants a single country but is unable to agree how this should be brought into existence. Meanwhile, the country is in turmoil, with brutal communal violence taking place across religious divides. At one point, Mountbatten's chief of staff, Lord Lionel "Pug" Ismay (Michael Gambon), reports to him: "There's been a massacre in Punjab. Half of Rawalpindi is on fire. Muslims burnt down Sikh and Hindu houses. Brutal reprisals have spread through Muslim streets." In these circumstances, although he is initially against dividing the country, Mountbatten is seen as forced to agree to Partition.[2] After telling his wife, Lady Edwina Mountbatten (Gillian Anderson), that "the country is burning" and, if power is not transferred soon, "there may be nothing left to transfer," he then goes further and decides to hand the country over as quickly as possible. Despite the British Prime Minister, Clement Attlee, having only recently given an already tight deadline for Indian independence of the end of June 1948, Mountbatten attempts to speed up the process still further and commits Britain to leaving by mid-August 1947.

According to one historian, Sekhar Bandyopadhyay, the resulting partition of India brought about the worst communal violence and human displacement the subcontinent had ever known. In his estimation, "about one million people were killed and seventy-five thousand or more women were raped," while "more than 10 million people were displaced and began to taste bitter freedom amidst the squalor of refugee camps."[3] People desperately attempting to return to their home areas on either side of the newly created borders were slaughtered, so that "trains full of dead bodies travelled across the border in both directions."[4][5] In the film, Mountbatten's valet, Jeet, believes both the woman he is in love with, Aalia, and her father, Ali (Om Puri), have been killed attempting to return from Delhi to Lahore by train. Crispin Bates is one among many others to suggest: "One explanation for the chaotic manner in which the two independent nations came into being is the hurried nature of the British withdrawal."[6] This is a line of argument explored by the film. Pages are shown being torn off a calendar as Mountbatten pushes the pace of change and around the country the violence increases.[7] At the same time, using the Viceroy's House as a parallel to the country as a whole, the household staff are told by Mountbatten: "Each one of you must choose which country will have your allegiance, India or Pakistan." The absurdity of the process is highlighted as everything in the Viceroy's House (again, paralleling the country)[8] is divided between the future countries of India and Pakistan.[9]

The darker line of argument pursued in the film is that the partition of the Indian subcontinent was actually planned by Churchill several years earlier.[10] *Viceroy's House* shows Churchill as having been able to influence British foreign policy even when he was no longer in office. In this respect the film draws heavily on Narendra Singh Sarila's revisionist account of Partition in the book *The Shadow of the Great Game—The Untold Story of India's Partition*, which as Ashvin Immanuel Devasundaram explains it, "indicts Winston Churchill as a villainous manipulator who masterminded a backroom deal with Muslim League leader Muhammad Ali Jinnah."[11] Following the line of argument in Sarila's book, the film puts forward the idea that Churchill promised to set up an independent Pakistan in return for it operating as a bulwark to Russian expansionism.[12] Furthermore, it suggests this was a deal about which Mountbatten knew nothing. Both Sarila and the film suggest Churchill's aim was to protect British oil interests in the Persian Gulf. Jinnah, according to Sarila, had agreed "to cooperate with Britain on defence matters if Pakistan was created."[13] Considering the global politics of the situation, Nisid Hajari suggests:

> Washington and London were both keenly aware that if India joined the Soviet camp, the country would pose a major threat cutting Britain off from

its eastern possessions. If Russian warships could steam out of Bombay or Karachi, they could easily blockade the vital Persian Gulf.[14]

## II

The idea of controlling Middle East oil supplies is one aspect of the film that allows Mark Kermode to suggest *Viceroy's House* is a film involved in "not so much signposting as trumpeting its contemporary references."[15] He highlights allusions not only to more recent efforts of western powers to control Middle East oil reserves but also to current refugee crises and Britain's decision to leave the European Union. In watching the film, he says, it is impossible "to avoid making connections with rushed Brexit deadlines as parties hurry towards a divisive future in double-quick time."[16][17] Many other reviews, however, focus more strongly and directly on what the film has to say about Churchill and Mountbatten. Kenneth Rosario claims the director set out "to whitewash the involvement of the last Viceroy of India, Lord Mountbatten, in the decision to divide India" by projecting him as "a pawn of a larger British conspiracy and a good man torn between bickering Indian politicians."[18] Ian Jack states the film has taken "a breathtaking liberty with the historical record."[19] The clear implication, he says, is that "when it comes to Britain's share of the blame for the bloodshed of 1947, Churchill, not Mountbatten is the culprit."[20] Jack adds that he cannot find any historian "who thinks this interpretation of events is anything other than a travesty."[21] Drawing attention to the strong focus the film has on the British perspective of events, Fatima Bhutto feels the implication of the film is that freedom is "not something fought and won by Indians" but rather is "a gift" from the Mountbattens and the empire they represented.[22] The British, she suggests, are represented as "serene and encouraging, weighed down with the heavy burden of soothing these wild, intemperate people."[23] The reality ignored by the film for Bhutto is that "the very foundations of the viceroy's residence were built on violence."[24] In response to these accusations, Gurinder Chadha has defended her film by saying: "My film does not ignore the freedom struggle—it celebrates that struggle . . . It does not ignore the colonial policy of divide and rule, but challenges it . . . Above all, it does not show the Muslim community as sole perpetrators of violence."[25]

Clearly, any filmmakers who approach the subject of Partition are entering a minefield of contending perspectives since they are creating a film that must necessarily have as its very essence the concept of division(s) between people. In particular, what is seen to be at stake in this film are separations between religions (Hindu, Muslim, Sikh, and Christian), classes (upper/aristocratic/princely and lower/servant), to some extent genders (Mountbatten and his wife and daughter, for example), and (most importantly) between colonizers and the colonized. Both the process of Partition and the film itself work to give, on the one hand, clarity to these already existing divisions and, on the other hand, fixity to the continued existence of these created borders between people. This process of bordering—the creation, reinforcement, and restoration of borders—is a prevalent feature of contemporary society. Even before Covid-19 exponentially magnified the socially, politically, and culturally sanctioned fear of others, borders were multiplying. In his book *Theory of the Border*, in which he asserts that what all borders have in common is that 'they introduce a division or bifurcation of some sort into the world,'[26] Thomas Nail states:

> We live in a world of borders . . . Despite the celebration of globalization and the increasing necessity of global mobility, there are more types of borders today than ever before in history. In the last twenty years, but particularly since 9/11, hundreds of new borders have emerged around the world.[27]

Nail reminds us that we should aim "to understand the historical (not idealist) conditions in which empirical borders emerge across different social contexts."[28] In other words, historical and social contexts are crucial to understanding the often apparently arbitrary, and yet very definitely real, boundaries that emerge between people. The key historical context with respect to the partition of India has been seen by many as the fact that:

> As part of the long standing "divide and rule" colonial strategy, the British had manipulated and exacerbated ethnic, religious, and tribal differences in most of their colonies to ensure their own survival in the face of resistance from emerging freedom movements.[29]

The writer and politician Shashi Tharoor believes "the horrors of Partition were the direct result of the deliberate British policy of communal division that fomented religious antagonisms to facilitate continued imperial rule."[30] He says the British approach involved "systematically promoting political divisions between Hindus and Muslims, defined as the monolithic communities they had never been before the British."[31] In defending her film and attempting to demonstrate that it was made with an acute awareness of historical context, Chadha pointed out the script for *Viceroy's House* highlights this concept of "divide and rule." She drew attention to the moment in the film when, as she quotes it, the Congress Party politician Nehru says to Mountbatten: "You have divided us and now you ask us for a solution."[32]

In her memory of it, Chadha is paraphrasing what Nehru actually says in the film, where he goes into more detail:

> You have done everything to foster hatred between our different communities: separate schools, textbooks, elections. That was always your policy: divide and rule. So, when you have divided us you ask me for a solution.

As might be expected, this aspect of historical context has always been highly contested. Writing twenty years ago, Bishwa Mohan Pandey said, "British historians have tried and are still trying to interpret issues related to partition to absolve the British of any responsibility for the division of the Indian sub-continent."[33] The classic British imperialist approach to this idea of "divide and rule," he said, was to suggest "Indian society was a divided society from the pre-colonial period and it was this division which culminated in partition."[34] Whether or not the antagonism between Hindus and Muslims pre-dated British rule or was essentially fomented by the British, Sekhar Bandyopadhyay says Churchill openly described this religious feud as the bulwark of British rule in India.[35]

## III

The battle lines with regards to Partition are, therefore, plainly drawn around the interpretation of historical context. We might all agree it is of critical importance to place an event such as Partition within an accurate historical context, but what would constitute a correct elucidation of history? This is a political decision. There are historical facts (just as there is scientific data), but the interpretation of facts (and data) requires a perspective to be taken on these facts (and data). Films that are historical dramas inevitably take part in a contestation of political perspectives in relation to any given period from the past. Such films unavoidably contribute towards both individual and collective understandings of the past. *Viceroy's House* presents Mountbatten, an actual historical figure who played a critical role in Partition, as a semi-heroic figure who was doing his best in difficult circumstances. According to the film, he genuinely wanted to achieve a positive outcome for India but was thwarted by the political maneuverings of others. In classical colonial terms, he might be seen as taking up the "white man's burden" and attempting to do his best by the poor native people he has to rule while nurturing them towards civilization and sufficient political competence to become an independent country.

However, from the historical record it would be equally possible to present Mountbatten as a duplicitous and untrustworthy character who made a series of errors of judgement and was actually only interested in getting out of the country as quickly as possible. Following this line of argument, Adil Najam, for example, suggests: "the one man whose job it was, above all else, to avoid the mayhem, ended up inflaming the conditions that made Partition the horror it became. That man was Lord Louis Mountbatten."[36] Najam goes on to explain his own (political) perspective on these historical events. He says:

> Mountbatten arrived in India in February 1947 and was given until June 1948—not 1947—to complete his mission. Impatient to get back to Britain and advance his own naval career, he decided to bring forward the date by 10 months to August 1947... How crucial were those 10 months? I would argue, they could have meant the difference between a simply violent partition and a horrifically genocidal partition.[37]

Stanley Wolpert has suggested: "Those ten additional months of postwar talks, aborted by an impatient Mountbatten, might have helped all parties to agree that cooperation was much wiser than conflict, dialogue more sensible than division."[38] Wolpert talks about "Mountbatten's hyperactive frenzy in accelerating the initially tight withdrawal schedule, mandated by Britain's cabinet to extend to June 1948";[39] while Bates describes the transfer of power into Indian hands as being "summarily advanced to August 1947 at the whim of ... Mountbatten."[40] Ayesha Jalal points out Mountbatten's instructions were "to avoid partition" and suggests a settlement with a federal system of provinces along the lines suggested by a group of Cabinet appointees sent out from Britain in 1946 was still conceivable when Mountbatten arrived in 1947.[41] And Mountbatten's biographer, Philip Ziegler, is clear about exactly how devious Mountbatten might be seen to be. According to him, "Field Marshal Templer once exploded across a dinner table, 'Dickie, you're so crooked that if you swallowed a nail you'd shit a corkscrew!'"[42][43]

It is certainly the case that when Mountbatten arrives at Viceroy's House in Delhi, along with his wife Edwina and daughter Pamela (Lily Travers), to take over as the final Viceroy who will usher in independence for India, he and his family enter a world of absolute privilege. We are shown servants working in the extensive gardens, servants brushing the tennis court, and servants cleaning and preparing rooms. A passing white man, a person of authority simply by virtue of race, is not working but is pointing out to servants what needs to be done next, and all the time copious amounts of food are being prepared. In another scene, the outgoing Viceroy's wife, Lady Wavell (Lucy Fleming), gestures towards an assembled array of servants, and announces: "This is the indoor staff: five hundred or something, I believe."

Mountbatten's aristocratic background is made clear in the film where the script identifies Queen Victoria as his great-grandmother. Ali, a Muslim who

*Colonialism and the Reshaping of History* 145

**Figure 9.2** A world of absolute privilege: the indoor staff assembled to greet the Mountbattens in *Viceroy's House*.

has campaigned for independence and spent time in gaol as a result, points out that, "He is the King's cousin: he has empire in his blood." Mountbatten himself highlights the fact that he is related to Tsar Nicholas II of Russia. Writing later and looking back at her family's time in India, Pamela Mountbatten discusses not only her father's links to British royalty but also the integration of British and Indian aristocracy. For instance, describing a visit to the Maharaja of Bikaner, she says this was

> a particularly enjoyable visit as my father had known the Maharaja for many years. They had first met when they were children, later at the coronation of King George V, and then when my father served on the staff of the Prince of Wales for his visit to India in 1921.[44]

Describing the life that was enjoyed during this visit, she says:

> There was an early-morning shoot of the famous imperial sandgrouse. Thirty thousand birds flew over our heads. They were difficult to shoot, flying very fast and swerving in all directions. That evening we gathered in the Durbar Hall of Lallgarh Palace where my father invested the Maharaja with the Grand Cross of the Star of India. The assembled nobles and courtiers looked magnificent in their red and yellow Durbar dress.[45]

Recognizing the links this Indian elite had with colonialism, Shashi Tharoor talks about "the complicity shown by the compromised Indian aristocracy with the colonial project."[46] Class, embodied in the structural "upstairs-downstairs" form of the film, is thus recognized by the film and the historical record as a key aspect of British rule in India. Even Mahatma Gandhi

(Neeraj Kabi), despite the austere simplicity of his presentation of self, is noticeably seen in the film to be part of the "upstairs" crowd.

## IV

What some observers have seen as being absent from the film is any real sense of the carnage on the streets that was occurring across India in 1946–7. Reconstructed newsreels document riots in various parts of the country, floods of refugees are shown streaming into Delhi to live in makeshift camps, and survivors report the chaos they have witnessed on their journeys, but the utter desperation and brutality experienced by so many is implied rather than visually expressed. Rosario described the "squeaky clean appearance" of the film, which meant the tragedy failed to "overwhelm, scare or infuriate" the viewer.[47] In overall terms, the primary historical events of mob violence that constituted Partition end up being presented in a palatable form for a mainstream audience.[48]

Chadha claims, "responsibility for the violence lay on all sides, and all communities were victims of the violence, irrespective of race or religion."[49] In other words, she puts forward the classic liberal response to the situation and, in so far as it goes, she is not incorrect in what she says. However, what this neglects, or succeeds in sidestepping, is any in-depth exploration of the politics of Partition. Bandyopadhyay tells us that by March/April 1947 "many Congress leaders had more or less reconciled themselves to the idea of conceding Pakistan and accepting freedom with partition as a preferable option to continuing communal violence."[50] Nehru himself is quoted as saying, "The plan for partition offered a way out and we took it."[51] In the film, only Gandhi will not accept the idea of dividing India into two countries: "Division does not create peace: it creates havoc," he asserts. But he is powerless to stop the violence that has begun to take hold of the country. And, in terms of politics, there the film leaves it: the passions unleashed are not simply unstoppable but also inexplicable it seems within the terms of rational reasoning.

However, what other writers documenting the period such as Yasim Khan tell us is that:

> Strikes were incessant and held by everybody from tram drivers and press workers to postmen and industrial workers in cotton mills, potteries and factories. In 1946 there were 1,629 industrial disputes involving almost two million workers and a loss of over twelve million man-days.[52]

Khan says there was a "terminal breakdown of power in the spring of 1946," so that "in the cities of North India militia groups, extremist parties and armed groups rapidly burgeoned."⁵³ "The dark underbelly of these organisations," he says, "was their exclusive, rigid, right-wing ideologies."⁵⁴ This was the political reality of the period in India: in a classic scenario of community disintegration, attitudes were becoming polarized between left-wing and right-wing ideologies in the face of the increasing emphasis placed by politicians seeking power on the divisions rather than the unity between people. Confronted by this divisive form of politicization, as Khan explains, "neutrality or political indifference was fast becoming an unrealistic and untenable option."⁵⁵ Amritjit Sinngh, Nalini Iyer, and Rahul K. Gairola reckon, even up until today, most communities in India, Pakistan, and Bangladesh have failed to overcome these "angers and resentments of the past."⁵⁶ In fact, they suggest, some groups in each of these countries seem determined to instigate even more menacing "tribalization of the population based on caste, class, and religious identity."⁵⁷ These authors point out it would be wrong "to equate Partition with the demand for Pakistan."⁵⁸ In his call for Pakistan, they say, the leader of the Muslim League, Jinnah, was in fact lobbying for "a stake in power for Muslims in India once the British left."⁵⁹ Following this line of thought, Bates says it is possible Jinnah "simply wished to use the demand for a separate state as a bargaining chip to win greater power for Muslims within a loosely federated India."⁶⁰ ⁶¹ However, this is to miss the significance of Jinnah's position: whatever his intention may have been, the effect was to embolden right-wing political forces with an essentially nationalistic fervor that is commonplace within such situations. In his inaugural address as Prime Minister of India, Nehru may have spoken about building "the noble mansion of free India where *all* [my italics] her children may dwell,"⁶² and, in his presidential address in Pakistan, Jinnah may have said people could "belong to any religion or caste or creed' and that this had 'nothing to do with the business of the state,"⁶³ but beyond the comfortably well-off, highly educated, middle-class circles inhabited by these politicians such statements held little weight.

It may be, as Sinngh, Iyer, and Gairola suggest, that "Partition is a tragedy of multiple narratives,"⁶⁴ but that does not mean these events are in some way beyond political analysis. *Viceroy's House* is a politically liberal text. The audience is supplied with important factual details about social conditions in India in the 1940s, in particular through the words ascribed to Edwina Mountbatten. She says to her husband, for example:

> Darling, did you know that ninety-two per cent of the population is illiterate and that one in five babies dies before they are four months old . . . India's problems are not just political, they are social and economic. Almost half the babies born here die before they are five: that cannot be the legacy the British leave India after three centuries.

But, of course, this is precisely the legacy the British Empire does leave India (along with a million dead in a horrendously chaotic transition to independence). We may see the Mountbattens—as representative Brits—doing their utmost to alleviate the misery of those who have ended up in refugee camps in Delhi, but we are also presented with at least some indications of the realities of imperialism. *Viceroy's House* provides us with woke representations of issues attaching to both women and race; this is a text that will resonate with supporters of the Me Too and Black Lives Matter movements. The central female characters—Edwina, Pamela, and Aalia—are all presented as strong, independent women; racist attitudes are confronted by the Mountbattens in the running of the Viceroy's household; and the religious divide is challenged (and defeated) in the relationship between Aalia and Jeet. However, just as with contemporary twenty-first-century movements agitating for social change that unless they are underpinned by a thoroughly coherent political analysis will flounder on the uncertainties and confusions of liberalism, so too with texts of all sorts, including this film. Thomas Carlyle famously asserted, "The History of the world is but the Biography of great men,"[65] and naturally those who see themselves as great men concur. If, however, as Shashi Tharoor suggests, there is a "moral urgency" attached to "explaining to today's Indians—and Britons—why colonialism was the horror it turned out to be,"[66] our grasp of history needs to be grounded in something much more than the foibles and whims (and, indeed, bursts of inspiration) of individuals. In the film, Edwina is able to quote back at him things Nehru has said; and so she reminds him he once said, "Without peace all other dreams vanish and are reduced to ashes," and that he went on to say, "The only alternative to coexistence is co-destruction"[67] These are impressively succinct proverbial sound bites that are admirable in their sentiments and have been interestingly woven into the script. However, the crucial point is that it is not just Mountbatten who is unable to see a peaceful route to independence—Nehru faces the same predicament. Both of them are confronted with the fact that their liberal responses are not only inadequate to deal with the political scenario with which they are faced but also leave them unable to comprehend the maelstrom within which they find themselves. The challenge for the filmmaker is not to show Partition as the unleashing of incomprehensible madness but to demonstrate the simple predictable political logic of events. In the film, Gandhi says, "What we need is not reason: we need a far greater force," and Edwina is immediately on his wavelength and fills in the missing requirement, "Love." But this is merely to demonstrate the similar vacuous nature of his philosophy at this juncture. Left like this, for the audience the world becomes a dangerous and unpredictable place where all you can do is imagine utopian, unattainable places. Aalia's fiancé, for example, says to her,

"Imagine life in Pakistan—no prejudice, no tension—a nation our children will be proud of."[68]

**Notes**

1. "Jewel in the crown" was a common phrase used in this regard. It was employed by Winston Churchill in a speech to the Indian Empire Society on 11 December 1930: "We have no intention of casting away that most truly bright and precious jewel in the crown of the King, which more than all our other Dominions and Dependencies constitute the glory and strength of the British Empire. The loss of India would mark and consummate the downfall of the British Empire." See Robert Rhodes James (ed.), *Winston S. Churchill: His Complete Speeches, 1897–1963, Volume 5: 1928–1935* (New York: Chelsea House, 1974), p. 4938. The phrase is widely quoted elsewhere; for example, see C. C. Eldridge, *The Imperial Experience: From Carlyle to Forster* (London: Macmillan, 1996), p. 179.
2. "The formal justification of a political partition is that it will regulate, that is, reduce or resolve, a national, ethnic or communal conflict." See Brendan O'Leary, "Partition," in Thomas M. Wilson and Hastings Donnan (eds.), *A Companion to Border Studies* (Malden, MA: Wiley-Blackwell, 2016), p. 29.
3. Sekhar Bandyopadhyay, *From Plassey to Partition: A History of Modern India* (New Delhi: Orient Longman, 2004), p. 460.
4. Ibid.
5. There is a lot of uncertainty around these figures but the scale of the violence and displacement is not in doubt. In *Revisiting India's Partition: New Essays on Memory, Culture and Politics* (Lanham, MD and London: Lexington Books, 2016), Amritjit Sinngh, Nalini Iyer, and Rahul K. Gairola suggest, "The summer of 1947 witnessed the migration of some fourteen million people and the deaths of at least one million" (p. xvi).
6. Crispin Bates, "The Hidden Story of Partition and its Legacies," BBC, 3 March 2011. Available at http://www.bbc.co.uk/history/british/modern/partition 1947_01.shtml (accessed 18 July 2020).
7. Mountbatten had a calendar printed showing the countdown to independence. ("Daddy has had a calendar distributed to most offices saying 'days left to transfer of power.'") See Pamela Mountbatten, *India Remembered: A Personal Account of the Mountbattens During the Transfer of Power* (London: Pavilion, 2007), p. 117.)
8. "The film chronicles the last six months of the British Raj in India, using the Viceroy's residence as a microcosm of all the political and social upheaval unfolding in that period." See Kennith Rosario, "*Viceroy's House* review: A soapy political saga," *The Hindu*, 17 August 2017. Available at https://www.thehindu.com/entertainment/movies/viceroys-house-review-a-soapy-political-saga/article19510228.ece (accessed 14 July 2020).
9. In debating which country will have the various English literary classics in the library, Mountbatten's daughter actually comments to her mother, "This is absurd."

10. In this way, *Viceroy's House* adds to the myth of Churchill largely endorsed by films considered in Chapter 7.
11. Ashvin Immanuel Devasundaram, "*Viceroy's House* is very watchable—but its account of Indian independence is limited," Queen Mary, University of London, 3 March 2017. Available at https://www.qmul.ac.uk/media/news/2017/hss/viceroys-house-is-very-watchable--but-its-account-of-indian-independence-is-limited.html (accessed 8 July 2020).
12. Mountbatten's Chief of Staff, Lord Hastings Lionel "Pug" Ismay, was Churchill's Chief of Staff during the period 1940–5, potentially providing Churchill's link to the on-the-ground events of Partition. See Larry Collins and Dominique Lapierre, *Freedom at Midnight* (London: Collins, 1975), p. 81.
13. Narendra Singh Sarila, *The Shadow of the Great Game—The Untold Story of India's Partition* (London: Constable, 2005), p. 10.
14. Nisid Hajari, *Midnight's Furies: The Deadly Legacy of India's Partition* (Boston and New York: Houghton Mifflin Harcourt, 2015), p. 8.
15. Mark Kermode, "*Viceroy's House* review—gripping political drama with a populist edge," *The Guardian*, 5 March 2017. Available at https://www.theguardian.com/film/2017/mar/05/viceroys-house-review-gurinder-chadha-gillian-anderson-hugh-bonneville (accessed 8 July 2020).
16. Ibid.
17. The origins of the film's production stretch back well before the Brexit referendum of 2016, but that is irrelevant since (as Kermode implies) the film only exists as a finished product in dynamic relationship to audiences after that vote.
18. Rosario, "*Viceroy's House* review: A soapy political saga."
19. Ian Jack, "The *Viceroy's House* version of India's partition brings fake history to the screen," *The Guardian*, 18 March 2017. Available at https://www.theguardian.com/commentisfree/2017/mar/18/the-viceroys-house-version-of-indias-partition-brings-fake-history-to-screen (accessed 14 July 2020).
20. Ibid.
21. Ibid.
22. Fatima Bhutto, "Fatima Bhutto on Indian partition film *Viceroy's House*: 'I watched this servile pantomime and wept,'" *The Guardian*, 3 March 2017. Available at https://www.theguardian.com/film/2017/mar/03/fatima-bhutto-viceroys-house-watched-servile-pantomime-and-wept (accessed 15 July 2020).
23. Ibid.
24. Ibid.
25. Gurinder Chadha, "My film has been wilfully misrepresented as anti-Muslim," *The Guardian*, 3 March 2017. Available at https://www.theguardian.com/film/filmblog/2017/mar/03/gurinder-chadha-defends-viceroys-house-film-fatima-bhutto (accessed 14 July 2020).
26. Thomas Nail, *Theory of the Border* (Oxford and New York: Oxford University Press, 2016), p. 2.
27. Ibid., p. 1.
28. Ibid., p. 12.

29. Sinngh, Iyer, and Gairola, *Revisiting India's Partition: New Essays on Memory, Culture and Politics*, p. xvi.
30. Shashi Tharoor, *Inglorious Empire: What the British Did to India* (London: Penguin, 2017), p. 148.
31. Shashi Tharoor, "The Partition: The British game of 'divide and rule': Before leaving India, the British made sure a united India would not be possible," *Aljazeera*, 10 August 2017. Available at https://www.aljazeera.com/indepth/opinion/2017/08/partition-british-game-divide-rule-170808101655163.html (accessed 16 July 2020).
32. Chadha, "My film has been wilfully misrepresented as anti-Muslim."
33. Bishwa Mohan Pandey, "An Attempt to Revive Imperialist Assumptions: A Historiographical Study of the Writings of P. N. S. Mansergh," *Proceedings of the Indian History Congress*, Vol. 61, 2000, pp. 605–11. Available at www.jstor.org/stable/44148133 (accessed 6 July 2020), p. 605.
34. Ibid.
35. Bandyopadhyay, *From Plassey to Partition: A History of Modern India*, p. 444.
36. Adil Najam, "How a British royal's monumental errors made India's partition more painful," *The Conversation*, 16 August 2017. Available at https://theconversation.com/how-a-british-royals-monumental-errors-made-indias-partition-more-painful-81657 (accessed 16 July 2020).
37. Ibid.
38. Stanley Wolpert, *Shameful Flight: The Last Years of the British Empire in India* (Oxford and New York: Oxford University Press, 2006), p. 2.
39. Ibid., p. 9.
40. Bates, "The Hidden Story of Partition and its Legacies."
41. Ayesha Jalal, *The Sole Spokesman: Jinnah, the Muslim League and the Demand for Pakistan* (Cambridge and New York: Cambridge University Press, 1994/1985), p. 250.
42. Philip Ziegler, *Mountbatten: The Official Biography* (New York: Fontana, 1986), p. 528.
43. Views of any historical figure will always be highly contested. In a foreword to a book written by her mother, India Hicks says that "despite his royal ties, my grandfather was a tough-minded realist, committed to those liberal principles which made him acceptable to Attlee's Labour party," and claims the fact was "no one foresaw the magnitude of the horrors that lay in wait." Mountbatten, *India Remembered: A Personal Account of the Mountbattens During the Transfer of Power*, p. 8.
44. Lady Pamela Hicks, *Daughter of Empire: My Life as a Mountbatten* (New York and London: Simon & Schuster, 2012), p. 155.
45. Ibid.
46. Tharoor, *Inglorious Empire: What the British Did to India*, p. xxvi.
47. Rosario, "*Viceroy's House* review: A soapy political saga."
48. To some extent it would be possible to counter this argument by reviewing the extensive high-angle long shots of refugee camps used towards the end of the film and by comparing individual shots to those found in stills from the period

such as that of a distraught boy sitting on the walls of Purana Qila in New Delhi in 1947 by Margaret Bourke-White. See Margaret Bourke-White, "The Great Migration: Five Million Indians Flee for Their Lives," *Life Magazine*, 3 November 1947, p. 118. It is worth considering this whole photo essay by Bourke-White, but for a quick overview, see "Partition, in pictures," *Hindustan Times*, n.d. Available at https://www.hindustantimes.com/static/partition/gallery/ (accessed 22 July 2020).
49. Chadha, "My film has been wilfully misrepresented as anti-Muslim."
50. Bandyopadhyay, *From Plassey to Partition: A History of Modern India*, p. 455.
51. Ibid., p. 454.
52. Yasmin Khan, *The Great Partition: The Making of India and Pakistan* (New Haven, CT and London: Yale University Press, 2007), p. 26.
53. Ibid., p. 50.
54. Ibid., p. 51.
55. Ibid., p. 68.
56. Sinngh, Iyer, and Gairola, *Revisiting India's Partition: New Essays on Memory, Culture and Politics*, p. xix.
57. Ibid.
58. Ibid., p. xxii.
59. Ibid.
60. Bates, "The Hidden Story of Partition and its Legacies."
61. Jinnah also says in the script (as quoted in Collins, *Freedom at Midnight*, p. 130): "India has never been a true nation: it only looks that way on the map." This would imply the move for Pakistan was more than a notional concept calling for recognition of Muslim ethnicity. With heavy irony he then adds, "The British divided Ireland to maintain peace. They're dividing Palestine. They must do the same here."
62. Jawaharlal Nehru, "Tryst with Destiny" speech, 15 August 1947. Available at https://soundcloud.com/university-of-cambridge/tryst-with-destiny (accessed 21 July 2020).
63. Quaid-e-Azam Muhammad Ali Jinnah, presidential address to the Constituent Assembly of Pakistan, August 11, 1947. Available at <http://www.pakistani.org/pakistan/legislation/constituent_address_11aug1947.html> (accessed 21 July 2020).
64. Sinngh, Iyer, and Gairola, *Revisiting India's Partition: New Essays on Memory, Culture and Politics*, p. xvi.
65. Thomas Carlyle, *On Heroes, Hero-Worship, and the Heroic in History*, 1840. Available at http://www.gutenberg.org/files/1091/1091-h/1091-h.htm#link2H_4_0007 (accessed 21 July 2020).
66. Tharoor, *Inglorious Empire: What the British Did to India*, p. xx.
67. These words, in fact, seem to have been spoken by Nehru seven years after Partition, with the first line used during an address to the UN General Assembly in New York on 28 August 1954 (see Lewis D. Eigen and Jonathan Paul Siegel (eds.), *The Macmillan Dictionary of Political Quotations* (London: Macmillan, 1993), p. 698)

and the second line given in *The Observer* on 29 August 1954 (see Michael C. Thomsett and Jean Freestone Thomsett (eds.), *War and Conflict Quotations: A Worldwide Dictionary of Pronouncements from Military Leaders, Politicians, Philosophers, Writers and Others* (Jefferson, NC and London: McFarland, 1997), p. 75, or see *The Indian Review*, 56, 1955, p. 27).

68. The script, of course, asks us to recognize the irony of this when looking at the troubled nature of twenty-first-century Pakistan.

# Part III

# Re-presenting Britain in the Twenty-first Century

The films dealt with in this section address a range of crucially important social issues for the period. However, each film received a limited theatrical release, meaning whatever perspectives may be offered on Britain in the twenty-first century will have come to the attention of an extremely restricted audience. As with previous sections, the main focus is on the socio-political and socio-economic contexts within which each film is framed.

CHAPTER 10

# Educated Elites and Plebeians: *The Sense of an Ending* (Ritesh Batra, 2017) and *Daphne* (Peter Mackie Burns, 2017)

## I

In common with art-house cinema in general, *The Sense of an Ending* (Ritesh Batra, 2017) is a film made by members of an educated elite for the purpose of being viewed by an audience from that same privileged minority.[1] This chapter will consider this film alongside another, *Daphne* (Peter Mackie Burns, 2017), that—although it was made on a tighter budget and, in terms of its characters and narrative structure, is entirely different—might also be described as having been created by filmmakers from the same formally learned strata of society with the expectation that their work will be watched by their intellectual peers. Each of these films immediately, obviously, and deliberately asserts itself to be cerebral and academically learned. Each aims to offer the audience a work that demands thought and careful reflection, and expects the viewer to bring with them a certain level of philosophical interest in the nature of the human condition and the formal characteristics of cinematic (and literary) cultural production. The audience should also display a curiosity regarding the relationship between text and reader, and be prepared to question their own perspectives, beliefs and self in the light of what they are viewing. While they can be enjoyed as simple stories, these films aim to offer the reader the potential for levels of analytical engagement beyond the direct impact of a narrative.

Both films pursue an intense focus on a single central character, scrutinizing their lives and in the process offering a psychological analysis of each. *The Sense of an Ending* examines a short period in the life of an older man in his sixties, Anthony "Tony" Webster (Jim Broadbent), as he remembers his time as a young man in the sixth form of his school and at university.[2] Through his story the film explores the way in which we all tell and retell the narrative of our lives to ourselves and to others in such a way as to edit it into something we deem an acceptable reconstruction of the past. *Daphne* considers a brief episode in the life of a young woman who has just reached her thirties. In her hedonistic pursuit of excess she reminds us of the classic stereotype of the intellectual "man about town." Her cynicism—she determinedly does not believe in love—cannot disguise her search for meaning in her life and in human existence. Both Tony and Daphne (Emily Beecham) are placed under the microscope at moments of existential confusion. Both seek to give some shape, form, structure, and ultimately meaning to their lives; and both therefore might be seen as appropriate subjects for a serious-minded, art-house audience. *The Sense of an Ending* adopts a format used before for art-house films in having characters (and actors) of a similar age to the likely profile of the audience and a narrative in which an older man (or a couple) look back at their life in such a way as to promote a nostalgic yearning for lost youth set alongside a determined defiance in the face of age (and death).[3] *Daphne* demonstrates the use of another formula, concentrating on the life of a vibrant young woman faced with a confusing world.[4]

The main characters in *The Sense of an Ending* have been to university either at Bristol or Cambridge, two of the highest-ranking higher education institutions in the country. Tony studied at the University of Bristol and at the time had a girlfriend, Veronica Ford (Freya Mavor)—played as an older woman by Charlotte Rampling. As a young man, Tony is friends with Colin Simpson (Jack Loxton), Alex Stuart (Timothy Innes),[5] and Adrian Finn (Joe Alwyn), who are in sixth form with him. Adrian goes to Cambridge University, where Veronica's brother, Jack (Edward Holcroft), is also an undergraduate. The indications are that Tony's main group of friends were all born around 1950 and would have been in the sixth form and then at university in the late 1960s. Historically, at this time less than 10 percent of the relevant population (i.e. each year group of seventeen-year-olds) obtained three or more A levels.[6] Without considering university, simply staying at school into the sixth form in this period put you in an elite stratum of society in terms of educational attainment. Attending university was truly elitist: in 1970, for example, just 51,000 students across the country gained an undergraduate degree. On the other hand, there was some evidence of social mobility in this period since this figure was up from 22,000 in 1960.[7] Participation in higher education in the UK increased from just over 3 percent of the relevant age-group population in 1950, to just over 8 percent in 1970, to more than 19 percent in 1990 and 33 percent in 2000.[8] And, while the numbers of people gaining a university education has clearly multiplied by the contemporary period in which *Daphne* is set, it is clear the central characters in this film are again from a certain elite group of young people. While Daphne works as a chef, she is obviously employed by a very upmarket establishment. She sits with her boss, for example, expressing euphoric delight as they allow their palate to explore the exceptional qualities of Banon, displayed to the audience as wrapped in chestnut leaves and tied with raffia. This is a goat's cheese from Provence likely to be knowingly esteemed by only a small percentage of any mainstream film audience.[9] With both films, the type of product on offer is clearly labeled as being of cultural relevance to an elite audience.

## II

But of course it is not only aspects of the product itself that mark these films as elitist, it is also the nature of the allocated space within society for these films to be screened and viewed. Art-house cinemas specialize in showing films that, to varying degrees, lie outside of the mainstream. The term "art-house" carries connotations of cultural status. The audience will be expecting works offering intellectual stimulation. Films put on in art-house cinemas are often made by independent production companies, but audiences will also be offered retrospectives of "classics" and specially curated "seasons" of related films. All of this helps designate the cinema space as one that is open to some and closed to others. Spectators attending such venues will be expected to be those who view themselves as requiring films that provide a critical space for audience reflection. They will be assumed to be the sort of viewers who anticipate their films being character-driven rather than plot-driven, to offer psychological depth and perhaps the use of interior monologues, and not to depend on dramatic action and spectacle for their impact. Art-house audiences might also be designated as "specialist cinema audiences" but their demographic characteristics will still be recognized as different "in important respects from commercial cinema audiences."[10] The Independent Cinema Office suggests that within these audiences there "are a noticeably higher proportion of people in education or with higher educational qualifications" and "older audiences tend to predominate but teenage audiences (14–20 years) rarely attend."[11]

David Bordwell designated art-house cinema "a distinct mode of film practice, possessing a definite historical existence, a set of formal conventions, and implicit viewing procedures."[12] He suggests art-house films often eschew clear narrative causation in favor of a form of ambiguity[13] that requires the audience to put in place a particular art-house "reading procedure."[14] The reader first looks for "realistic motivation" but may ultimately have to look to "authorial motivation" to make sense of the viewing experience.[15] He says, "art cinema motivates its narratives by two principles: realism and authorial expressivity,"[16] and suggests, where characters in classical narratives "have clear-cut traits and objectives, the characters of the art cinema lack defined desires and goals."[17] Characters "may act for inconsistent reasons," or they "may question themselves about their goals."[18] Choices are "vague or nonexistent" and the narrative has "a certain drifting episodic quality."[19] Alongside this, Bordwell claims, "art cinema foregrounds the author as a structure in the film's system," so that "the author becomes a formal component, the overriding intelligence organizing the film for our comprehension."[20] There seems little need to update these characteristics but what should be restated is that these features require a certain approach to the screening of these films, what Bordwell denotes above as a specialist "reading procedure." Furthermore, using the word "art" sets in play a set of particular meanings generally viewed as being open only to a restricted group within society.[21] The term "art-house" also informs us not only that a distinctive approach will be taken to the making of the film but also that a specific arrangement of distribution and exhibition will be in place. Specialist distributors will handle the publicity and marketing of these products, aiming to connect the film to its intended audience, and the films will not be shown in mainstream venues but in generally smaller art-house outlets. These sorts of films are often described as "artistic ventures in cinema, driven largely by authorial vision and by creative value over profit,"[22] or as frequently being made "by people who are more concerned with film as a serious art than a business."[23] But, while this may be true, such films are still generally expected to be commercial, that is they remain products that are expected to find a niche within the market and create a return for investors.

*The Sense of an Ending* grossed $1.5 million at the box office in the UK, $1.3 million in the United States, and overall around the world it took $5 million.[24] By comparison, *Daphne* was not released in the US, and took just $148,000 at the UK box office and $210,000 worldwide.[25] *The Sense of an Ending* opened in 107 cinemas in the UK and at its widest release was playing at 171 venues—at its peak in the US it was playing at 282 cinemas.[26] *Daphne* opened in only twenty-three cinemas in the UK and after four weeks was left playing at only three venues.[27] Set against the release pattern adopted for *The Sense of an Ending*, the small scale of cinema exhibition available to *Daphne* shows something of the range of products screened even within the art-house circuit in the UK. As a point of contrast, *Dunkirk* (2017) opened in 3,720 cinemas in the US, eventually went to more than 4,000 cinemas, and took $50 million in its opening weekend.[28] In the UK, *Dunkirk* opened in 638 cinemas and eventually played in 690 cinemas.[29] Ten weeks after it was released, *Dunkirk* was still playing to more cinemas than even *The Sense of an Ending* ever reached, let alone *Daphne*.[30] Art-house films play at very few cinemas and take very limited amounts at the box office, as we see with *The Sense of an Ending*, or they play at almost no cinemas and take absolutely miniscule amounts at the box office, as we see with *Daphne*. However, what each of these films does manage is to be exhibited to a highly select group of punters.

In questioning who might go to see *The Sense of an Ending* or *Daphne* in the UK, we need, primarily, to be aware of the fact that the nature of the cinemas screening these products means the audience is already highly selected, and limitations on the budget for marketing and publicity mean the audience is still further restricted. Structural limitations within the industry itself mark out these films as not for the "ordinary" cinema-going public. However, we should also note this does not mean art-house projects such as these are likely to be especially radical, or challenging to the status quo. Catherine Fowler suggests that whereas *counter-cinema* positioned itself as "radically other," *art cinema* simply "presents itself more as an alternative to classical narrative cinema."[31] And such films certainly remain part of the industry, a segment of the film business. Fowler says art cinema is "tied up in commercial discourse," is typically produced to be exported, and "exists via a whole different, yet equally significant commercial circuit."[32]

Jon Barrenechea links "art-house" film to what the UK Film Council describes as "specialised" cinema, that is "films that do not sit easily within a mainstream and highly commercial genre."[33] He points out how small a part of the market is represented by "the arthouse sector," saying this accounts for "just seven per cent of all tickets sold" and that it "struggles to compete with the commercial multiplexes."[34] He adds that "the majority (69 per cent) of specialized and arthouse films are shown in single-screen, independently-owned cinemas," but suggests that "by focusing on atmosphere, service, quality and comfort, the arthouse industry can establish a strong market presence."[35] Discussing the success of one particular exhibition company in the UK, the Picturehouse cinema chain, he says: "Their strategy involves opening in university cities, often in historic buildings that have been remodelled to fit extra screens and cafe/bar space, programming a very wide variety of films and adopting keen marketing strategies."[36]

All of this helps to further define the sort of audience we might expect to find watching both *The Sense of an Ending* and *Daphne*. This is a comfortably well-off middle class, probably with some experience of higher education and with some appreciation of a variety of aspects of elite culture—reading literary fiction, visiting art galleries, and attending the theater, for example. In his review of *The Sense of an Ending*, the *Guardian* film critic Peter Bradshaw concludes that "this is an upscale piece of Britfilm hardback cinema which is intensely aware of its blue-chip origins. It never entirely relaxes."[37] The problem with the film for Bradshaw seems to be that it lacks clarity; that it is too obscure, too hard to understand. He is exasperated that the film "never delivers the strong, clear storytelling impact that we appear to be leading up to, and the final discovery is a bit opaque: it has to be inferred, and key events are not shown in the flashbacks."[38] Then again, these are, of course, exactly those features that place *The Sense of an Ending* firmly within the bracket of art-house cinema. The critic wants something more definite, something that has the crucial defining characteristics of mainstream cinema. The implication of a review for *The Observer* from another critic, Rex Reed, is that he revels in the very aspects of this film Bradshaw has found to be a problem:

> Literature on the screen is not everyone's favourite style of filmmaking, but when a good novel is intelligently rendered . . . nothing thrills me more . . . This is a mature, poignant, intricately detailed film . . . In this time of dominant mediocrity, I don't know if there is an audience for such a thoughtful and perceptive exception . . . [39]

Reed is clear that on three counts this is an elitist piece of work. Firstly, this is a film that rises above the "mediocrity" found elsewhere; secondly, it is unmistakably aimed at an audience with a high level of cultural discernment; and thirdly, it is a work that very few filmmakers could have created.

## III

Both *The Sense of an Ending* and *Daphne* unashamedly display their literary and cultural credentials. *The Sense of an Ending* is adapted from the novel of the same name by Julian Barnes and includes references to the poets Dylan Thomas and Philip Larkin.[40] The contemporary philosopher Slavoj Žižek is frequently mentioned in *Daphne* and there is some referencing of the originator of psychoanalysis, Sigmund Freud.

In *The Sense of an Ending*, when Tony is invited to his girlfriend's home he talks pretentiously about being interested in poetry and wanting to become a poet when he leaves university. Remembering something his friend, Adrian, has said about finding Dylan Thomas to be "one of the most humane poets of the twentieth century," he claims Thomas is his favorite poet. Veronica's father, David Ford (James Wilby), and her brother, Jack, immediately satirize the morose, death-riddled nature of Thomas' poetry. Her father labels him "the gloomy Welshman," and Jack recites a faux quotation from Thomas' work in suitably melancholic tones. His supposed quote ("And the winds did bloom, / And the brides in the wooed field / Did sew the coming summer frost") is actually a constructed parody but Tony is not familiar enough with Thomas' poetry to be aware of this. For those members of the art-house audience who are sufficiently academic, this is a mildly amusing moment in the film and a telling contribution to the revelation of Tony's character by the filmmakers. It is also the case that the choice of Thomas as Tony's professed favorite poet is entirely thematically apt for the film. Thomas' poetry is, as Veronica's father and brother indicate, famously obsessed by death.

Among his most well-known poems would be "And Death Shall Have No Dominion"[41] and "Do Not Go Gentle Into That Good Night."[42][43] We should remember this is a film with a suicide as its central event. The idea of taking your own life is first brought into focus by the death of the student Robson, who kills himself during Tony's sixth-form days, but this is merely the prelude to the occurrence around which the whole plot revolves, the suicide of his best friend, Adrian. This is also a film in which the central character succinctly documents for us their movement through youth, to middle age, and to old age ("Time delivers us all too quickly into middle age and then old age"), with the clear implication that this is the inevitable human trajectory towards death, or a sense of an ending, on which we are all embarked.[44]

In the film, Veronica's mother, Sarah Ford (Emily Mortimer), counters Tony's advocacy of Thomas by saying she is "partial to a little Larkin" and goes on to quote the opening lines to "Aubade," a poem by Philip Larkin:

> I work all day, and get half-drunk at night.
> Waking at four to soundless dark, I stare.
> In time the curtain-edges will grow light.[45]

In this case, the choice made here by the filmmakers is not only of a poet who is appropriate to the themes of the film but also of a poem that is similarly apposite. Sarah's voice trails off into sadness after the three lines quoted above, but if we know the poem we are aware that the lines that follow are:

> Till then I see what's really always there:
> Unresting death, a whole day nearer now,
> Making all thought impossible but how
> And where and when I shall myself die.
> Arid interrogation: yet the dread
> Of dying, and being dead,
> Flashes afresh to hold and horrify.
>
> The mind blanks at the glare. Not in remorse
> —The good not done, the love not given, time
> Torn off unused—nor wretchedly because
> An only life can take so long to climb
> Clear of its wrong beginnings, and may never;
> But at the total emptiness for ever,
> The sure extinction that we travel to
> And shall be lost in always.

Larkin is at least as preoccupied with death as Thomas, and this poem is entirely in tune with the general tenor of the character of Tony as portrayed in the film by Broadbent. On several occasions we see Tony waking in the morning with the light coming through slightly parted bedroom curtains. Later in Larkin's poem we find the lines:

> Slowly light strengthens, and the room takes shape.
> It stands plain as a wardrobe, what we know,
> Have always known, know that we can't escape,
> Yet can't accept.

And, although this is about inescapable death, with regard to Tony it is also a description of the process he goes through in the film in coming to terms with his past—slowly "light" is thrown on the past and that past "takes shape" until what he has "always known" and "can't escape" and "can't accept" becomes "plain" to see.[46]

"Aubade" was first published in 1977,[47] and so judged on the basis of period authenticity its use would be deemed an error on the part of the filmmakers, since Tony's university days would seem to be set several years earlier than this. If we require a logical explanation for what could appear a blunder we might bear in mind that Tony is an unreliable narrator, his memory or his construction of the narrative of his life is not necessarily accurate—his friends have to remind him that it was he who introduced Veronica and Adrian, for instance. On this basis, we cannot be sure about the veracity of any of the flashbacks in the film. Tony may be ascribing lines from a poem to a character after the event, lines that in fact could not have been uttered because they were not as yet in the public domain. Or maybe this sort of

**Figure 10.1** Tony (Jim Broadbent) waking to the morning light coming into his bedroom in *The Sense of an Ending* (Ritesh Batra, 2017).

approach to analyzing the film is all too literal. Both the film and the novel are about the creation of personal narratives but also about the nature of storytelling. The film is a fiction, and the filmmakers are able to assemble their exploration into the ways in which we create shape and meaning in our individual lives in whatever way they choose; maybe in such a way as to remind us that this is a fiction and that we are always surrounded by what are necessarily imagined inventions. For the novel, and in among a whole range of actual poets, philosophers, and writers, Barnes invented an entirely fictitious French philosopher or historian, "Patrick Lagrange." In a sixth-form history class, Adrian quotes him as saying, "History is that certainty produced at the point where imperfections of memory meet the inadequacies of documentation."[48] As with the use of "Aubade" in the film script, there is potentially a logical explanation in that Adrian could have invented both "Lagrange" and this supposed quotation; but again as with the film script, this could serve to remind us that this is a fiction and that the author is free not just to embellish but to invent anything and everything. The question then becomes: where does this place us as a reader or viewer wishing to ground the text in some reality, to stabilize the possibilities in order to construct "the sense of an ending," or some finality, or certainty? We are left with ambiguity, uncertainty, and unreliability. We can be sure of nothing, and maybe this is appropriate for the human experience of life.[49]

In *Daphne* the key recurring cultural reference is to Slavoj Žižek. Although the central character spends her time drinking, taking drugs, and picking up men for casual sex, her real interests seem more cerebral. She reads and quotes Žižek, returns time and again to the topic of what she sees as the falsity of the human concept of "love," and challenges the psychoanalyst at the start of their first meeting with the question, "Do you think that it's true that we are all just matter, that we just die and that's it, or the whole heaven and hell thing? That those are our two basic choices?"[50] She cites Žižek as saying, "Internet dating is consumerism masquerading as love,"[51] and claims "love" is simply "a necessary illusion to bind us all together to propagate our shitty species." Despite the fact that her boss, Tom (Osy Ikhile), says she is just trying to sound cool by referencing Žižek, there is no doubt she is, as Peter Bradshaw describes her, "an articulate adult."[52] In fact, it is Žižek who effectively summarizes Daphne's philosophical positioning of herself in this film:

> Remember what hysteria is? To simplify it, from a psychoanalytic standpoint, society confers on you a certain identity. You are a teacher, professor, woman, mother, feminist, whatever. The basic hysterical gesture is to raise a question and doubt your identity. "You're saying I'm this, but why am I this? What makes me this?" . . . Male patriarchal ideology constrains women to a certain

position and identity, and you begin to ask, "But am I really that?" ... So, hysteria is this basic doubting of your identity.[53]

On the face of it, Daphne is super-confident: for example, in ordering the man she has just picked up in a pub to "Go and wait for me outside." However, it is her doubt and uncertainty that are often revealed as her face is momentarily held by the camera after she has made an apparently self-assured comment such as proclaiming she does not believe in love, or it is her lost emptiness we see as her face is held in tight close-up when she is having sex performed on her. We repeatedly see Daphne in long shot walking within a constricted space within the frame, perhaps between a row of cars and a set of railings; or we view her alone in the centre of the frame within an empty space, perhaps within a corridor; or the camera holds her so that she is unable to escape within a lengthy tracking shot; or we observe her as a fragmented image perhaps reflected in a series of mirrors or through bars; or we are shown her in boxed spaces within the frame, perhaps in a doorway, or between a wall and railings.

If the character of Daphne is self-absorbed, through its intensity of focus and the particularities of its cinematography the film magnifies this self-preoccupation. And, if the concept of narrative is important for *The Sense of an Ending*, the idea of performance is equally significant for *Daphne*. Žižek has suggested that:

> Our fundamental striving is not to observe, but to be part of a staged scene, to expose oneself to a gaze—not a determinate gaze of a person in reality, but of the non-existing pure Gaze of the big Other.[54]

**Figure 10.2** In *Daphne* (Peter Mackie Burns, 2017), we repeatedly find Daphne (Emily Beecham) alone within boxed spaces inside the frame.

We must surely conclude Daphne's central subject is not the nature of love, real or otherwise, but herself. As we have said, Tom accuses her of simply trying to "sound cool" in all her talk about Žižek. In fact, is she not "always performing, playing a role for a foreign gaze, imagined or real"?[55] And then again, at the same time as we view the film Daphne is also the actor, Beecham, performing within the film frame. All of which drives us back to ourselves and reminds us that, as Žižek has it, "When we perform there is always a frame that defines our activity as performance."[56] And, with regard to our viewing of the film that, again as Žižek has it, the frame "implies gaze, the gaze which observes the scene through the frame, the gaze for which the scene is performed."[57] The nature of existence in Žižek's terms is being played out before us. Furthermore, Daphne's mother, Rita (Geraldine James), demonstrates that the questions Daphne is wrestling with are not peculiar to her (or her generation): "You are born, you work, you have a child, and you die. It's not enough. I want more than that than," she says. And in this she echoes Žižek's description of himself: "Slavoj Žižek was born, writes books, and will die."[58] Like her daughter (and every generation), Rita is at a loss as to how to proceed: "I want . . .," she says, unable to end her sentence, before following this with another inconclusive effort, "That's why I'm trying to, you know . . ."

## IV

Both *The Sense of an Ending* and *Daphne* are films of some philosophical depth. Both play well to an educated audience with a particular form of cultural capital at their disposal. Each of them exposes a profound division within the nation's film audience, and a similar level of separation within our society as a whole. Looking at elite groups within UK society, the Social Mobility Commission concludes that "while just 19% of the working age population are educated to the level of bachelor's degree or above, 84% of the elites we have examined are," and that "while only 6% of the population attended the Russell Group[59] for an undergraduate degree, almost half of our elites have done so."[60] In *The Class Ceiling: Why It Pays to Be Privileged*, Sam Friedman and Daniel Laurison say, "inequality—particularly at the top end of the income distribution—has mushroomed, climbing, by many measures, towards levels not seen since the 1930s,"[61] and conclude that "much of what is routinely categorised as 'merit' in elite occupations is actually impossible to separate from the 'following wind' of privilege."[62]

## Notes

1. At its widest release, *The Sense of an Ending* was screened at 171 cinemas in the UK, while *Daphne* played in just twenty-three cinemas.

2. The young Tony Webster is played by Bill Howle.
3. See, for example, *Another Year* (Mike Leigh, 2010) and *Le Week-end* (Roger Michell, 2013), both featuring Jim Broadbent.
4. See, for example, the very different films *Happy-Go-Lucky* (Leigh, 2008) and *Fish Tank* (Andrea Arnold, 2009).
5. The older Colin Simpson and Alex Stuart are played by Peter Wight and Hilton McRae.
6. In 1965–6, for example, only 6 percent of the relevant population group gained three or more A levels. See Paul Bolton, "Education: Historical Statistics," House of Commons, 27 November 2012, p. 19. Available at researchbriefings.files.parliament.uk>documents/SN04252/SN04252.pdf (accessed 30 October 2020).
7. Ibid., p. 20.
8. Ibid., p. 14.
9. See Catherine W. Donnelly (ed.), *The Oxford Companion to Cheese* (Oxford and New York: Oxford University Press, 2016), p. 59.
10. Anon., "How to start a cinema—Understanding audiences—Different films, different people," Independent Cinema Office. Available at https://www.independentcinemaoffice.org.uk/advice-support/how-to-start-a-cinema/understanding-audiences/ (accessed 2 November 2020).
11. Ibid.
12. David Bordwell, "The Art Cinema as a Mode of Film Practice," *Film Criticism*, 4 (1), 1979, p. 56. Available at JSTOR, www.jstor.org/stable/44018650 (accessed 24 October 2020).
13. Ibid., p. 60.
14. Ibid.
15. Ibid.
16. Ibid., p. 57.
17. Ibid., p. 58.
18. Ibid.
19. Ibid.
20. Ibid., p. 59.
21. For a fuller exploration of the term "art," see John White, *European Art Cinema* (London and New York: Routledge, 2017), pp. 6–8.
22. Pamela Hutchinson (ed.), *30-Second Cinema* (London: Ivy Press, 2019), p. 138.
23. Thomas Sobchack and Vivian C. Sobchack, *An Introduction to Film* (Glenview, IL and Boston, MA: Scott, Foresman, 1987), p. 284.
24. Anon., "*The Sense of an Ending* (2017)," *The Numbers*. Available at https://www.the-numbers.com/movie/Sense-of-an-Ending-The#tab=box-office (accessed 30 October 2020).
25. Anon., "*Daphne*," *Box Office Mojo*. Available at https://www.boxofficemojo.com/release/rl1038648321/weekend/ (accessed 30 October 2020).
26. Anon., "*The Sense of an Ending* (2017)."
27. Anon., "*Daphne*."

28. Anon., "*Dunkirk* (2017)," *The Numbers*. Available at https://www.the-numbers.com/movie/Dunkirk(2017)#tab=international (accessed 3 November 2020).
29. Ibid.
30. Ibid.
31. Catherine Fowler (ed.), *The European Cinema Reader* (London and New York: Routledge), p. 88.
32. Ibid.
33. Jon Barrenechea, "British Arthouse Cinemas," in Emma Bell and Neil Mitchell (eds.), *Directory of World Cinema: Britain* (Bristol and Chicago: Intellect, 2012), p. 185.
34. Ibid.
35. Ibid., p. 186.
36. Ibid., pp. 186–7.
37. Peter Bradshaw, "*The Sense of an Ending* review—an upscale bit of Britfilm hardback cinema," *The Guardian*, 6 April 2017. Available at https://www.theguardian.com/film/2017/apr/06/the-sense-of-an-ending-review-jim-broadbent-julian-barnes (accessed 30 October 2020).
38. Ibid.
39. Rex Reed, "*The Sense of an Ending* Is a Powerful, Moving Portrait of Memories Past," *The Observer*, 14 March 2017. Available at https://observer.com/2017/03/sense-of-an-ending-movie-review-jim-broadbent/ (accessed 30 October 2020).
40. The novel refers to writers (e.g. George Orwell), poets (e.g. Ted Hughes and T. S. Eliot), the occasional composer (Antonín Dvořák and Peter Ilyich Tchaikovsky), and the occasional philosopher (Friedrich Nietzsche), but does not mention Dylan Thomas and Philip Larkin. They have been introduced by director Ritesh Batra and screenwriter Nick Payne. As with the role of the daughter, Susie Webster (Michelle Dockery), being expanded, this signals both a recognition that the change of medium places new demands on the material and a determination by the co-creators to bring their own stamp to the film.
41. The first verse concludes: "Though they go mad they shall be sane, / Though they sink through the sea they shall rise again, / Though lovers be lost love shall not; / And death shall have no dominion." The reference in the title is to Romans 6: 9, King James Bible. Available at https://www.kingjamesbibleonline.org/Romans-Chapter-6/#9 (accessed 3 November 2020).
42. The opening to this poem: "Do not go gentle into that good night, / Old age should burn and rave at close of day; / Rage, rage against the dying of the light."
43. See Daniel Jones (ed.), *Dylan Thomas: The Poems* (London: Dent, 1971), pp. 49–50 and pp. 207–8.
44. It is also the case that there may be a defiantly more hopeful note within the film and within the choice of Dylan Thomas. Although Jack's "quote" is made up, it does echo elements of an actual poem by Thomas. In "The White Giant's Thigh," Thomas has the lines: "Who once were a bloom of wayside brides in the hawed house / And heard the lewd, wooed field flow to the coming frost." This is a poem about "love that's evergreen," the urgent creative sex drive that continues

through generation upon generation. See Marlene Chambers, "1. Thomas' The White Giant's Thigh," *The Explicator*, 19 (1), October 1960, pp. 1–3. Available at DOI: 10.1080/00144940.1960.11482139 (accessed 30 October 2020).
45. Anthony Thwaite (ed.), *Philip Larkin: Collected Poems* (Victoria and London: The Marvell Press and Faber & Faber, 2003) pp. 190–1.
46. The poem ends with the line, "Postmen like doctors go from house to house," that might be worth considering regarding the recurring use of the character of the postman in the film.
47. Philip Larkin, "Aubade," *The Times Literary Supplement*, 23 December 1977, p. 1491.
48. Julian Barnes, *The Sense of an Ending* (London: Jonathan Cape, 2011), p. 17.
49. In examining literary and cultural references in this film, it would also be possible to explore some of the ways in which Frank Kermode's book of literary criticism, *The Sense of an Ending: Studies in the Theory of Fiction*, operates as a springboard for the novel and, therefore, the film. On page five, for example, Kermode discusses "fictions of the End—about ways in which, under varying existential pressures, we have imagined the ends of the world." On page 140, he suggests "truth would be found only in a silent poem or a silent novel." And on page 164, "The free imagination makes endless plots on reality." In a direct link to the film that bypasses the novel and in language that conjures Tony Webster's situation, Kermode also mentions Larkin (on page 179): "In our perpetual crisis we have, at the proper seasons, under the pressure perhaps of our own end, dizzying perspectives upon the past and the future, in a freedom which is the freedom of a discordant reality. Such a vision of chaos or absurdity may be more than we can easily bear. Philip Larkin, though he speaks quietly, speaks of something terrible:

> Truly, though our element is time,
> We are not suited to the long perspectives
> Open at each instant of our lives.
> They link us to our losses—"

Frank Kermode, *The Sense of an Ending: Studies in the Theory of Fiction (with a New Epilogue)* (Oxford and New York: Oxford University Press, 2000/1966).
50. In contributing to the book *Žižek and Performance*, Žižek described himself in this way: "Slavoj Žižek was born, writes books, and will die." Broderick Chow and Alex Mangold (eds.), *Žižek and Performance* (London: Palgrave Macmillan, 2014).
51. In *Living in the End Times*, Žižek discusses "self-commodification" and says "through internet dating or marriage agencies, each prospective partner presents themselves as a commodity." Slavoj Žižek, *Living In the End Times* (London and New York: Verso, 2011), pp. 413–14.
52. Peter Bradshaw, "*Daphne* review—Emily Beecham takes a stylish plunge into sex, drugs and drink," *The Guardian*, 28 September 2017. Available at https://www.theguardian.com/film/2017/sep/28/daphne-review-emily-beecham-geraldine-james-pete-mackie-burns (accessed 30 October 2020).

53. Mike Bulajewski, "Getting a Grip on Slavoj Žižek (with Slavoj Žižek)," 27 June 2018, JSTOR Daily. Available at https://daily.jstor.org/getting-a-grip-on-slavoj-zizek-with-slavoj-zizek/ (accessed 1 November 2020).
54. Slavoj Žižek, *The Year of Dreaming Dangerously* (London and New York: Verso, 2012), p. 247.
55. Ibid., p. 246.
56. Chow and Mangold, *Žižek and Performance*, p. 241.
57. Žižek, *The Year of Dreaming Dangerously*, p. 241.
58. See note 50.
59. The Russell Group of twenty-four leading UK universities includes both the University of Bristol and the University of Cambridge.
60. Anon., *Elitist Britain 2019: The educational backgrounds of Britain's leading people*, The Sutton Trust/Social Mobility Commission (London: Sutton Trust, 2019).
61. Sam Friedman and Daniel Laurison, *The Class Ceiling: Why It Pays to Be Privileged* (Bristol: Policy Press, 2019), p. 7.
62. Ibid., p. 27.

CHAPTER 11

# Migration in an Age of Ideological Confrontation: *God's Own Country* (Francis Lee, 2017)

## I

Francis Lee's debut feature film is set in his own physical and experiential backyard. The location for *God's Own Country* is Lee's home area of the Yorkshire Dales and the subject matter explores the experiences of a gay man living in the area. During the course of the film, Johnny Saxby (Josh O'Connor), who is in his early twenties, inherits the responsibility of maintaining a small hill-farm. His mother left home when he was young ("I don't really remember. She left and . . . We just got on with it") and he has been brought up by his father, Martin (Ian Hart) and his grandmother, Deirdre (Gemma Jones). When the film opens, his father has had a stroke and during the course of the film he will have a second, which means Johnny is expected to take over the farm. The burden this entails is clear from the manner in which his grandmother describes the situation: "It's all on your shoulders now," she says.

Johnny feels the pressure of his obligations to his family and to maintaining the farm. When a friend, Robyn (Patsy Ferran), points out he is not as much fun as he used to be, Johnny's response is that she is referring to a time before he had to "join the real world." His father and "Nan" both believe what you have to do when faced with hardship of any sort is to "get on with it." Johnny himself has adopted the same phrase: when Robyn asks how his father is coping with his illness, Johnny's reply is, "He's gettin' on with it, you know." The problem is Johnny has no real idea how to "get on with" the situation in which he finds himself. He feels trapped by the small rural community he has lived in all his life. When Robyn returns to the village with her university friends, Johnny says, "I thought once you lot escaped to your fancy colleges and that, you'd never come back," and it is his use of the word "escaped" that is most telling. He feels he has been left behind in this rural backwater and that anyone who is going to university will be bringing with them a sense of cultural, even colonial, superiority. He accuses Robyn of bringing her friends "to gawp and laugh at the natives."

Into this countryside setting and into Johnny's life, Lee introduces a Romanian migrant worker, Gheorghe Ionescu (Alec Secăreanu), and what follows is a gay romance between Johnny and Gheorghe. However, as we follow the development of this relationship we should not lose sight of the fact that at base this film is a story of a young person—whether he is gay or not, to some extent does not matter—who believes he is stuck within a small community and a claustrophobic family, both of which are limiting his possibilities for self-development; nor should we lose sight of the significance of the catalyst for change in Johnny's life arriving in the form of a migrant worker. Lee has put in place from the outset a series of potential conflicts. Some of these points of tension are recurring features of human life: the development of the father–son relationship as the child comes into adulthood and the friction between the supposed simplicity of a rural existence and the imagined sophistication of a more urban way of life. Others reflect more specific conflicts within UK society in the early twenty-first century: between a resident population and migrant workers, and between homophobic elements of the population and the LGBT+ community. It is these last two areas of interest that will provide the main focus of attention here.

Gheorghe is the only person to respond to an advert asking for a seasonal worker to help with lambing on the hill-farm and Johnny's first words to this "outsider" when he picks him up from the railway station are aggressively blunt: "You a Paki or summat?" In the same vein, on hearing Gheorghe is Romanian, Johnny straightaway wants to know if he is a "gypsy." The casual racism that might be found within a whole range of quite enclosed social locales but here within a small rural community is immediately apparent. Johnny's words are direct and seemingly designed to be provocative. His grandmother's words, however, when describing a doctor who has spoken to her at the hospital regarding her son's second stroke are, perhaps, simply the norm for her generation within this neighbourhood: "Doctor's just been round. Young coloured lass. Nice little thing." In *The Rise of the Right: English nationalism and the transformation of working-class politics*, Simon Winlow, Steve Hall, and James Treadwell discuss the "growing fear of and hostility towards otherness among the broad white working class."[1] They classify racism in the UK today as "a post-imperial racism" rooted in "the absolute decline of traditional working-class work, security and status in the west."[2] Traditional racism, they say, was mainly a result of an imperialist colonial ideology, the racism of "imaginary superiority."[3] Whereas, what we have today is the racism of "imagined inferiority."[4] Johnny is a specific character imagined as existing within a specific community but he is also someone who might be recognized by Winlow, Hall, and Treadwell, who claim more and more people in the UK today "feel lost, rootless and set apart from the world."[5]

In *Historicizing Fear: Ignorance, Vilification and Othering,* Travis Boyce and Winsome Chunnu suggest: "While xenophobia is propagated in many western and central European nations in an attempt to get far-right candidates into office, such efforts have recently proven most successful in the United Kingdom."[6] These authors say when the UK voted to leave the European Union in the Brexit referendum of 2016, the leave vote "was marketed to British, Scottish and Irish voters with a shrewd combination of messages springing from racial hatred and xenophobia."[7] They claim these racist attitudes "were fundamentally grounded in working-class anxieties about losing jobs to immigrants."[8] Johnny fixates on a particular form of racism prevalent in the UK over successive generations, repeatedly calling Gheorghe "gypsy" or "gypo": "You doing any work today, gypsy, or what?" / "Get your ass into gear, gypo." Gheorghe eventually responds to these provocations by attacking Johnny, pinning him to the ground, and saying, "Do not call me that. I know what you're doing. I will fuck with you. Do we understand each other?"[9] To focus on one aspect of what is said here, we might want to ask what exactly Johnny is "doing" in repeatedly goading Gheorghe in this way. Is there something beyond provocation at work? As a gay man, Johnny is himself what might be described as "other" and it may be that one thing he is doing is transposing his "otherness" onto someone else, offloading his own sense of social marginalization. It may also be the case that beyond Johnny's sense of "otherness" resulting from being gay in a small rural community, the way in which he baits Gheorghe reflects something of the wider "working-class anxieties" identified by Boyce and Chunnu. Johnny's racism may be a response to his own queer marginalization but may also arise as a result of his class position in contemporary UK society as one of those feeling left behind and socially marginalized.

The choice of "gypsy" and "gypo" as Johnny's chosen racial slurs might be expected to resonate especially strongly with Gheorghe as a Romanian. A report on racism in Romania in 2008 stated that the Roma were the most discriminated against group in the country, adding that these people were "caught in a vicious circle of poverty, reinforced by discrimination and social exclusion."[10] It has been suggested that though they were recognized as an ethnic minority in 1991, "Roma in Romania continue to be seen as foreigners."[11] According to Roma activist Valeriu Nicolae, "life for the majority of Roma in Romania is a daily struggle for survival and nothing else."[12] A European Commission report from 2020 identifies the Roma[13] as Europe's largest ethnic minority and states, "many of the continent's estimated 10–12 million Roma continue to face discrimination, antigypsyism and socio-economic exclusion in their daily lives."[14] Ruxandra Trandafoiu suggests the enlargement of the

*Migration in an Age of Ideological Confrontation* 175

**Figure 11.1** Gheorghe (Alec Secăreanu) responds to the provocations of Johnny (Josh O'Connor) and pins him to the ground in *God's Own Country* (Francis Lee, 2017).

European Union in 2007[15] to take in Romania and Bulgaria gave rise "to new forms of both racism and xenophobia (or xeno-racism) directed at Romany Gypsies and 'audible' Eastern European minorities."[16] Employing the concept of "otherness," she describes "audible minorities" as "people whose physiognomies are undifferentiated from the general European type, but whose accents give them away as the 'other.'"[17] Although *God's Own Country* focuses on the UK, and indeed, on a very specific location within the UK, through the introduction of Gheorghe it manages to suggest the importance of the issues it deals with for the whole of Europe. In his foreword to Ian Hancock's *We Are the Romani People*, Ken Lee identifies the continuing prevalence within the contemporary period of "antigypsyism" and "stereotypical images of 'The Gypsies,'" while also highlighting the brutality with which these people have been treated in the past.[18] Lee specifically highlights "centuries of slavery in Romania" alongside the more well-known "attempted Romani genocide under the Nazis."[19] Johnny's use of racist language and Gheorghe's determined response need to be seen in this wider Romani context but also against the more all-encompassing background of the contemporary pervasiveness of racism more generally throughout Europe. This in turn needs to be seen against the backdrop of the trend across Europe to attempt to strengthen borders and the rising popularity of right-wing politics.[20]

## II

The concept of race may be an entirely spurious arrangement of distinctions between people without any scientific basis in biology but it remains a powerful force for the creation of divisions within society, and a force being unleashed with growing confidence within contemporary Europe. As David Gillborn explains it in *Racism and Education: Coincidence or Conspiracy?*, "race" is "far from being a fixed and natural system of genetic difference," but is rather, "a system of socially constructed and enforced categories that are constantly recreated and modified through human interaction."[21] Racism is singular in the sense that within whatever time and place we find it, it always employs a range of human characteristics in order to erect a structure of domination. However, it is plural in the sense that its specific configuration is always the product of a particular society at a particular historical moment. It is never random, or "accidental,"[22] and it is linked to a range of political positions that sustain popular belief in the existence of fixed racial identities. It is certainly the case that politicians on the extreme right "trade in these beliefs,"[23] but it is also the case that there is a tendency for many countries not controlled by right-wing politicians to foster commonplace assumptions that take for granted "the constructed nature of the minority/majority relations"[24] found within their society. Liberal democracies generally fail to offer any determined challenge to such glaring inequalities. As a result, David Gillborn, for example, is able to debate "the racist nature of the education system" and to discuss "race inequality" as "a fundamental axis of oppression" in western societies like the United States and the UK.[25]

It is Gheorghe's position as a migrant that brings race issues to the fore. Johnny takes to labeling him as "gypsy" because of his outsider/migrant status. In recent decades across Europe, migrant workers have been seen as a vital ingredient in strengthening national economies.[26] Low-skilled, seasonal migrant workers have been viewed as a critical flexible resource, particularly within various agricultural sectors. High-skilled, more settled migrant workers have been seen as crucial within many parts of the economy, particularly within new technology, where it is important to maintain a competitive edge within a global marketplace. At the same time, migrants have been consistently "perceived as outsiders who take jobs, sponge off welfare benefits and threaten social cohesion."[27] In a range of countries, populist politicians have "contributed to anti-immigrant feelings, spreading the idea of an 'invasion' of migrants and refugees and of their links with the terrorist threat."[28] It is undeniably the case that at the current time, "racism, xenophobia and hostility towards migrants are on the rise in Europe."[29] Gheorghe's role within *God's Own Country* cannot escape taking its place within this context. On meeting him, Johnny's grandmother, Deirdre, immediately offers the observation that his use of English is "very good"; and to his reply that his mother teaches English in Romania she simply responds, "Fancy." One of the Saxby family's assumptions about the migrant who is coming to work for them, that he will not be able to speak much English,[30] has been overthrown only for a further potential division between Gheorghe and the Saxbys to immediately open up: Gheorghe is well educated and seems to come from a family that is similarly literate. The grandmother's single word response, "Fancy," announces her refusal to be impressed by any of this. Johnny's father, Martin, is direct and firm with Gheorghe when he first meets him, asserting that they are "not running a charity for waifs and strays," while Johnny is almost gleeful in telling Gheorghe the caravan he will be staying in is a "shite-hole." And yet, despite these immediately apparent antagonisms, what the film actually shows is how open the family are to someone who appears to arrive in their life from another world entirely. Deirdre has immediately invited him into the house so that she can cook him something to eat. Martin comes across as blunt but is actually asking after Gheorghe's well-being. He enquires whether he has more work to go to when he leaves and when he hears that he has, his full response is: "Good, cos we just need someone for the week, lad. We're not running a charity for waifs and strays, like." It is undeniably to-the-point but the use of "lad" at the end of the first sentence and "like" at the end of the second softens the overall effect. Ultimately, what the film presents to us is the way in which "the migrant" is just another person. The "othering" that is achieved through the use of the label of "migrant" dissipates as a result of simple human interaction. This is most obvious in the relationship between Gheorghe and Johnny. Their story is a gay romance but perhaps more importantly, this is Johnny, a representative native of one place, accepting a migrant as just another human being in the most intimate way possible. There are also a series of moments demonstrating Gheorghe's competence as a shepherd. In the first we are shown in some detail the way in which Gheorghe helps with the birth of a lamb, massaging it and clearing mucus from around its mouth to start it breathing, before the camera lingers on Martin. What we are shown is Martin not only acknowledging a good job is being done by Gheorghe but also feeling himself to be in the presence of a fellow farmer.

Two years before this film was made, more than a million refugees and asylum-seekers—many, but not all of them, coming originally from Syria—crossed the Mediterranean into Europe.[31] One year before this film was made, 52 percent of those voting in the UK's Brexit referendum opted to leave the European Union to a considerable extent because of concerns over immigration.[32] Discussing Brexit, Winlow, Hall, and Treadwell suggest, "anyone with any recent first-hand experience of the old working class's precarious existence and hardening attitudes must have seen this coming."³³ Summarizing the position in the UK, they say:

> For many ordinary working people, growing diversity and continued inward migration is inextricably bound up with the context of their own declining fortunes. For them, migrants are first and foremost economic competitors. They make it harder to get and keep a job, and they place downward pressure on wage levels . . . Talk of the overall net economic benefits of high levels of immigration cut no ice.³⁴

While they recognize migration is "an inherently divisive issue," Haas, Castles, and Miller say there is little evidence migrants take jobs from locals nor that migration is the main cause of poorer working conditions, welfare provision, and public services.³⁵ They flag up the overall benefits identified by Winlow, Hall, and Treadwell, concluding that "most evidence suggests migration has positive impacts on overall growth, innovation and the vitality of economies and societies."³⁶ The problem as they see it is that "the benefits of migration are not equally distributed" across societies.³⁷ Businesses and the well-off gain most while those on lower pay, who often experience "a deterioration of working conditions, real wages and social security as a result of economic deregulation and globalization,"³⁸ end up enjoying "few, if any, direct economic benefits from migration."³⁹

Over successive generations and for a range of reasons, many Romanians have chosen to become migrants, and there are various estimates, or ways of calculating, how many people this might amount to. Ruxandra Trandafoiu suggests at any time up to 10 percent of Romania's population (more than two million people) could be elsewhere in Europe.⁴⁰ Taking into account twentieth-century migrations, she says, the extended Romanian diaspora amounts to ten million people,⁴¹ so that "a third of all Romanians now live outside their nation-state."⁴² Felicia Nica and Madalina Moraru say, in 2017, "the number of Romanian emigrants reached 3.58 million, which represented 18.2% of the Romanian population."⁴³ They also point out the Romanian diaspora is such a recognized facet of Romanian life that these people have their own representation in the Romanian Parliament ("two Senators and four Deputies are elected to represent the interests of three to five million Romanians living abroad").⁴⁴ Trandafoiu feels Eastern European migration as a whole is something more than "purely 'labour' or 'work' migration"⁴⁵ and puts forward the idea that emigration is "a political act,"⁴⁶ and that "among all the possible political acts, emigration stands out as one of the most radical."⁴⁷ Oana Romocea believes many Romanians nurtured aspirations to become more like Western Europe since well before the fall of communism in 1989.⁴⁸

Reflecting the intense reality of migration for Romanians, Gheorghe expresses his feelings about his country of birth to Johnny in these bleak terms: "My country is dead. You can't throw a rock in most towns without hitting an old lady crying for her children who have gone." This clearly reflects the well-documented extent of the Romanian diaspora outlined above. However, he also speaks of Romania with a sense of nostalgic longing: "In my country spring is the most beautiful: the sun, the flowers, the smells." These two sentiments ("My country is dead" and "In my country spring is the most beautiful") that might seem to be at odds with each other may in fact accurately reflect something of migrant consciousness. Trandafoiu speaks of "diasporic reflexivity," which she describes as "the ability to provide complex and continuous identity reflections as a result of the coexistence of the self within multiple spaces of interaction."[49]

## III

All the sub-textual indications are that Gheorghe has undergone the same economic hardships experienced by farmers working marginal land in Britain and it is these conditions that have forced him to become a migrant worker. He has barely arrived at the family farm before he is, in effect, suggesting Martin and his son need to diversify and should consider starting to make cheese.[50] Later, when Johnny proposes Gheorghe should stay with him and help to run the farm, Gheorghe's immediate response is to ask, "And how would we work on the farm?" Essentially, he wants to know what the business model would be, or how they would make a small hill-farm profitable within the current economic environment; but unable to see any possibility other than simply carrying on with things as they are, Johnny is confused and can only respond, "How do you mean?" Gheorghe has to point out that the farm "can't go on like it has," and it is at this point that we get the clearest indication of what it is that has pushed him to become a migrant worker. "I've been through this before," he says, "on my farm. I can't go through that again. It will not survive, believe me." Even within the semi-protected economic space of the European Union (and, maybe, a post-Brexit Britain), Gheorghe knows this type of farm will find it difficult to survive in the face of neo-liberal globalization without finding new niche markets. In January 2020, *The Guardian* newspaper highlighted the case of a Romanian farmer who "like all Romanian shepherds with small and medium-sized flocks" was "struggling in a market dominated by a few live animal exporters, big farmers and hypermarkets." The paper quoted him as saying, "The sheep trade has become a mockery . . . I can't find workers any more—young people see that it's all going downhill."[51][52] This film might correctly be classified within the genre of queer cinema but, be that as it may, the lives of the characters we see on screen are largely being determined by global economic forces. Johnny's farm has no future if he does not adapt to global economics, and it is his relation to the farm (or to no farm) that will decide his future as it has dictated his past and his father's life before that. Gheorghe's farm in Romania has failed to meet the expectations of profitability placed on it by the market. His life as a migrant worker has been shaped by this "failure." Romania's level of population fluidity over recent decades, again, has been determined largely by the market. The influx of migrant workers into the UK may to some extent be regulated by government policies but is also the inevitable outcome of the intensification of globalization.[53][54] We can sometimes forget the extent to which everything within a country is geared towards "developing" the economy and the role migration plays in this. In October 2020, the UK government reduced the minimum salary a migrant coming to Britain would need to earn under the post-Brexit immigration system from £35,800 to £25,600. Oxford University's Migration Observatory saw this as the end of the government's attempt to get net migration down below 100,000 a year.[55] As one writer expressed it recently, looking at the continuing importance of migrants to a dynamic economy:

> As the UK economy struggles back to life after lockdown one thing is certain: migrants will play a vital role in the rebuilding process . . . They always do . . . They don't uproot themselves from their families and their homelands lightly . . . migrants have a unique mindset and a burning desire to succeed. They drive innovation and economic development.[56]

The increasing importance of migration to European economies in recent decades has been one factor "in the rise of anti-immigrant and anti-Islam parties and a subsequent move to the right of the entire political spectrum."[57] Following on from this, "anti-immigrant sentiment and migrant scapegoating by politicians and opinion makers" has created "a climate where far-right and racist attacks have flared up."[58] Eva A. Duda-Mikulin says, "migrants have been increasingly cast as scapegoats—the cause of social and economic problems in the UK and as a drain on society," and links this not only to "rising English nationalism" but also to "economic austerity" and "cuts to public services."[59] She relates all of this to the Brexit vote, which she claims arguably "all boils down to immigration."[60] She sums up the situation in this way:

> People have been migrating since the beginning of time, but the issue of migration has now been elevated to a key national concern and is one of the most contentious and divisive matters in the UK and beyond. Migration

has become a dirty word in itself . . . The UK wishes to retain its trade deal agreements while at the same time it wants to fortify itself from the rest of Europe.[61]

She connects this to "an increase in racially motivated hate crime" in the UK.[62] And this is what we see represented on screen towards the end of *God's Own Country*, when Gheorghe is goaded by a customer sitting at the bar in the village pub. The man flicks beer at Gheorghe. Gheorghe responds by saying, "Please don't do that." The man mimics his voice in an exaggerated manner, saying, "Pleez don do zat." Gheorghe stands and with a single confident, swift, flowing movement twists the man's arm behind his back and forces his face down onto the bar. The landlady's reaction from behind the bar is to shout at Gheorghe, "Hey! Get the fuck out of my pub, you dirty little bastard, or am I calling t' pigs?" Both the man's attempt to imitate Gheorghe's accent and the landlady's verbal attack on Gheorghe (rather than both men) would seem to be racially motivated. Although it is also possible to suggest the whole incident offers an example of homophobia. Gheorghe has been at the bar with Johnny who is well-known locally, and certainly Robyn seems to be aware he is gay. Either way (and Gheorghe's sexuality and ethnicity could also be seen to operate as joint motivations for the confrontation), what is presented to us amounts to the seeds of hate crime. Duda-Mikulin says the narrative that saw migrants as the cause of many ordinary people's problems in the UK and was employed in the campaign to leave the EU, "resulted in an increase in racially motivated hate crime."[63] It was widely stated hate crime increased in the UK in and around the Brexit vote. A report in *The Observer*, for example, said, "The number of homophobic attacks more than doubled in the three months after the Brexit vote."[64] Of course, it is likely things are at least as bad and may be even worse for sexual (as well as racial) minorities in many other parts of Europe.

Adela Moraru reported in 2010 that in Romania societal attitudes towards homosexuality were "dominated by intolerance, especially in rural areas."[65] She highlighted a Gallup study from 2003 that reported, "45% of respondents said homosexuals should not be treated the same as others in society; 37% thought homosexuality should be criminalized; and 40% thought homosexuals should not be allowed to live in Romania."[66] Another study from 2009 indicated Romania was among the most intolerant of European countries with respect to homosexuality. In this investigation, more than 60 percent of participants said they did not want to have a homosexual as a neighbour and almost 80 percent believed homosexuality was "not justifiable."[67] A report from the Danish Institute for Human Rights in 2009 stated that in Romania descriptions of homosexuality as a "vice" or "sin against nature" occurred both in print and online.⁶⁸ Summarizing the situation, this report said: "Anti-gay prejudice and stereotypes are widespread in Romania, and it appears that expressions of homophobia remain legitimate and respectable."⁶⁹ When, quite early on in the film, Johnny says to Gheorghe, "Bet you wish you'd stayed in Romania," he is clearly not speaking with any knowledge of the prejudices to be found in that country nor with any appreciation of how these things might be mirrored across the continent. By contrast to the man at the bar, what we see from other characters in the film is generally a profound tolerance of both Johnny and Gheorghe's "difference." Robyn is plainly aware of Johnny's homosexuality but is not at all bothered by it, and although little is put into words by Johnny's father and grandmother, what is demonstrated is again an acceptance of difference. His grandmother finds a used condom and simply flushes it down the toilet. His father observes Johnny and Gheorghe laughing and larking with each other as they work at "muck-spreading," and nods his head in acceptance when Johnny tells him that Gheorghe is the one thing that will make him happy. He even tells his son he is proud of him. Gheorghe teaches Johnny gentleness through the physicality of their relationship (and the empathy with which he responds to the animals on the farm) but this tenderness reverberates beyond their relationship: Johnny reaches out and touches his father's finger when he is unconscious in hospital following his second stroke, and then when Johnny is bathing him his father in turn touches his hand and uses that simplest phrase of all, "Thank you." In a sense, the nature of the sexuality at the heart of the film is unimportant, rather it is the expression of sensitivity within human relationships that is crucial.

## IV

Hate crime is on the rise throughout Europe, fuelled by the increased advocacy of right-wing political views. Homophobia, racism, anti-migrant sentiment, anti-gypsyism: all these perspectives are finding increasing acceptance. At the same time, "migration has become inevitable in the contemporary world and, due to globalisation, it is likely to accelerate."⁷⁰ This, in turn, in recent decades has provided further oxygen for the growth of nationalism and a rejection of "otherness." *God's Own Country* stands against this trend. It provides positive images of both sexual and ethnic difference. Within a world that seems to be closing in on liberalism, it posits more hopeful possibilities. Talking about the landscape around them, Gheorghe says to Johnny, "It's beautiful here," but Johnny cannot really see that beauty, and neither can we because the camera has (like Johnny) had its head cast down throughout the film to this point, focusing intently on the claustrophobic day-to-day grind of work without pleasure and with no sense of more hopeful horizons. It is only when Gheorghe charges off up the fell and Johnny pursues him to the top that he is (and we are, as the camera looks up) able to appreciate the beauty of distant vistas leading him on to new possibilities.

Ultimately, what we have is a film with a happy ending; a film that defies the state of Europe in order to offer hope for something better and more caring. The danger might be, however, that we end up with something approaching what Trandafoiu describes as "diasporic idealization."[71] She suggests the reality is that "migration and foreignness lead to discrimination in both majorities *and* minorities" (my italics).[72] Gheorghe is good and right and true throughout. Notice, for example, the way in which Hollywood hero-like he is able to deal with the provocation he receives in the pub. This is a film beneath which the reality of the divided state of the UK (and Europe) flows like a turbulent subterranean river. What we have is a story that suggests maybe something like "love conquers all," while the reality for experiences of "otherness" is that something much more substantial within both a political and socio-economic sense is necessary if such issues are to be addressed. In the face of increasingly confident right-wing politics, attacks on migrants and homophobia are unlikely (distressingly) to be dealt with simply through tenderness and "love." At the same time, Winlow, Hall, and Treadwell suggest these issues are not going to be resolved by blaming people who voted for Brexit for the rise of the right. Instead, they advise we need to ask ourselves

**Figure 11.2** With Gheorghe's guidance, Johnny is able to look up and see the beauty of the landscape around him for the first time in *God's Own Country*.

one crucial question: "Why at this point in our history are so many people so keen to cut immigration?"[73] The simple fact of the matter regarding Brexit, they say, is that

> many of those who live in the deindustrialised zones of Wales and the north of England couldn't see any economic benefit in remaining in the EU... Many of those we spoke to worked very hard for terrible rates of pay. Their jobs were insecure and they were cut adrift from mainstream civil society.[74]

What Lee *is* powerfully aware of is the way in which, faced with such tough daily strictures on their lives, ordinary people simply get on with enjoying life. In a moment which deliberately echoes a scene in the British New Wave film about working-class lives, *The Loneliness of the Long Distance Runner* (Tony Richardson, 1962), Lee shows Johnny and Gheorghe watching TV and revelling joyously in their blossoming relationship. The presenter on TV is talking about the funeral of Winston Churchill, ceremonial Ministry of Defence uniforms, members of the Royal Family, World War Two and the Blitz, but the two young men have absolutely no interest in these ideas that are usually seen as such significant markers of Britishness, being entirely absorbed in the intensity of their complicity.

## Notes

1. Simon Winlow, Steve Hall, and James Treadwell, *The Rise of the Right: English nationalism and the transformation of working-class politics* (Bristol: Policy Press, 2017), p. 205.
2. Ibid., p. 206.
3. Ibid.
4. Ibid.
5. Ibid.
6. Travis D. Boyce and Winsome M. Chunnu (eds.), *Historicizing Fear: Ignorance, Vilification and Othering* (Louisville: University Press of Colorado, 2019), p. 6.
7. Ibid.
8. Ibid. They also point to "exaggerated stories about the benefits available to people coming to the United Kingdom from other countries" being circulated and point out that: "These myths about the effects of immigration are commonly held all over western and central Europe." See Boyce and Chunnu, *Historicizing Fear: Ignorance, Vilification and Othering*, p. 6.
9. They are lying as close as lovers and, particularly as a result of this proximity, elements of this speech obviously carry additional impact for the viewer in retrospect.
10. Delia-Luiza Niṭă, "ENAR Shadow Report 2008: Racism in Romania," European Network against Racism (ENAR), October 2009, p. 3. Available at http://cms.

horus.be/files/99935/MediaArchive/national/Romania%20-%20SR%202008.pdf (accessed 2 December 2020).
11. Ioana Szeman, *Staging Citizenship: Roma, Performance and Belonging in EU Romania* (New York and Oxford: Berghahn, 2018), p. 3.
12. Quoted in Cristian Tileaga, *The Nature of Prejudice: Society, Discrimination and Moral Exclusion* (London and New York: Routledge, 2016), p. 43.
13. The report explains that "Roma" is an umbrella term encompassing diverse groups, including Roma, Sinti, Kale, Romanichels, Boyash/Rudari, Ashkali, Egyptians, Yenish, Dom, Lom, Rom, and Abdal, as well as various Traveller populations. See Anon., "EU Roma strategic framework for equality, inclusion and participation for 2020–2030," European Commission, 7 October 2020, p. 1. Available at https://ec.europa.eu/info/sites/info/files/union_of_equality_eu_roma_strategic_framework_for_equality_inclusion_and_participation_en.pdf (accessed 2 December 2020).
14. Ibid.
15. Poland, Hungary, Czech Republic, Slovakia, Slovenia, Estonia, Latvia, and Lithuania had joined the EU in 2004.
16. Ruxandra Trandafoiu, *Diaspora Online: Identity Politics and Romanian Migrants* (New York and London: Berghahn, 2013), p. 17.
17. Ibid.
18. Ken Lee, "Foreword," in Ian Hancock, *We Are the Romani People* (Hatfield: University of Hertfordshire Press, 2002), p. xi.
19. Ibid.
20. See, for example, Eva A. Duda-Mikulin, *EU Migrant Workers, Brexit and Precarity: Polish Women's Perspectives from Inside the UK* (Bristol: Policy Press, 2019), p. 4.
21. David Gillborn, *Racism and Education: Coincidence or Conspiracy?* (London and New York: Routledge, 2008), pp. 2–3.
22. Ibid., p. 4. Gillborn refers to "the non-accidental nature of racism as a structure of domination patterned historically, culturally, socially, and economically."
23. Ibid., p. 3.
24. Ibid., p.2.
25. Gillborn, *Racism and Education: Coincidence or Conspiracy?*, 2008, p. 1.
26. Stefania Marino, Judith Roosblad, and Rinus Penninx, *Trade Unions and Migrant Workers: New Contexts and Challenges in Europe* (Cheltenham and Northampton, MA: Edward Elgar, 2017), p. 1.
27. Ibid.
28. Ibid.
29. Ibid.
30. After telling Gheorghe the size of the flock on the farm, Johnny's father, Martin, has already asked, "Do you understand me?"
31. Hein de Haas, Stephen Castles, and Mark J. Miller, *The Age of Migration: International Population Movements in the Modern World*, 6th edn. (London: Red Globe Press, 2020), p. 2.
32. Ibid.

33. Winlow, Hall, and Treadwell, *The Rise of the Right: English Nationalism and the Transformation of Working-Class Politics*, p. 201.
34. Ibid., p. 205.
35. De Haas, Castles, and Miller, *The Age of Migration: International Population Movements in the Modern World*, p. 2.
36. Ibid.
37. Ibid.
38. Ibid.
39. Ibid.
40. Trandafoiu, *Diaspora Online: Identity Politics and Romanian Migrants*, p. 7.
41. Ibid.
42. Ibid.
43. Felicia Nica and Madalina Moraru, "Diaspora Policies, Consular Services and Social Protection for Romanian Citizens Abroad," in Jean-Michel Lafleur and Daniela Vintila (eds.), *Migration and Social Protection in Europe and Beyond (Volume 2): Comparing Consular Services and Diaspora Policies*, IMISCOE Research Series (Cham, Switzerland: Springer Nature, 2020) p. 414. Available at https://doi.org/10.1007/978-3-030-51245-3 (accessed 2 December 2020).
44. Ibid., p. 413.
45. Trandafoiu, *Diaspora Online: Identity Politics and Romanian Migrants*, p. 18.
46. Ibid., p. 24.
47. Ibid.
48. Oana Romocea, "Facets of migrant identity: ethical dilemmas in research among Romanian migrants in the UK," in Ulrike Ziemer and Sean P. Roberts (eds.), *East European Diasporas, Migrations and Cosmopolitanism* (London and New York: Routledge, 2013), p. 124.
49. Trandafoiu, *Diaspora Online: Identity Politics and Romanian Migrants*, p. 23.
50. The irony is while Martin (in a broad rural accent) is asking Gheorghe if he can understand what he is saying, it is he who fails to understand Gheorghe's point. When Gheorghe asks about milk, Martin thinks he is asking if they have any dairy cattle when he is in fact querying why they don't milk the sheep.
51. Paula Erizanu, "'A whole sheep for £18': how live exports are hurting farmers in Romania," *The Guardian*, 22 January 2020. Available at https://www.theguardian.com/environment/2020/jan/22/a-whole-sheep-for-18-how-live-exports-are-hurting-farmers-in-romania (accessed 2 December 2020).
52. For a further account of hardships faced by Romanian sheep farmers, see also Teofilia Nistor, "Sheep farming in Romania," Radio Romania International, 4 April 2017. Available at https://www.rri.ro/en_gb/sheep_farming_in_romania-2562363 (accessed 2 December 2020).
53. The Organisation for Economic Co-operation and Development, a group of European countries committed to "democracy" and the "market economy," reported "a sharp upswing" in Romanians entering the United Kingdom in 2014, "with flows almost doubling to 37,000" and with the number reaching 56,000 in 2015. Their understanding of this was that the "lifting of work

restrictions on Romanian citizens in the United Kingdom in 2014 likely contributed to this upsurge." See Anon., "Talent Abroad: A Review of Romanian Emigrants," OECD (OECD Publishing: Paris, 2019), p. 82. Available at https://doi.org/10.1787/bac53150-en (accessed 2 December 2020).
54. Judy Fudge and Petra Herzfeld-Olsson discuss tensions within the EU between ambitions to protect the pay and conditions of migrant workers and the reluctance of individual countries to accept anything that might interfere with the "flexibility" of their labor markets. At heart the debate is about the extent to which the market should be curbed and regulated, and the extent to which a more neo-liberal approach should prevail. See Judy Fudge and Petra Herzfeld-Olsson, "The EU Seasonal Workers Directive: When Immigration Control Meet Labour Rights," *European Journal of Migration and Law*, 16 (4), 2014, pp. 439–66. Available at https://kar.kent.ac.uk/44227/1/FudgeandHerzfeldOlssonSeasonalWorkersDirectiveFinal%2028%20Sept.pdf (accessed 2 December 2020).
55. Mattha Busby, "Government reduces minimum salary for migrants to settle in UK," *The Guardian*, 24 October 2020. Available at https://www.theguardian.com/world/2020/oct/24/migrants-to-uk-now-need-to-earn-only-20480-after-home-office-climbdown (accessed 2 December 2020).
56. Yash Dubal, "Migrant workers will be critical to the UK's economic rebirth," *Personnel Today*, 2 June 2020. Available at https://www.personneltoday.com/hr/migrant-workers-will-be-critical-to-the-uks-economic-rebirth/ (accessed 2 December 2020).
57. De Haas, Castles, and Miller, *The Age of Migration: International Population Movements in the Modern World*, p. 1.
58. Ibid., p. 3.
59. Duda-Mikulin, *EU Migrant Workers, Brexit and Precarity: Polish Women's Perspectives from Inside the UK*, p. 4.
60. Ibid., p. 15.
61. Ibid.
62. Ibid., p. 4.
63. Ibid.
64. "Hate crimes against lesbian, gay, bisexual and transgender (LGBT) people increased 147% during July, August and September compared to the same period last year, according to the LGBT anti-violence charity Galop. Statistics from the police have already documented a spike of hate crimes against ethnic minorities and foreign nationals. Few analysts predicted a rise in hate crime based on victims' sexual orientation, however." See Mark Townsend, "Homophobic attacks in UK rose 147% in three months after Brexit vote," *The Observer*, 8 October 2016. Available at theguardian.com/society/2016/oct/08/homophobic-attacks-double-after-brexit-vote (accessed 2 December 2020).
65. Adela Moraru, "Social perception of homosexuality in Romania," *Procedia—Social and Behavioral Sciences*, 5 (2), 2010, pp. 45–9. Available at https://www.researchgate.net/publication/232415423_Social_perception_of_homosexuality_in_Romania (accessed 2 December 2020).

66. Ibid., p. 45.
67. Ibid., p. 46.
68. Anon., "The social situation concerning homophobia and discrimination on grounds of sexual orientation in Romania," Danish Institute for Human Rights, March 2009. Available at https://fra.europa.eu/sites/default/files/fra_uploads/389-fra-hdgso-part2-nr_ro.pdf (accessed 2 December 2020), p. 3.
69. Ibid., p. 4.
70. Duda-Mikulin, *EU Migrant Workers, Brexit and Precarity: Polish Women's Perspectives from Inside the UK*, p. 8.
71. Trandafoiu, *Diaspora Online: Identity Politics and Romanian Migrants*, p. 18.
72. Ibid.
73. Winlow, Hall, and Treadwell, *The Rise of the Right: English Nationalism and the Transformation of Working-Class Politics*, pp. 203–4.
74. Ibid.

CHAPTER 12

# Rural Poverty: *Dark River* (Clio Barnard, 2017) and *The Levelling* (Hope Dickson Leach, 2016)

## I

There are some clear parallels between these two films from different directors. In *Dark River* a strong central female character, Alice Bell (Ruth Wilson), returns to the family home, a rundown sheep farm in the Yorkshire Dales, following the death of her father (Sean Bean). In *The Levelling* a similarly independent central female character, Clover Catto (Ellie Kendrick), returns to her family home, a struggling dairy farm on the Somerset Levels, following the death of her brother, Harry (Joe Blakemore). Both films offer closely observed, psychological explorations of the central character, and both place this psychological examination against a rural, small-farm backdrop. In *Dark River*, Alice must renew her relationship with her brother, Joe (Mark Stanley), who has been left to run the farm for the past fifteen years, and to nurse their father through his final illness.[1] In *The Levelling*, Clover is forced to renegotiate her relationship with her father, Aubrey (David Troughton), who she despises for what she remembers as the harsh manner in which he raised his children.

Reviews of each of these films have primarily seen them as studies of the psychology of family relationships.[2] Both films have an absent mother whose death has been critical to the development of relationships within the family and whose presence in absentia is vital to the narrative. In both films our understanding of each strand of the triangular relationship between father, son, and daughter steadily grows as we move through the film. And although they may offer some element of hope in their endings, both films view the family essentially as a dysfunctional space—a place of division and anguish. Dickson Leach said she saw the devastating flooding that could occur on the Somerset Levels if drainage channels were not maintained as a metaphor for what could happen within a family if channels of communication were not kept open.[3] Early in *The Levelling*, as someone delivers news of her brother's death and asks if there is anything they can do to help, Clover's immediate bitter riposte is: "Can you make it my father instead of my brother? Can you make that happen?" But gradually she begins to realize the memory she has of events, the narrative she has developed for herself over the years, may not be the only possible version of the past.[4]

> CLOVER: I hated boarding school.
> AUBREY: You didn't: Harry hated boarding school.
> CLOVER: He never went: he got to stay here.
> AUBREY: He did. He went for a term: cried the whole time . . . You loved it there.

Early in *Dark River*, as Alice tells her male boss she has had news of the death of her father she flinches from his attempted consoling touch on her arm. This is our first indication of the sexual abuse she has suffered as a young woman at the hands of her father. When she returns to the family home but cannot sleep in the house and experiences flashbacks to her earlier life on the farm,[5] the full extent of her trauma becomes clear.

> ALICE: You told me not to tell anyone. Did you think it was something I ought to be ashamed of?
> JOE: No, I was trying to protect you. Why did you never say owt to him?
> ALICE: I were a child. He told me to keep quiet . . . I were a child.

These are films about family dislocation: fathers divided (in, admittedly, vastly different ways) from daughters and sons, daughters and sons divided from fathers (and mothers), and brothers and sisters divided from each other. These are films about the resurfacing of past events caused by the loss of a family member, but also (to be more hopeful) the opportunity for the renewal of remaining family relationships that such bereavement can create. The central characters in each must return to their family home in the countryside in order to address those half-buried elements from their past that made them leave in the first place.

Both sets of filmmakers create central protagonists who are highly capable women, well able to hold their own within a man's world. The opening scene in *Dark River* shows Alice proficiently making her way in a male-dominated world as the only woman in a team of sheep-shearers. Later she is seen as the only woman at a farmers' market, confidently herding her sheep through the auction ring. And yet, although she is adept within what are classically all-male spaces, her vulnerability is also clear from the outset; before she travels home, for example, an extreme long shot shows her minute within the frame as she stands beside the sea alone with her thoughts. Similarly, early in *The Levelling*, when Clover helps to milk the cows, despite the fact that her father continually feels the need to correct what she is doing and she may not

**Figure 12.1** In *Dark River* (Clio Barnard, 2017), Alice (Ruth Wilson), here walking her sheep through a market sales-ring, appears well able to hold her own in a man's world.

have done this for some time, it is clear she is highly competent within this space. And, again, it is the cinematography that reveals a further side to this; when she enters the family home, Clover is shown as small within the frame, boxed within a doorway in the depth of a long shot. Both characters have to move haltingly towards a point at which they are able to find some accommodation with their family history. While in the final analysis consolingly recognizing that the family may also be a space capable of offering a certain solace in the face of the complexities of life, both films present the family as an arena of contestation and conflict. However, rather than pursuing in more detail the psychological journeys of Alice and Clover, it is those components of film construction more normally seen as little more than a backdrop to the events of the film that will mainly occupy our attention here—the geographical locations and rural settings, and the economic and political contexts within which these family ruptures occur.

## II

*The Levelling* opens with images of an excavator dredging a river and a handpainted sign reading: "Save Our Village: Dredge the River." The reference being made is to actual flooding experienced by people living on the Somerset Levels in the winter of 2013–14 that became the subject of extensive national news coverage. There are repeated allusions to this event in the script. Clover's family home has been flooded so that it is no longer habitable,[6] Harry refers to having to deal with "two hundred cattle in four feet of water at two o'clock in the morning," and a family friend mentions in passing the difficult year everybody in the area has had. *Dark River* does not contain indications of such a specific event but the setting of the rugged hill-farming country of the Yorkshire Dales is emphasized through repeated shots of the landscape. This is harsh, marginal agricultural land that includes rough, moorland grazing that successive images, particularly towards the end of the film, portray as frequently saturated. When Alice arrives at her family home she hesitates before pushing open the door into this well-known childhood space and revealing to us a rundown, old-fashioned interior. For Clover in *The Levelling*, there is a similar moment of uncertainty on the threshold before she shoulders open the door to enter the family home and once again we are shown a dilapidated interior. Neither film presents us with well-to-do farmers running profitable agri-businesses, quite the reverse; the background to these films is rural poverty and the economic precariousness of more traditional farming practices. This is the type of farming discussed at length by James Rebanks in two books, *The Shepherd's Life: A Tale of the Lake District* (2016) and *English Pastoral: An Inheritance* (2020). In the first of these books, he talks of the struggle that has always been faced by the rural poor: "My grandfather belonged to an agricultural family struggling by generation to generation, occasionally making it into the ranks of the relatively established farmers, before sinking back into being tenants, or farmworkers, or in the workhouse, or worse."[7] But, at the same time, Rebanks also presents a powerful awareness of the heritage that goes with an agricultural family's close association with their land and with a specific place. "I have always liked the feeling of carrying on something bigger than me," he says, "something that stretches back through other hands and other eyes into the depths of time."[8] In this way he expresses the dual characteristics of the primary social context employed by both Dickson Leach and Barnard in their films; what both directors reveal to us are people facing an all-too-real rural poverty while retaining their own rich understanding of the natural world. In the opening pages of *The Shepherd's Life*, Rebanks articulates this connection to the land in these terms:

> There is no beginning, and there is no end. The sun rises, and falls, each day, and the seasons come and go. The days, months and years alternate through sunshine, rain, hail, wind, snow and frost. The leaves fall each autumn and burst forth again each spring. The earth spins through the vastness of space. The grass comes and goes with the warmth of the sun. The farms and the flocks endure, bigger than the life of a single person . . . I smile at the thought that the entire history of our family has played out in the fields and villages stretching away beneath that fell, between Lake District and Pennines, for at

least six centuries, and probably longer. We shaped this landscape, and we were shaped by it in turn.[9]

This may sound a somewhat romanticized view of the countryside but that is not what Rebanks is about. Like both Dickson Leach and Barnard, he refuses to adopt an idealized perspective on the countryside. In *English Pastoral: An Inheritance*, he says:

> My inheritance is an ancient one, the chance to live and work on a piece of much-loved land ... In the most practical and real way imaginable, I began to think about how we shaped the earth. I would have to work out how we could create a farm that would keep us, and regenerate our land and its ecosystems as best we could ... But how? What sort of future could we shape for our children? I was already determined that I would not intensify and scale-up, take huge financial risks or make factories out of our fields. But nor could I see how to manage our land entirely for nature, producing less, without going broke. I knew that if we farmed in more sustainable ways—and no one wanted to pay us to do that—then we would just go bankrupt. The applause of middle-class people who "care about the environment" isn't worth much when the bank manager says "No."[10]

Dickson Leach and Barnard present the viewer with the realities of attempting to maintain traditional farming in the contemporary world. The vulnerability of tenant farmers to market fluctuations—essentially to globalization and the industrialization of farming methods—is made clear in both films. This is the reality faced by small-scale farmers across the UK. A report on farming in the Teesdale area issued a few years before these films were released makes clear the hardship facing farmers in that area. According to this document, difficult economic circumstances "led to situations where farmers couldn't afford to pay bills or mend broken equipment, had to forego basics (such as food) and lower their input costs (e.g. reduce the amount or quality of feed given to livestock)."[11] It went on to say that,

> While the widely accepted definition of poverty is having a household income which is 60% or less of the average, and the Minimum Income Standard 2012 found a single working-age adult living in a village needed to earn at least £19,820 ... upland farmers in Teesdale had an income of £12,600 (with some earning much less, just £8,000 a year).[12]

The report listed a number of characteristics exhibited by farmers who found themselves in "farm poverty." It said they were often operating without adequate insurance, were unable to pay into a pension scheme, had no savings or few savings to draw on, and depended on working at other jobs to balance the farm budget. The report added that many farmers "felt vulnerable to decisions made by their landlord and bank, and some were exhibiting mental health and personal well-being issues."[13]

A major part of the plot for *Dark River* revolves around the passing of the tenancy of the family farm from one generation to the next: both Alice and her brother, Joe, apply to take on their father's tenancy. However, it is made very clear that it is the owners of the land and their agents who have all the power in tenancy contractual agreements. Looking at the current state of the farm, the agent comments dismissively to Joe, who has been working the farm under his father's tenancy: "We do expect our tenants to do a better job of maintaining our properties." Both the reality of who legally owns the property and the subordinate position of tenant farmers are made blatantly clear in such a sentence: the land and buildings are "*our* properties," i.e. they do not belong to the tenants, and there is even a sense of ownership over the tenants themselves in that they too are denoted as "our tenants." In an article in *The Financial Times*, Barnard is quoted as saying: "Tenant farmers have a rough deal."[14] This film makes it clear that profit margins for tenant hill-farmers are so tight that, as indicated in the report on farmers in Teesdale quoted above, it is often necessary for the tenant to undertake a second job. Joe has taken on work driving for a haulage contractor; and in order to make the point, the filmmakers have Joe pull into the farmyard in the company's lorry on several occasions. Attempting to persuade Joe to sell up the tenancy, another employee of the land agent says to him: "These farms aren't making any money anymore, are they; sold quite a few of them on to property developers. There's a hundred grand in it for the tenant." The perilous position of not only tenant farmers but anybody farming marginal land in the UK is made apparent at every narrative turn. According to an article in *The Guardian*:

> At least one-quarter of all farming families live on or below the official poverty line . . . The levels of borrowing that farmers require in order to run their businesses is mind-boggling; it's not uncommon for farmers to have debts well into six figures.[15]

A 2017 report from the Social Mobility Commission that aimed to assess "the education, employability and housing prospects" of people living in England in order to highlight whereabouts in the country people from disadvantaged backgrounds were most and least likely to make social progress,[16] found there was a major problem not only in the old industrial areas of the country that were now economically depressed but also in certain rural areas. The report identified more than seventy largely rural areas in which over 30 percent of people earned below the voluntary living wage.[17] Average wages in the worst-performing area of West Somerset were £312 a week, which was less than half that being achieved in the best-performing areas of Wandsworth, Richmond upon Thames, and Westminster.[18] What the report called "new social mobility coldspots" were found to be concentrated "in remote rural or coastal areas" as well as in former industrial areas.[19] Many of these places, it was pointed out, combined poor educational outcomes for young people from disadvantaged backgrounds with weak labor markets that had a greater share of low-skilled, low-paid employment than elsewhere in England.[20] West Somerset was found to be the worst part of the country for social mobility,[21] and in this area more than 40 percent of people earned less than the voluntary living wage, the highest levels in the country.[22] The report pointed towards "the growing sense that we have become an 'us and them' society" and "the sense of political alienation and social resentment" felt in many parts of the country.[23]

## III

The stories we are presented with in both *Dark River* and *The Levelling* give expression to the marginalized socio-economic position many people from rural communities feel themselves to occupy. Alongside this, they are also explicitly set within the context of modern industrial-scale farming, commercial attitudes towards the land and agriculture, and chemical exploitation of the land through the use of fertilizers and pesticides. When, in *Dark River*, Alice is preparing to lay poison for the rats that have been one of the concerns of the land agent, Joe intervenes and points out there are barn owls with young fledglings nesting in the building in which she is about to place the poison. Maybe it is at this point we begin to become more aware of the way in which the soundtrack uses birdsong as an accompaniment to the images of fields and moorland we are frequently shown. The key moment in the thematic underpinning of the whole film occurs when Alice and Joe clash over whether to cut silage from the meadow in order to feed the sheep, or whether they should leave this field so that it develops as a hay meadow later in the year. Joe becomes both passionate and eloquent in putting forward the case for something other than a purely profit-driven approach to farming. He says:

> When you cut it for silage all you end up doin' is killin' everything that's under it. In an acre of hay meadow you've got 400 million insects, 600 million mites, two million spiders, and moths, butterflies, bees, voles, shrews.

In her highly respected book, *Silent Spring*, the person frequently seen as having offered a crucial early alarm-call regarding humanity's treatment of the natural world, Rachel Carson, warned in the 1960s that, "The rapidity of change and the speed with which new situations are created follow the impetuous and heedless pace of man rather than the deliberate pace of nature."[24] She was not the only person at that time counseling against the unfettered exploitation of the land. Ruth Janette Ruck, for example, a hill-farmer in Wales, cautioned that, "Though scientific knowledge has tamed Nature, it may yet despoil the natural world. Meanwhile the hills remain precariously unspoilt for all who can lift their eyes to them."[25] Almost sixty years later, Barnard is raising the same sort of questions about our relationship with the land. In *English Pastoral: An Inheritance*, Rebanks is more direct and forceful in his expression of the same idea: "The last forty years on the land were revolutionary and disrupted all that had gone before for thousands of years—a radical and ill-thought-through experiment that was conducted in our fields."[26] Raising issues within the same arena of debate, we find that in *The Levelling* Clover is vegetarian and her childhood bedroom has several posters relating to the environment and animal welfare. Partly this is an expression of her youthful revolt against her father, but it is also the case that particular subjects are being deliberately placed before the viewer for further consideration. In his foreword to a later book by Ruck, John Lewis-Stempel comments: "Disciples of Big Farming say that these old ways of agriculture are uneconomical... which is odd criticism from an industry only kept afloat by billions of pounds in subsidies."[27] Ruck, he says,

> ... does not romanticize her life, but she is alive to the benefits, such as free-range kids who can swim in the stream, and surroundings which are "a constant inspiration" in their beauty. The phrase she uses about her style of farming is "soul-rewarding." Is there any soul at all in modern agriculture? Any esteem at all for livestock on slats in factory units?[28]

In a review of her film in *The Financial Times*, Barnard quotes the ecologist Timothy Morton as saying, "Putting something called nature on a pedestal and admiring it from afar does for the environment what patriarchy does for the figure of woman. It is a paradoxical act of sadistic admiration."[29] For Barnard, there is some sense in which her central character has been abused in a similar fashion to the way in which the land has been exploited. Violent male attitudes of dominance and oppression towards women can also be seen in man's approach to the natural world. Seeing beauty in nature is a shallow cover for exploitation (as is the worshipping of "beauty" in women). Environmental and feminist agendas come together, so that violence and abuse within both arenas is perhaps seen to originate from the same wellspring. Barnard says:

> You can't shy away from the things you see in the countryside—like dead things . . . I hope this doesn't sound crap but, it's birth, sex and death—that's the reality . . . The countryside isn't a park or a weekend retreat. I grew up in a place where all my neighbours were tenant farmers, and every one of them has gone. It has become a grouse-rearing community for the richest people in the world to come and shoot . . . You have to acknowledge the countryside for what it is. What it means to raise an animal, what it means to chop down all the trees on the moors and turn them into land for grouse shooting—we have to think about what the land really means.[30]

Early on in *Dark River*, Alice finds a sheep that has escaped from a field into a road and has broken its leg. She talks to the animal and soothes it but knows the reality of what has to happen next. The knacker[31] is called to kill the sheep with a captive-bolt shot to the head and then we are shown the dead body being winched into the back of a truck. Before the animal is killed, Alice holds it and talks soothingly to it: "It's all right. Be over soon. All right." In *The Levelling*, having been away to university, Clover has to be reminded of the reality of rural life on a stock farm: a calf is born but it is a male and has to be "culled" as being of no use on a dairy farm. Aubrey asks his daughter to shoot it, and we have to watch as Clover takes the shotgun and cartridges from the gun-cabinet, before we view her in a static shot and in slow motion maneuvering the calf out of the frame to the right, hugging, almost cuddling the animal as she does so. We see her in close-up and hear her cocking the gun before we cut to a static shot of the empty farmyard, over which we hear the gun going off. The action is stretched out in such a way as to allow us to reflect on what we are seeing.[32] In this way both films explore what Barnard refers to above as the "reality" of rural farming life. Nature is not soft and gentle but harsh and brutal. If it has beauty it is not a chocolate-box beauty. The reality of the countryside is that when a sheep breaks its leg it needs to be killed. If there is beauty it is the beauty of Alice's words to the sheep facing its final moments: "It's all right. Be over soon."

In *The Levelling*, a significant strand of the plot revolves around the contemporary threat to cattle farms posed by tuberculosis (TB) and the debate as to whether this disease might be passed to cattle via badgers. Here again the theme in both films of the economic vulnerability of small farms is linked with an environmental issue. A friend of her brother, James (Jack Holden), explains to Clover the dire financial straits the farm is in. "You know they're broke, don't you?" he says to her, "The house is a wreck. Their insurance

**Figure 12.2**  Clover (Ellie Kendrick) prepares to shoot a young calf in *The Levelling* (Hope Dickson Leach, 2016).

fucked up. The land is still full of glass and all kinds of shit from the floods." And then, when a government department Animal Health lorry arrives to take the "reactor cattle,"[33] it becomes clear the herd is infected with TB and that this has been one of the final pieces of news that has pushed Clover's brother, Harry, towards the act of taking his own life. Harry has inherited a farm with so many problems that in the end he can see no way out other than suicide. And this is not that unusual. The number of dairy farms in the UK fell from almost 36,000 in 1995 to only just over 12,000 in 2019, a 66 percent reduction.[34] And in 2018, farming journals in particular highlighted the fact that on average one agricultural worker a week was taking their own life in the UK.[35] In looking at suicide rates in the countryside, Cameron Stark says, "Rural areas are not the idyllic areas of popular imagination . . . Two distinct themes arise from the literature on rural suicide in the UK. Suicide rates in some areas are higher than expected, particularly in the most rural parts of the UK. Some occupational groups have a higher than expected proportion of deaths from suicide, of which farmers are the best known—and most researched—example."[36] In their book *The Changing World of Farming in Brexit UK*, Matt Lobley, Michael Winter, and Rebecca Wheeler point out that suicide "is the part of the problem which is visible but under which lays a much greater body of depression, stress and anxiety."[37]

## IV

Both these films highlight divisions within families and show us individuals divided against themselves, but beyond this both films show a nation economically, socially, and politically divided against itself. There are many constituencies within the UK population that feel they have been ignored and ultimately abandoned by politicians and government departments. One such group is the rural poor and another is small farmers. Many of these people feel themselves to be isolated from the rest of society, and certainly from the power centres of society. Aubrey's cryptic aside to his daughter, "My very own refugee camp," when she finds him living in a static caravan rather than the family house in *The Levelling*, carries much more heft than we might at first realize. Furthermore, the fact that throughout the film locals are seen to be attempting to help Aubrey by digging a drainage ditch by hand with spades and wheelbarrows merely reinforces their impotence in the face of the social and economic waters swirling around them. In what has frequently been seen as a vote reflecting the increasing marginalization of certain sectors of the UK population, more than 60 percent of voters in both Sedgemoor and West Somerset in the 2016 referendum voted to leave the European Union.[38] In 2015, the *Somerset County Gazette* reported West Somerset was officially one of the poorest regions in the country.[39] Looking at Joe's words in defence of his hay meadow, and extrapolating out from just one small region of the UK, we might even see a whole western way of life in conflict over its future direction. Of course, it remains highly debatable where the answer to these sorts of tensions may be found. For example, if we take flooding as a specific aspect of a much wider concern for the environment that is being raised in these films and return to the poster we see in *The Levelling* which is demanding "Save Our Village: Dredge the River," we have to admit this gut response from local people may not be the answer. Discussing the very floods Dickson Leach says offered her an apt backdrop to the struggles of her family on the Somerset Levels, George Monbiot quotes an Environment Agency presentation as saying, "Dredging of river channels does not prevent flooding during extreme river flows."[40] Monbiot explains that, "A river's capacity is tiny by comparison to the catchment from which it draws its water. You can increase the flow of a river by dredging, but that is likely to cause faster and more dangerous floods downstream when the water hits the nearest urban bridge."[41] *Dark River* and *The Levelling* may not offer solutions, but they identify crucial divisions within UK society, highlight critical social and environmental dilemmas for the country, and put into play what the filmmakers see as important issues that need to be addressed.

## Notes

1. The title is not only a potent image for the sense of menace running through the film but also alludes to a recurring image in the work of the most famous poet

associated with this region, Ted Hughes. Susan Bassnett, for example, refers to "the imagery of dark water that recurs so often in Hughes's poetry" (see Susan Bassnett, *Ted Hughes* (Liverpool: Liverpool University Press, 2009), p. 50). In "The Dark River" (1979), Hughes includes phrases such as, "behind encircling horizons,/A happy hell, the arguing, immortal dead,/" that are entirely apt for this film (see Paul Keegan (ed.), *Ted Hughes: Collected Poems* (London: Faber & Faber, 2012), p. 455). In a poem celebrating the innocence of his young daughter, "Full Moon and Little Frieda" (1967), Hughes sees a herd of cows as they move along a lane between hedges as "a dark river of blood" (Keegan, *Ted Hughes: Collected Poems*, p. 182).

2. Some, like Mark Kermode talking about *The Levelling*, have recognized the importance of the background elements—the regional settings and the economics. He refers to the way Dickson Leach's "quietly overwhelming feature debut addresses grand upheavals (personal, regional, economic) in deceptively understated and fiercely truthful fashion." See Mark Kermode, 'The Levelling review—a tremendous debut from Hope Dickson Leach,' *The Observer*, 14 May 2017. Available at https://www.theguardian.com/film/2017/may/14/the-levelling-review-mark-kermode-somerset-hope-dickson-leach (accessed 15 November 2020). Others, like Joseph Walsh, have recognized something similar in *Dark River*. He confidently asserts: "Make no mistake, *Dark River* is a deeply political film." See Joseph Walsh, "Director Clio Barnard on *Dark River* and the drama of rural life," *Financial Times*, 16 February 2018. Available at https://www.ft.com/content/2aed47a8-f48d-11e7-a4c9-bbdefa4f210b (accessed 15 November 2020).

3. "What happens to a family who don't talk and then find themselves in difficult situations and how do they get beyond that? . . . The rivers, the man-made channels that it was so essential to maintain and look after—in order to make the countryside work, for life on The Levels to sustain itself—had been neglected and led to disaster . . . This felt like a poignant external representation of the family drama I was developing.' Hope Dickson Leach, "Writer Director's Statement," *The Levelling* DVD cover, Peccadillo Pictures, 2016.

4. See Chapter 10 for the exploration of a similar theme in *The Sense of an Ending* (2017).

5. The young Alice is played by Esme Creed Miles and the young Joe by Aidan McCullough.

6. Beyond the grounding in realism this brings to the text, it is (of course) also a metaphor for the state of their family life.

7. James Rebanks, *The Shepherd's Life: A Tale of the Lake District* (London and New York: Penguin, 2016), p. 6.

8. Ibid., p. 285.

9. Ibid., pp. 2–3.

10. James Rebanks, *English Pastoral: An Inheritance* (London and New York: Allen Lane, 2020), pp. 186–7.

11. Anon., "Challenges Facing Farmers: A report into upland farming and farming families in Teesdale," Upper Teesdale Agricultural Support Services and Rose Regeneration (London: Oxfam, n.d.), p. 3.

12. Ibid.
13. Ibid.
14. Walsh, "Director Clio Barnard on *Dark River* and the drama of rural life," 2018.
15. Tobias Jones, "The harsh lives of the forgotten rural poor," *The Guardian*, 24 February 2013. Available at https://www.theguardian.com/commentisfree/2013/feb/24/rural-poverty-invisible (accessed 21 November 2020).
16. Anon., *State of the Nation 2017: Social Mobility in Great Britain*, Social Mobility Commission, November 2017, p. iii.
17. Ibid., p. iv. The voluntary living wage is slightly higher than the national minimum wage and is something employers sign up to pay on a voluntary basis.
18. Ibid.
19. Ibid., p. v.
20. Ibid.
21. Ibid.
22. Ibid., p. 118.
23. Ibid., p. viii.
24. Rachel Carson, *Silent Spring* (London and New York: Penguin, 2000/1962), p. 24.
25. Ruth Janette Ruck, *Place of Stones* (London: Faber & Faber, 1961), p. 227.
26. Rebanks, *English Pastoral: An Inheritance*, p. 6.
27. John Lewis-Stempel, "Foreword," in Ruth Janette Ruck, *Along Came a Llama* (London: Faber & Faber, 2020/1978), p. xiv.
28. Ibid., pp. xiv–xv.
29. Timothy Morton, *Ecology without Nature: Rethinking Environmental Aesthetics* (Cambridge, MA: Harvard University Press, 2007), p. 5.
30. Walsh, "Director Clio Barnard on *Dark River* and the drama of rural life."
31. The knacker, or knackerman, is a local person responsible for the culling and removal of dying and injured animals.
32. Of course, returning to the more usually taken analytical approach to this film, this event has a further impact in that it replicates the action Clover's brother has taken to end his own life.
33. A reactor is an animal that has failed a test for bovine TB (p. 6). If there is any suspicion of TB in any cows in a herd the whole herd loses its "Official TB Free" status (p. 2). See "Dealing with TB in your herd. What happens if TB is identified in your herd?" Animal Health and Veterinary Laboratories Agency, 2014. Available at https://assets.publishing.service.gov.uk/government/uploads/system/uploads/attachment_data/file/347050/TBYHS-03.pdf (accessed 21 November 2020).
34. Elise Uberoi, "UK Dairy Industry Statistics," House of Commons Library Briefing Paper, No. 2721, 1 May 2020, p. 4.
35. John Swire, "More than one farmer a week in the UK dies by suicide," *Farm Business*, 15 February 2018. Available at http://www.farmbusiness.co.uk/news/more-then-one-farmer-a-week-in-the-uk-dies-by-suicide-2.html (accessed 21 November 2020). Anon., "More than one agricultural worker in UK commits suicide a week, figures show," *Farming UK*, 14 February 2018. Available at

https://www.farminguk.com/news/more-than-one-agricultural-worker-in-uk-commits-suicide-a-week-figures-show_48613.html (accessed 21 November 2020).
36. Cameron Stark, "Suicide in rural areas," in Stephen Palmer (ed.), *Suicide: Strategies and interventions for reduction and prevention* (London and New York: Routledge, 2008), p. 63.
37. Matt Lobley, Michael Winter, and Rebecca Wheeler, *The Changing World of Farming in Brexit UK* (London and New York: Routledge, 2019), p. 171.
38. Anon., "EU Referendum Results," BBC News. Available at https://www.bbc.co.uk/news/politics/eu_referendum/results (accessed 21 November 2020).
39. Anon., "Beautiful but with serious deprivation: Scale of West Somerset rural poverty laid bare," *Somerset County Gazette*, 22 October 2015. Available at https://www.somersetcountygazette.co.uk/news/13886398.beautiful-but-with-serious-deprivation-scale-of-west-somerset-rural-poverty-laid-bare/ (accessed 21 November 2020). The report said 40 percent of workers in West Somerset were earning under the living wage, the highest percentage in England, and went on to highlight the number of people working on temporary or zero-hours contracts, or in seasonal jobs.
40. George Monbiot, "Dredging rivers won't stop floods. It will make them worse," *The Guardian*, 13 January 2014. Available at https://www.theguardian.com/commentisfree/2014/jan/30/dredging-rivers-floods-somerset-levels-david-cameron-farmers (accessed 21 November 2020).
41. Ibid.

CHAPTER 13

# Urban Poverty: *Sorry We Missed You* (Ken Loach, 2019)

## I

During more than fifty years of making films and TV dramas, Ken Loach has never lost sight of the fact, nor allowed his audience to lose sight of the fact, that for him "class" is the fundamental issue determining the nature of society. Critics approaching his work are left with no choice other than to acknowledge "his remarkably consistent concern with the lot of the working class."[1] In an interview with Lorenzo Marsili, he is referred to as "one of the greatest narrators of working-class consciousness and its transformations under neoliberalism."[2] As Loach explains it:

> I believe class is fundamental. It just changes shape as the demands of capital for a different kind of labour force change. But it's still the labour force. And it's still being exploited and it's still providing surplus value even more intensely than before. More important, if we don't understand class struggle, we don't understand anything.[3]

*Sorry We Missed You* (2019) is exclusively focused on the white working class. There are ways in which we might argue some wider areas of identity such as gender, disability, sexuality, race, ethnicity, and other elements are relevant (if only by omission, or light-touch focus), but essentially this film offers an intense single emphasis on a social group that has been the target for considerable criticism within the media recently (but also historically). The supposedly blinkered perspective of the white working class has, for instance, been blamed by many for the 2016 referendum vote to leave the European Union.[4] According to the research agency Ipsos MORI, "Younger, more middle class, more educated and BME voters chose to remain; older, working class, less educated and white voters opted to leave."[5] In an article in *The Guardian* just before the referendum, John Harris said:

> ... make no mistake: ... the foundation of the Brexit coalition is what used to be called the proletariat ... In Stoke, Merthyr, Birmingham, Manchester

and even rural Shropshire, the same lines recurred: so unchanging that they threatened to turn into clichés, but all the more powerful because of their ubiquity. "I'm scared about the future"... "No one listens to us"... "If you haven't got money, no one cares." And of course, none of it needs much translation. Instead of the comparative security and stability of the postwar settlement... what's the best we can now offer for so many people in so many places? Six-week contracts at the local retail park, lives spent pinballing in and out of the benefits system, and retirements built on thin air?[6]

In his book *Chavs: The Demonization of the Working Class*, Owen Jones argued there was now "a widespread middle-class image of the working-class teenager" as "Thick. Violent. Criminal. 'Breeding' like animals."[7] Setting out to answer the question, "How has hatred of working-class people become so socially acceptable?"[8] Jones saw the notion of "chavs" as "an attempt to obscure the reality of the working-class majority."[9] Throughout his career, Loach has set out to offer the audience an insight into what he sees as the actual "reality of the working-class majority." He repeatedly attempts to offer a corrective to any notion of the working class as thick, or violent, or criminal, or animal-like. What we are given in *Sorry We Missed You* is the hard-working working class, the caring working class, the family-orientated working class. The most obvious feature of both central characters, the married couple, Ricky (Kris Hitchen) and Abby (Debbie Honeywood), is their ordinariness. Ricky is a heavily under-pressure delivery driver in today's gig economy. Abby is a care worker, with a daily routine of going from house to house to get people up, feed them, and put them to bed. On the one hand, they are carefully individualized characters who, through the performances the actors give and the ways in which they are filmed, are clearly defined as such. On the other hand, they are also every(wo)man characters, representative of "the working-class majority." Their caring natures, their essential gentleness and kindness, and their good humor are echoed in their children and in many of the people they meet. We see, for example, the caring attitude of their son, Seb (Rhys Stone), as he says goodbye to his (girl)friend at the bus station when she leaves for Blackpool, and we see the imaginative creativity of his witty response when he and his friends are caught spraying a billboard with graffiti. We are shown little moments where the daughter, Liza Jane (Katie Proctor), clears away the plates for her parents when they are asleep together on the settee, or where she attempts to get her brother out of bed to go to school. We view scenes oozing with humanity, in which Abby is in the home of Mollie (Heather Wood), one of the "clients" she regularly helps. Ricky is not educated nor, in socialist terms, is he politically aware; see, for example, the way in which he breaks ranks with the other drivers in the depot when offered the chance to take over a more lucrative delivery route. However, time after time, and despite all that is kicking off in his life, Loach and his writer, Paul Laverty, show the viewer that he loves his family and is in turn loved by his family. It is that love—that essential gentleness and kindness, that is, for Loach, the gentleness and kindness of the working class as a whole—that is tested and pushed further and further towards the brink as the plot of the film develops.

In discussing plot we need to be aware that what is driving the story forward are the politics and economics of the situation in which the family finds itself. There *is* a narrative in which events happen: Ricky does hit his son, for example, and is beaten up on a housing estate during the course of his work. Characters do interact with each other in a variety of ways that move the story on. However, the most crucial aspect of all of this is that scene after scene serves to demonstrate how the difficulties being experienced by this (representative) family are the result of political and economic contexts. Ultimately, it is global economics and politics that cause events to happen in the way in which they do and determine the nature of much of the character interaction we see. The life of the (representative) family the writer and director have chosen to follow exists within both national and international socio-economic contexts. Stage by stage, the nature of the global economics that are shaping the life experience of Ricky (and the rest of his family) becomes clearer. For Loach, this is the crux of the matter. In his interview with Marsili, mentioned above, he explained his understanding of all of this:

> Politics lives in people, ideas live in people, they live in the concrete struggles that people have. It also determines the choices we have—and the choices we have in turn determine the kinds of people we become. How families interact is not some abstract concept of mother, son, father, daughter; it has to do with economic circumstances, the work they do, the time they can spend with each other. Economics and politics are related with the context in which people live their lives, but the details of those lives are very human, often very funny or very sad and in general full of contradiction and complexity.[10]

For Loach, it is clear you and your family can only live your life within the political and economic limits within which you find yourself. You may desperately attempt to live your life with resilience, determination, and good humor, but forces beyond your control will finally determine the way things turn out. Ricky just cannot understand the maelstrom within which he finds himself: "You know, I never thought it would be this difficult, Abby. It just seems to me everything's outta whack, you know what I mean." And his wife is similarly nonplussed: "It just seems like the more we work, the more hours we do, we just sink further and further into this big hole." As Peter Bradshaw expresses it in a review, as with Loach and Laverty's previous film, *I, Daniel Blake*, this film "depicts the human cost of an economic development that we are encouraged to accept as a fact of life."[11] Loach has said that for him and the team he works with, it is "a constant dilemma" deciding how to "tell the story of a working class family, tragically destroyed by economic and political circumstances" without leaving the audience in despair.[12] What Loach and Laverty show us in their film is exactly what researchers have consistently documented in recent years. As Rob Lambert and Andrew Herod explain it in *Neoliberal Capitalism and Precarious Work: Ethnographies of Accommodation and Resistance*, for instance:

> the impact on workers' lives of such work, work which is generally low-paid, unstable and lacking in much physical and legal protection, stretches far beyond the workplace. Thus, those who are subjected to it often find that the long and/or unpredictable hours they must work make it difficult to schedule time with friends and family, whilst the low levels of remuneration make it difficult to plan for marriage and children, or for purchasing a home or even for simply living without having to rely upon government assistance or charity.[13]

## II

It is apparent, then, that the divisions we will find within any film directed by Loach are always going to be class divisions caused by economic and political circumstances. At the same time, over the period he has been making films and TV dramas from the 1960s to the present day, the specifics of the economic and political context will have changed. *Sorry We Missed You* reflects in this regard some of the key aspects of the current historical moment. Primarily, Loach and Laverty are investigating the changing face of work for people in the UK (and by extension for people across the globe). For many the nature of employment has changed drastically within the last thirty or forty years. With globalization there has been a drive towards creating what is described as an increasingly "flexible" workforce. Regulations protecting employees' rights, defending their levels of pay, their terms and conditions, their entitlement to holiday pay and sick pay, for example, have been seen to hamper the ability of businesses to respond to changing market conditions. By finding alternative approaches to the direct employment of permanent workers, companies have found methods to deregulate the employer–employee relationship. *Sorry We Missed You* takes this context and shows the impact it has on an individual worker and his family. When Ricky goes for a job with a delivery company, the depot manager, Maloney (Ross Brewster),[14] explains the situation to him:

> You don't work for us: you work with us. You don't drive for us: you perform services. There's no employment contracts. There's no performance targets. You meet delivery standards. There's no wages but fees... No clockin' on: you "become available." You sign up for us: you become an owner-driver franchisee, master of your own fuckin' destiny.

Ricky has to buy his own van, has to pay for any necessary repairs to this vehicle, has to be available to work or provide an alternative driver, and has to pay fines for any breaches of "standards" or for failing to be "available." He is provided with a handset scanner, which he has to pay for if it is lost or damaged, and with this he has to document the parcels he puts on his van. Maloney tells him: "Once you scan a parcel onto your van, it's yours, it's in the system. We can track it every inch of its journey from here to the doorstep." But it is not only the company that knows where he is and where the parcels are, it is also the customer. As Ricky explains to his daughter, "The customer always knows where I am. They track every parcel, don't they, to the front door, to the back door, even if I put it in the garden shed they know where it lands." Effectively, the film is displaying a key aspect of what has become known as the "gig economy."

George Morgan and Pariece Nelligan identify this term as having "recently entered the vernacular to describe the trend away from standard employment contracts."[15] More workers, they say, are now "living like musicians—working precariously from gig to gig."[16] They go on to explain:

> The word "job" is losing its Fordist connotation of regular-waged work and is increasingly used to describe a particular remunerated task—such as would be performed by an independent tradesperson/artisan... Companies like Uber use a business model that treats those who work for them as subcontractors rather than employees and thus avoid the obligations—for example, to provide sick leave and holiday leave—that employers traditionally carry.[17]

As Jeremias Prassl explains the gig economy:

> Humans have always provided services to their employers and customers... As workers, however, they enjoy significant legal and economic protection in return, from minimum wage and unfair dismissal laws, to social security and pensions... Once work itself becomes the service or commodity, however, such responsibilities can be avoided, lowering prices for consumers and increasing employers' profits.[18]

He says the gig economy sells humans "as a service" and ignores "traditional employment law protection."[19] In the process, workers become "independent entrepreneurs" and work is "rebranded as entrepreneurship."[20] Prassl reminds us of the reality to which Loach is also attempting to alert us: "Beneath the shiny surface of our phones, tablets, and computers, behind the frictionless apps that allow us to order all kinds of products and services, someone, somewhere, is doing work."[21]

Morgan and Nelligan suggest the term "gig economy" has effectively come to stand for "worker precariousness." And this is something Izabela Florczak and Marta Otto, among others, have picked up on. They suggest, "one of the largest and fastest growing problems in Europe is labour market dualization, that is, an increasing divide between insiders in permanent employment and outsiders in precarious work or unemployment."[22] Those in "precarious work" are identified as a "heterogeneous new class of workers"[23] known as "the precariat."[24] Loach and Laverty are concerned to take the viewer into the world of this "precariat," bringing the term alive as real people living real family lives.[25]

As a worker with too many clients to be able to deal with in the time available, like Ricky, Abby "suffers the same squeeze of exploitation."[26] It is her conversations with Mollie, one of those she cares for, that function to widen the audience's awareness of the historical economic contexts that have given rise to the current situation. At one point Mollie shows Abby some photos of her when she was younger. She had been one of those responsible for feeding striking workers and pickets during the Miners' Strike of 1984–5. This has always been a key event for Loach in his understanding of how the present has been shaped by the recent past. In the UK the defeat of the miners represented the final moment of triumph for the neo-liberalist policies advocated by Margaret Thatcher's government in Britain and Ronald Reagan's administration in the United States. The National Union of Mineworkers, traditionally the strongest union in the country, was crushed, undermining union power in general and opening the way for creating an increasingly "flexible" workforce in all areas of business. Loach carefully employs the camera to record a moment of empathy between Mollie and Abby, emphasizing the humanity at the heart of Mollie's story about her past and attempting to create a scene that is something other than didactic. Jacob Leigh discusses the way in which Loach works to create "the sense of authenticity."[27] When Abby in turn shows Mollie some of her family photos, the history is fleshed out further. Abby is pictured with Ricky outside a house with a "sold" sign. This was the house they were about to buy ten years ago when "the Northern Rock crash happened."[28] We learn that it was at this point that "Ricky lost his job in the building trade," and that since then he has only been able to go "from job to job," essentially joining the precariat. Abby herself, she tells Mollie, is on a "zero-hours contract"[29] and just gets paid for the number of visits she manages. Naively remembering days of less precarious employment when some workers were able to claim for the time it took them to get to work, Mollie asks, "What about your travellin' time?" Her final comment to Abby on the hours she works drives home the point of the extent to which some people's terms of employment have deteriorated since the Miners' Strike and since the global financial crash of 2007–8 that brought down Northern Rock:[30] "Seven-thirty in the morning until nine at night! Whatever happened to the eight-hour day?" she says. The political point Loach and Laverty are making is clear, some would say too clear. This final comment ends the scene and in effect leaves the audience with a request for them to consider this idea of the long-term erosion of terms and conditions of employment.

In the preface to *The Precariat: The New Dangerous Class*, Guy Standing—in effect, endorsing exactly what Loach and Laverty show the viewer in *Sorry We Missed You*—says, "Those in the precariat have lives dominated by insecurity, uncertainty, debt and humiliation."[31] He claims this is "the first class in history expected to labour and work at a lower level than the schooling it typically acquires."[32] Standing explains the "neo-liberal model": under this political approach to the economy, he says, the emphasis is on the belief that national economic growth will occur with increased "market competitiveness."[33] The principle being followed, he says, is that "everything should be done to maximise competition and competitiveness, and to allow market principles to permeate all aspects of life."[34] A key theme is that "countries should increase labour market flexibility, which came to mean an agenda for transferring risks and insecurity onto workers and their families."[35] As globalization has proceeded, he adds, governments and corporations have "chased each other in making their labour relations more flexible" and the number of people in "insecure forms of labour" has multiplied.[36] Adrianna Kezar, Tom DePaola, and Daniel T. Scott explain it is not only low-skilled work that has been affected by neo-liberalism. This approach to economics has impacted all sectors of the economy, they say, including higher education.[37] They point out that by 2018, "academic capitalism and neoliberal policies had become the dominant regime" in universities.[38] They call attention to the fact that "the majority of all non-management university workers, both academic and non-academic, are employed on a part-time, temporary, or contingent basis, sometimes called 'at will,' 'on-demand,' or 'just-in-time' hiring."[39] The tension between the political perspectives at stake is made clear by Callum Cant who, in talking about a specific employer that has been one of those companies helping to redefine the nature of employment, says: "To hear CEO Will Shu talk about Deliveroo, you would think it was a company defined by innovation, entrepreneurship, and flexibility. But from the point of view of workers, it's more about low pay, precarious conditions, and conflict."[40] In a phrase that corresponds to Maloney's concept in *Sorry We Missed You* that a worker signing up to his company becomes "an owner-driver franchisee," Cant describes those working for Deliveroo as being defined by "independent contractor status."[41] He emphasizes the fact that without employment status, "workers lose out on a range of legally enforceable rights,"[42] and adds:

> We had no rights to statutory sick pay, holiday pay, or pensions, no right to maternity or paternity pay, no right to vote to force Deliveroo to accept trade union representation, no right to be protected from unfair dismissal, and so on. Almost the entire handbook of employment law goes out of the window when employment does.[43]

## III

*Sorry We Missed You* may be a fiction but in its attention to detail it documents the day-to-day reality of work. Loach often positions the camera at a distance from the action, capturing the space and location as much as the human interactions taking place before the camera.[44] This is particularly so in the depot, where frequently workers crisscross within the space between the camera and the main character(s).[45] Similarly, when we see Ricky out on the road driving, it is the space around him and the nature of the location that is as important to Loach as his central character. Often these moments do little or nothing to move the story forward but they are crucial in documenting the experience of work. Ricky's work involves driving, driving, and more driving, while all the time coping with heavy traffic which, like fellow workers in the depot, repeatedly crisscrosses through the space between the camera and Ricky in his van. All of this is as important to the film as the moments where Ricky is shown dropping parcels off to customers, because conveying a sense of the relentless nature of the work is as important to Loach and his team as the development of the plot. Ricky's workplace is only briefly the depot: for most of the day it is the main roads, side roads, streets, and culs-de-sac of Newcastle and its environs.

At the same time, we are also shown all the various facets of Abby's workaday world. We see her on the bus, at bus stops, and walking along very ordinary streets, as well as at various clients' homes. What we notice with Abby, in particular, but also with Ricky, is that in addition to carrying out their work they are via their mobile phones attempting to organize and

*Urban Poverty* 211

**Figure 13.1** In *Sorry We Missed You* (Ken Loach, 2019), from a quite distant observational camera we frequently see Ricky (Kris Hitchen) driving his white delivery van through heavy traffic.

retain control over their family life. Abby, for example, leaves a message for her daughter:

> Your pasta's in the fridge. Heat it up in the microwave, ok. Leave your project out and I'll look at it when I come in. Fifteen minutes on your computer, that's it. I want all your homework done tonight and get into bed for quarter to nine, right. I'm not sure when I'll be in. I'll be as quick as I can. Your dad's gonna be in late though. I'll see you later on, ok. Love you loads.

How ordinary, how dull, are lines such as these? And yet, as with the recurring shots of Ricky in traffic, such dialogue is absolutely crucial to the authenticity Loach and his team are aiming to achieve. Not only that, but in point of fact, of course, a little speech like this tells the viewer so much not only about Abby and her relationship with her daughter but also about the life of this family (and, to use our earlier phrase, the lives of "the majority of the working class")—the pressures they are under and the efforts they make to hold it all together. The representation of the working class found in *Sorry We Missed You* shows a whole class as hard-working, caring, and determinedly juggling family and work commitments, while suffering work conditions that make it almost impossible to survive.[46] The film shows a family disintegrating as a direct result of the pressure created by work. Loach and Laverty may indicate this all stems from the global dominance of neo-liberalism, but the family themselves have no comprehension of any of this. Ricky is frequently dazed and mystified by events. "I just don't know what to do, Abby," he says, as he sits at the bottom of their bed looking bewildered. Moments of closeness, such as when Liza Jane accompanies Ricky on a delivery shift, or when they all share a takeaway, or when they travel as a family in the van to see one of Abby's clients, only serve to emphasize more clearly what Loach sees as the brutality of the system under which these people are forced to live their lives. And it is no better for others: Abby finds one of her clients, Rosie (Sheila Dunkerley), hiding in a wardrobe scared that a strange man[47] has been in her house, and another, Ben (Christopher John Slater), refusing to get out of bed because he says he is sick of sitting in his chair all day doing nothing.

Perhaps the theme most often repeated in *Sorry We Missed You* is the idea of choice, of being able to exert control over your own life. As was mentioned above, Maloney tells Ricky that in becoming a driver for this company he will become "master of his own destiny." When Rosie, who we have just mentioned, knocks a plate of food Abby has made her onto the floor she is trying to find a way of exerting some sort of control over events. Similarly, Ben in refusing to get out of bed is doing the same thing. When Ricky tries to discuss his son's future with him, he urges Seb to keep going to school and working hard because this is what will give him "choices" in life. Abby chips in, adding: "We've talked about this: you could go to university." But Seb's response is that following that route will just mean he ends up "fifty-seven grand in debt" like a friend he knows and still working in a job with poor prospects. In reply, Ricky asserts there are "some good jobs out there" if Seb would just "knuckle down" and give himself "some options." The whole conversation, that becomes an argument, revolves around the idea of choice and the concept of individuals having the freedom to choose between various options. Lambert and Herod discuss precarious work in just these terms. They write:

> zero-hour contracts and other efforts to remove worker protections so as to encourage flexibility... are often justified with arguments that draw upon Adam Smith to contend that both employer and employee are free to come to the marketplace to negotiate a price for which they will buy and sell labour—both parties, it is asserted, have the freedom to walk away from a bad deal.[48]

Seb's rejection of school amounts to the fact that it feels pointless since even if he works hard it will not open a range of attractive future possibilities for him, i.e. that he will not have the freedom to select from various options. When Seb is later interviewed by a police officer after being caught shoplifting, the officer tries the same approach of urging Seb to "get through school" and "get a job" because then he can have the things he wants. The problem is all Seb can see waiting for him if he follows that route is ending up like his father as a "skivvy." The film implies the traditional "social contract" that says if you work hard at your education you will end up with a "good" job and enjoy the rewards has broken down.[49] Depressingly, what the film shows us is that however hard people might work and however much good nature they may bring to the task, they are always in the clutches of the capitalist system: as individuals, ordinary people are powerless to control the political and economic forces dominating their lives. In *The Creativity Hoax: Precarious Work and the Gig Economy*, Morgan and Nelligan suggest: "Contemporary neo-liberalism offers a paradox: it presents us with an apparent abundance of choice and implores us to take charge of our fate ... Yet at the same time we face a future riddled with risk and precarity."[50] This is surely Ricky's experience. A little later in the same book, Morgan and Nelligan write: "In return for being emancipated from Fordist job-for-life monotony, workers must embrace vocational uncertainty and the state of radical bewilderment generated by fast-burn capitalism."[51] Again, a state of "radical bewilderment" would seem to be entirely apt for what is captured in Hitchen's performance as Ricky.

The nature of the gig economy and precarious employment does not simply underpin *Sorry We Missed You* but is at its heart. Throughout his career, Loach has been consistent in saying he and whatever team he is working with

**Figure 13.2** A static shot from behind his boss, Maloney (Ross Brewster), means we are forced to watch Ricky as he almost begs for time off in *Sorry We Missed You*.

want "to move our audience to new conclusions and insights about society and their lives."[52] We mentioned above a scene that ends with a question from Mollie, "Whatever happened to the eight-hour day?" that is actually a question to the audience. This is a very deliberate attempt to encourage the viewer to enter the ideational space of the film and epitomizes what Loach's process is about. The spectator is repeatedly asked to reflect on what they are witnessing. There are, for example, static shots that refuse to allow us to cut away when we would like to: when Ricky is in Maloney's office asking for a week off, the camera is behind Maloney so all we can see is his back and we are forced to watch Ricky as he moves further and further towards begging. There are also shots at the end of scenes that are momentarily held in order to demand the audience should at this point ponder what they have just witnessed. When after a family confrontation, first Ricky leaves the room and then Seb, we are presented with a shot of a blank white door and wall before the camera reveals Abby and then holds her in the shot as she sits at the family dining table in a bare room, sobbing. At such points the claims being made on the viewer would seem clear.

**Notes**

1. Wendy Everett, "Ken Loach and the Geographies of Class," in Nicole Cloarec, David Haigron, and Delphine Letort (eds.), *Social Class on British and American Screens: Essays on Cinema and Television* (Jefferson, NC: McFarland, 2016), p. 167.
2. Lorenzo Marsili, "Ken Loach: If We Don't Understand Class Struggle, We Don't Understand Anything," *Political Critique*, 30 October 2018. Available at http://politicalcritique.org/world/uk/2018/ken-loach-class-struggle/ (accessed 20 December 2020).
3. Ibid.
4. There has been much debate about the truth or otherwise of this claim. Danny Dorling, for instance, points out, "The proportion of Leave voters in the lowest two social classes (D and E) was just 24%," and, "The Leave voters among the middle class were crucial to the final result because the middle class constituted two thirds of all those who voted." See Danny Dorling, "Brexit: the decision of a divided country," *The BMJ*, 2016, p. 354. DOI: https://doi.org/10.1136/bmj.i3697. See also Wendy Bottero, *Sense of Inequality* (London and New York: Rowman & Littlefield, 2020), for a succinct summary of the main arguments around this. She explains, "While the outcome of the UK's EU referendum has been blamed on the working class in the deindustrialised north of England, most people who voted Leave lived in the more advantaged south, with 59% of Leavers coming from the middle classes" (p. 8).
5. Anon., "How Britain voted in the 2016 EU referendum," Ipsos MORI, 5 September 2016. Available at https://www.ipsos.com/ipsos-mori/en-uk/how-britain-voted-2016-eu-referendum (accessed 20 December 2020).

6. John Harris, "Britain is in the midst of a working-class revolt," *The Guardian*, 17 June 2016. Available at theguardian.com/comentisfree/2016/jun/17/Britain-working-class-revolt-eu-referendum (accessed 20 December 2020).
7. Owen Jones, *Chavs: The Demonization of the Working Class* (London and New York: Verso, 2020/2011), p. 4.
8. Ibid., p. 2.
9. Ibid., p. 7.
10. Marsili, "Ken Loach: If We Don't Understand Class Struggle, We Don't Understand Anything."
11. Peter Bradshaw, "*Sorry We Missed You* review—Ken Loach's superb swipe at zero-hours Britain," *The Guardian*, 16 May 2019. Available at theguardian.com/film/2019/may/16/sorry-we-missed-you-review-ken-loach (accessed 20 December 2020).
12. Marsili, "Ken Loach: If We Don't Understand Class Struggle, We Don't Understand Anything."
13. Rob Lambert and Andrew Herod, *Neoliberal Capitalism and Precarious Work: Ethnographies of Accommodation and Resistance* (Cheltenham and Northampton, MA: Edward Elgar, 2016), p. 3.
14. We might note this character's name rhymes with "baloney"!
15. George Morgan and Pariece Nelligan, *The Creativity Hoax: Precarious Work and the Gig Economy* (London and New York: Anthem Press, 2018), p. 6.
16. Ibid.
17. Ibid.
18. Jeremias Prassl, *Humans as a Service: The Promise and Perils of Work in the Gig Economy* (Oxford: Oxford University Press, 2018), pp. 3–4.
19. Ibid., p. 4.
20. Ibid.
21. Ibid., p. 6.
22. Izabela Florczak and Marta Otto, "Precarious work and labour regulation in the EU: current reality and perspectives," in Jeff Kenner, Izabela Florczak, and Marta Otto (eds.), *Precarious Work: The Challenge for Labour Law in Europe* (Cheltenham and Northampton, MA: Edward Elgar, 2019), p. 2.
23. Migrant workers, dealt with in Chapter 11, would clearly form a sizeable proportion of this group.
24. Florczak and Otto, "Precarious work and labour regulation in the EU: current reality and perspectives," p. 2.
25. Loach and Laverty would approve of the way in which Florczak and Otto point out "virtually all forms of employment can be seen as precarious, yet they differ in the type/form and degree of precarity." See Florczak and Otto, "Precarious work and labour regulation in the EU: current reality and perspectives," p. 6.
26. Steven Mears, "*Sorry We Missed You*," *Film Comment*, 56 (2), March/April 2020, p. 70.
27. Jacob Leigh, *The Cinema of Ken Loach: Art in the Service of the People* (London: Wallflower Press, 2002), p. 10.

28. Northern Rock was a British bank taken into public ownership in 2008 during the global financial crisis of that year. Eric Helleiner sums up the situation around this worldwide economic meltdown: "Global industrial production, world trade, and the value of world equity markets all fell more rapidly in the first ten months after April 2008 than they had during the same period after the start of the Great Depression." See Helleiner, *The Status Quo Crisis: Global Financial Governance after the 2008 Meltdown* (Oxford and New York: Oxford University Press, 2014), p. 1.
29. The Office for National Statistics recorded: "Numbers on zero hour contracts have gone from 143,000 (or 0.5 per cent of the workforce) in 2008 to 1,068,000 in 2020 (or 3.3 per cent of the workforce)." See Anon., "EMP17: People in employment on zero hours contracts," Office for National Statistics, 11 August 2020. Available at https://www.ons.gov.uk/employmentandlabourmarket/peopleinwork/employmentandemployeetypes/datasets/emp17peopleinemploymentonzerohourscontracts (accessed 20 December 2020).
30. In their preface to *Precarious Work: The Challenge for Labour Law in Europe*, Jeff Kenner, Izabela Florczak, and Marta Otto discuss "the worldwide shift to more insecure jobs since the global financial crisis" and the increasingly commonplace practice "of using more 'flexible' forms of employment without the whole spectrum of rights associated with the standard employment relationship of regular, full-time work." See Jeff Kenner, Izabela Florczak, and Marta Otto (eds.), *Precarious Work: The Challenge for Labour Law in Europe* (Cheltenham and Northampton, MA: Edward Elgar, 2019), p. xi.
31. Guy Standing, *The Precariat: The New Dangerous Class* (London and New York: Bloomsbury Academic, 2016/2011), p. x.
32. Ibid.
33. Ibid., p. 1.
34. Ibid.
35. Ibid.
36. Ibid., p. 7.
37. Adrianna Kezar, Tom DePaola, and Daniel T. Scott, *The Gig Academy: Mapping Labor in the Neoliberal University* (Baltimore, MD: Johns Hopkins University Press, 2019), p. 2.
38. Ibid.
39. Ibid., p. 16. Like Florczak and Otto, who point out work is always to some extent precarious (see note 24), these writers make it clear what the fuller picture reveals: "Industries have a long history of trying to contain production costs by replacing full-time, permanent workers with short-term, contingent ones." See Kezar, DePaola, and Scott, *The Gig Academy: Mapping Labor in the Neoliberal University*, p. 16. Lambert and Herod highlight the same thing. They say "there are myriad examples of precarity operating within the period of the so-called Fordist mode of economic regulation." See Lambert and Herod, *Neoliberal Capitalism and Precarious Work: Ethnographies of Accommodation and Resistance*, p. 18.
40. Callum Cant, *Riding for Deliveroo: Resistance in the New Economy* (Cambridge: Polity Press, 2020), p. 2.

41. Ibid., p. 71.
42. Ibid.
43. Ibid.
44. Everett describes Loach's use of "a distant, observational camera." See Everett, "Ken Loach and the Geographies of Class," p. 169.
45. Leigh discusses the way Loach "takes a camera to places rarely seen in mainstream cinema fiction." See Leigh, *The Cinema of Ken Loach: Art in the Service of the People*, p. 12.
46. Forty years ago, Loach was clear the effort he was making was to present on the screen "people as they really are." See Leonard Quart, "A Fidelity to the Real: An Interview with Ken Loach and Tony Garnett," *Cinéaste*, 10 (4), Fall 1980, p. 29.
47. Another carer, but one she doesn't know.
48. Lambert and Herod, *Neoliberal Capitalism and Precarious Work: Ethnographies of Accommodation and Resistance*, p. 23.
49. As with work not being precarious only now but always having been precarious, so too it might be the case that this informal "social contract" is not only a myth now but has always been a myth.
50. Morgan and Nelligan, *The Creativity Hoax: Precarious Work and the Gig Economy*, p. 11.
51. Ibid., p. 22.
52. Quart, "A Fidelity to the Real: An Interview with Ken Loach and Tony Garnett," p. 28.

CHAPTER 14

# Conclusion: Liberal Consensus Politics, Economics, and Class

## I

Way back in history, before Covid-19, even before the Brexit vote, a former British Prime Minister, David Cameron, claimed at the Conservative Party Conference of 2009: "We are all in this together."[1] The patent untruth of this utterance would seem to be clear. According to any measure we might propose, the UK is currently a severely divided nation, and has been in the process of becoming an increasingly divided nation over recent decades. A recently published history of Britain states, "progress in socio-economic equality went into reverse as neo-liberalism became hegemonic from the 1980s."[2] The author, Pat Thane, contends this has led to "inequalities comparable with those in 1900."[3] Were we to appraise the situation in social, economic, political, or cultural terms, we would be forced to conclude the gulfs between various sectors of society have been widening rather than narrowing since the final years of the twentieth century. In this book we have examined ways in which this reality of a deeply fissured society might have found expression within British cinema. The UK is presently a nation of strongly entrenched social, economic, political, and cultural elites, and the overall contention here has been that certainly in the films we have explored we find narratives driven by crucial aspects of a currently profoundly divided nation. In a sense, the notion of Britain as a divided nation is nothing new. Thane tells us, in terms of inequality, we can see "strong similarities and continuities between the early twentieth and early twenty-first centuries" in the UK, and throughout the 1900s and into the 2000s there have been "profound, lasting divisions and inequalities."[4] It is also the case that films have frequently been seen to be reflecting the politics of the period in which they were made. In the preface to *Fires Were Started: British Cinema and Thatcherism*, for example, Lester Friedman says cinema of the 1980s produced

... a diverse series of pictures proving an intimate, often quite uncomfortable, look into the modern British consciousness moulded by Thatcher and her policies.[5]

Ultimately, both the thought of a nation as divided and the idea of films as being anchored in the expression of divisions among characters are truisms. All nations are necessarily divided in a variety of ways, including through differences in income, education, gender, sexuality, ethnicity, and religion. The concept of the nation is of an extensive united community, but naturally in reality a nation is always divided. The question is the extent to which any nation may be deemed united and the extent to which it must necessarily be seen as divided at any particular moment in history. At the same time, all narratives, whether in films or within other cultural products, depend on the existence of conflict, tension, and division. Division between individuals or groups leads to conflict but also creates sufficient energy for the dynamism of change to take place. This is true both of film narratives and societies. It would be possible to write about division as expressed within any group of films from any society in any period. However, it would not always be so easy to write about a society as a divided nation; although unity or division within a society will be ever-present, the degree of unity or the depth of division will vary. What the concept of division might offer is a useful approach for thinking about films and society. The representations of a nation to be found in its films will always give a sense of the levels of agreement or dislocation to be found in that society.

The fact is that from 1945 into the 1970s, the gap between rich and poor in the UK was narrowing, before this trend was dramatically reversed from the 1980s. Highlighting the present gulf between rich and poor, Thane says, in 2017 at least 500,000 people a week needed free food from voluntary food banks, and adds that this situation would have been "unimaginable a few decades earlier."[6] In 2009–10, Thane claims, "about 16.5 per cent of the UK population (10 million people)" were officially classified as poor and this included almost 20 percent of children.[7] A recent think-tank investigation suggested the richest 10 percent of the UK population currently owns more than 50 percent of the country's net personal wealth, while the richest 1 percent owns 20 percent of the nation's wealth.[8] This report concluded that "in the past 40 years trends in falling inequality have faltered or even reversed" right across "high-income Western economies."[9] So the UK is not unique: this is a phenomenon being experienced across the western world. In the preface to her book about what she sees as the latest phase of capitalism, a period she describes as "surveillance capitalism," Shoshana Zuboff suggests that around the globe we now find "concentrations of wealth, knowledge, and power unprecedented in human history."[10]

It might be logical to expect huge left-behind sections of the population in the UK suffering in the wake of the 2007–8 financial crisis to react against Cameron's claim that "We're all in this together," and support a re-energized package of welfare reforms designed to help all those suffering under difficult economic circumstances; but that is not what has happened. Instead, in a more complicated process, not only was Cameron rejected by the public and effectively a different version of Conservatism chosen (when Britain voted to leave the European Union in 2016), but a little later the socialist alternative offered by the leader of the Labour Party, Jeremy Corbyn, was also rejected by the electorate. The referendum in 2016 ended the UK's membership of the European Union and, although it did not happen immediately, essentially set up the possibility of Boris Johnson (who in defiance of Cameron had campaigned to leave the union) becoming leader of the Conservative Party. In the previous year a vote for a new leader within the Labour Party moved that organization to the left when it was won by Jeremy Corbyn. Then, in the election of December 2019 (after having fared better than expected in the general election of 2017, increasing the Labour vote to 40 percent), Corbyn's socialist platform was decisively rejected by voters and the Conservatives under Johnson gained a massive eighty-seat majority in the House of Commons.

This series of events from 2015 to 2019 were the latest moves in a succession of shifts in the make-up of British politics since the election of Margaret Thatcher in 1979. Her election had signaled the end of guaranteed government support for the welfare state, which in electoral terms had been an obligatory policy position for every administration since 1945. Thatcherism introduced neo-liberalism to British politics; the belief that the best way to create prosperity for all was to ensure global market forces were unconstrained. Each subsequent alteration in the British political landscape would be consistent in at least one feature: neo-liberalism was to remain unchallenged. Famously, Thatcher asserted there was no such thing as "society" (although in the nationalistic sense she strongly supported the notion of there being a British people with very distinctive qualities).[11] What she was questioning was that concept of "society"—the idea of a community of individuals within which each person feels a sense of responsibility for the well-being of all the others in the group—that had been the guiding principle underpinning welfare provision since 1945. As Thane explains it, Thatcher "challenged sentiments of collective social responsibility, inherent in the idea of a 'welfare state.'"[12] Consistently, from 1979 through a series of administrations, UK government policy was built around an endorsement of globalization, privatization, and deregulation as the essential features of a vibrant economy. Global trade might be seen as having a lengthy history taking us back (from a Eurocentric/western perspective) at least to the fifteenth and sixteenth centuries, but commentators have suggested there are various distinctively different aspects attaching to the current period of global business activity. Zuboff describes the way in which under contemporary capitalism, rather than simply having our labor exploited by big business, every facet of our existence is now (inescapably) subject to capitalism's project.[13] What she calls "surveillance capitalism," she says, "feeds on every aspect of every human's experience."[14] Slavoj Žižek claims the defining feature of what he calls "postmodern capitalism" is "the direct commodification of our experience itself."[15] As he explains it,

> I buy my bodily fitness by way of visiting fitness clubs; I buy my spiritual enlightenment by way of enrolling in courses of transcendental meditation; I buy the satisfactory self-experience of myself as ecologically aware by purchasing only organic fruit; and so on.[16]

Theodore Martin recognizes the "new historical conditions of global capitalism,"[17] but also views the contemporary period as "crisis-ridden."[18] He describes the present as "an age defined from every angle by inequality, immiseration, dispossession, and disaster."[19] From this perspective, neoliberalism is seen as a capitalist process that has led to increased depths of division within society.

Interestingly though, even as all of this has been happening, from a certain angle it remains possible to suggest that rather than becoming increasingly divided, UK society has in fact become more cohesive in a progressive liberal sense. A recent report, *Divided Britain? Polarisation and fragmentation trends in the UK*, suggests that although a traditional left–right split in political beliefs on economic issues is still visible, the divide in attitudes on issues such as gay marriage or abortion is now much more dependent on whether you are socially liberal or conservative in your outlook rather than what your party political allegiance may be.[20] This report quotes a British Social Attitudes Survey from 2018 that found divides were narrowing "on a range of issues, such as sex before marriage, same-sex relationships, abortion and gender equality."[21] The data shows, for example, that "since the mid-1980s, views on traditional gender roles have seen a marked shift, going from a topic that split the population, to one where only 8 per cent agree that it's 'a man's job to earn money' and 'a woman's job to look after the home and family.'"[22] Attitudes towards homosexuality are also becoming increasingly liberal, to the point that: "Two-thirds now say that sex between two adults of the same sex is 'not wrong at all'—an increase of almost 50 percentage points over the last 35 years."[23] Thane has identified the same phenomenon, pointing out that social and cultural change was not just down to politics and that "profound changes in attitudes to the family and sexuality, for example, developed largely independently of, sometimes in opposition to, the aims of politicians."[24] From this perspective it seems that in the UK "the Left has now fragmented in its cultural values on a socially liberal–socially conservative scale."[25] Presumably, it would also be possible to say the same about the Right.

## II

All of this may help us make sense of the key thematic ideas and socio-economic divisions we have found in the films we have examined in preceding chapters. To take one example, the first film we considered, *Mary Queen of Scots* (Josie Rourke, 2018), is about the division between England and Scotland but also the way in which Scotland is internally riven.[26] Within Scotland brother is set against sister, political leader against loyal follower, and Catholic against Protestant. There are extreme and dangerous religious divisions not only between the two kingdoms but also within each realm. In England there is the ever-present threat of Catholic plots, and in Scotland a zealous, firebrand style of Calvinism is set against the Catholicism of Mary. The patriarchy on display is not only concerned to police the strict hierarchical social division between men and women but also any transgression of stereotypical, socially authorized expressions of gender and/or sexuality. Male violence is performed (almost ritually) against anybody challenging patriarchal social norms; but the film also suggests the existence of a strong natural bond of sisterhood between women standing in defiance of patriarchy. In other words, there is a concentration in this film on social issues, such as patriarchy, homosexuality, and transgender issues, about which there has been a growing liberal consensus in the UK in recent decades. Similarly, positioning religious tolerance in opposition to religious fanaticism would realize a comparable sense of accord; and even the echoes of Brexit in the discord between nations is likely to sit comfortably with an art-house audience. What we do not find are class issues: "ordinary" people are seen going about their business in places, but only as a background tapestry to the playing out of the lives of "great" men and women.

As with *Mary Queen of Scots*, so with *Fanny Lye Deliver'd* (Thomas Clay, 2019), in which the main focus is on the oppression of women under patriarchy. Here again we are shown the strength of women; we see sexual oppression being confronted, and religious fundamentalism is set against the freedom to question what is meant by "God." In contrast to *Mary Queen of Scots*, we might also argue that class hierarchies are challenged in this film and that there is some sense of history being written from below. In *The Favourite* (Yorgos

Lanthimos, 2018), we find a representation of British political machinations among an elite that can be seen as having similarities to today. The main focus may be on powerful women who are able to compete in a male world and to some extent challenge patriarchy, but we are also given some sense of social inequality, with the lives of the servant class being set out against those of the aristocracy and a mercantile class. In the background, it could be argued, issues to do with imperialism and the slave trade are to some extent brought into focus. However, overall, the subjects of class and economics are largely ignored other than in showing the tension between "old money" and "new money" (the landed/propertied class set in opposition to mercantile/city-based wealth). *Peterloo* (Mike Leigh, 2018), on the other hand, immediately takes up a working-class perspective, demonstrating from the outset the extent to which these people are subject to the caprice of the aristocracy, the political class, the industrialists, the courts, and the police. This is a film that very clearly and deliberately offers "history from below."

Within the films covered in Part II, *Downton Abbey* (Michael Engler, 2019) adopts a singular line of approach, suggesting British class society is defined in a positive rather than negative way by its internal divisions. The UK is viewed as a unique social organization that functions with tremendous efficiency and with a vital awareness on the part of the aristocracy of the need to appreciate the contributions of all members of society. Issues such as the working-class struggle for a living wage, the brutality of the experience of poverty, and British imperialism are fantastically sidestepped. And this is a line also pursued by *Darkest Hour* (Joe Wright, 2017) in its celebration of British unity under a heroic wartime leader and its elevation of the concepts of patriotism and nationalism. As with several previous films in this book, this is an endorsement of a model of British history that perceives its role as being that of telling the stories of great men (and women) that have made the country what it is. A certain version of Second World War history focused around a Churchillian bulldog spirit is activated as a touchstone for contemporary British attitudes, and the reality of the historical record (as, for example, in the case of Churchill's racism) is ignored in an attempted manipulation of the contemporary audience. Running alongside this, as with *Downton Abbey*, the viewer is provided with a very particular representation of royalty and concept of the Crown.

As has happened at more than a few points earlier in this book, we are again left to consider the nature of history and historical drama. What is the role of history as a subject? How should we understand the genre of historical drama as functioning within society? Possibly, as with Lanthimos' use of a fish-eye lens to produce distorted images in *The Favourite*, so our perspectives on the past inevitably always include a level of distortion. We see the past through our own determinedly personal but necessarily ideologically polished lens, or through the ideologically biased lens given us by society. There is a tendency for the films considered in previous chapters to focus on the upper echelons of society or the elite middle classes. Only *Peterloo* and *Sorry We Missed You* are absolutely, determinedly focused on the working class. Clearly, both in deciding which events should be represented in film and in determining how those events should be represented, political choices are being made. *Darkest Hour* focuses on Churchill as the heroic, single individual, battling against the odds. The film reinforces ideas of Britain/England as an island under siege faced with a threatening problem emanating from continental Europe. Churchill is presented as a man who is comfortable among the working class and at home in a multicultural Britain; these things, at least, would seem to be a travesty of the historical reality. In a newspaper article, Simon Schama argued statues commemorating historical figures or events do not do history any favours since they set history in stone whereas the subject is actually about continual debate.[27] Statues, he says, frequently "shut off debate through their invitation to reverence."[28] Perhaps films are also capable of creating "statues" out of figures and/or events from the past. One thing we might conclude would be that every age rewrites, and in the process reshapes, the past in its own image; but this would be to oversimplify. An "age" does not exist as a single monolithic expression of a period in time. There may be a dominant version of the past that is seen as being etched in a particular "age," but understandings of any period of history remain multifaceted and highly contested.

In *Where Hands Touch* (Asante, 2019) and *A United Country* (Amma Asante, 2016) in Part II, race is obviously the key issue. Once more, this is one of those social issues around which a liberal consensus has developed (despite the fact that the contemporary reality on the streets and within various sectors of social provision may still be somewhat different): the majority would not find the open expression of racist views acceptable. The more thought-provoking area of interest here may be that of personal identity. Both these films forcibly demonstrate the constrictions placed on the free development of your own personal identity by the socio-economic and political contexts into which you are born. In an age that tends to suggest simple, straightforward personal choices enable you to be whoever you want to be, these films suggest the importance of recognizing the intimidating power of restrictive historical contexts. As with *The Favourite* from Part I, the next film, *Viceroy's House* (Gurinder Chadha, 2017), explores political maneuvers within the corridors of power. In line with what we have seen to this point, women in the film are shown to be strong and independent, i.e. notions of patriarchy are challenged. There is also a sub-plot love story involving people of different, powerfully antagonistic religions. Following the pattern found in other films examined here, *Viceroy's House* therefore closely pursues liberal-consensus attitudes. However, the perspective on history that is given and the evaluation of the efforts of the elite ruling class once again might be seen to support the status quo: the political class, whether British or Indian, does its best to direct and control native populations that are simply incapable of responding in a rational manner.

Moving to Part III, *The Sense of an Ending* (Ritesh Batra, 2017) and *Daphne* (Peter Mackie Burns, 2017) are both films that target an educated, middle-class, elite audience. Individuals struggle with the angst-ridden issues of life without any sense of their own privileged elitism. The central narrative plank of homosexuality in *God's Own Country* (Francis Lee, 2017) is, yet again, one of those areas around which unanimity has developed in recent decades: a previous source of severe division within society is now something the majority of the general public feels much more relaxed about. As with patriarchy that we have seen challenged in a series of these films, this does not mean the subject of homosexuality is not a valid issue to be "put out there" by films, but it does mean it is an issue that is likely neither to court controversy nor challenge the status quo. More interesting is the manner in which this film deals with the related ideas of migrant labor, xenophobia, and nationalism, because these matters have as their unavoidable backdrop the issue of global economics and the relationship of growing nationalism to neo-liberalism. *Dark River* (Clio Barnard, 2017) and *The Levelling* (Hope Dickson Leach, 2017) raise economic issues relating specifically to rural poverty (but also, by extension, to other regions of the UK that may feel themselves to be economically left behind). Yet again, there is a feminist perspective that focuses on strong, independent women, but there are also ways in which these two films ask us to consider wider issues relating to globalization and contemporary capitalism. Like *Peterloo*, *Sorry We Missed You* (Ken Loach, 2019) adopts a (white) working-class perspective and (again, like *Peterloo*) provides a positive portrayal of these "ordinary" people. Class divisions are fundamental to the film's narrative. *Sorry We Missed You* does not simply raise the idea of neo-liberalism but explores in detail the gig economy and precarious work, aspects of the contemporary economy that are directly attributable to neo-liberalism. The audience is presented with the concrete reality of what the destruction of carefully regulated terms and conditions of employment means for "ordinary" working people.

## III

So, there are certain divisions within UK society about which there is a societal consensus. For example, patriarchy is seen as existing, as being unacceptable, and as being something that should be combated. What we have is a liberal consensus; this is also a cross-party consensus, bridging political organizations such as the Conservative Party, the Labour Party, and the Liberal Democrats. There are other divisions in society, however, that are more contentious and about which there is no consensus; for example, inequalities of wealth and the economic way forward. Around these divisions, rather than consensus we have strong political disagreement.

It is easy to include in films ideas about which there is general agreement among the public: it is not so straightforward to make films that present more controversial ideas, notions that polarize attitudes. In the first situation, as a filmmaker you are swimming with the tide not only of public opinion but also of political opinion within your society. In the second instance, you are dividing society in the very act of filmmaking. The films we have examined do not often directly address economic issues: to do so involves displaying partisanship on an issue about which the country is, rather than divided, polarized. *The Favourite* has been heralded for its use of three female leads but not for the way in which it implicates the role of imperialist economics in the politics of the period. *Fanny Lye Deliver'd* is praised for its use of strong female characters but not for the way in which it could be seen to advocate the complete overthrow of social hierarchies. There is currently social consensus on the importance of having the freedom to express your own personal identity, on being able to articulate sexual difference, on the importance of religious tolerance, on the unacceptable nature of racism, as well as on the importance of challenging patriarchy. These things, therefore, at the moment represent safe ground for filmmakers. When filmmakers begin to approach issues such as the existence of hierarchies of wealth and privilege, the accompanying unacceptable presence of elite cliques, and the existence of left-behind groups in society, they may begin to display attitudes that are contrary to the beliefs of at least half of the population. This immediately becomes more controversial filmmaking. The real interest in the films considered here, therefore, comes in exploring the attitudes displayed towards class, nationalism, and imperialism, as well as more specific issues relating to neo-liberalism such as the role of migrant labor, the gig economy, and the precarity of work.

In these ways this book has been interested in exploring film in relation to history and politics, examining film representations in relation to the major axes of socio-economic division within contemporary society. In an era in which socio-economic change is driven by the increasing pace of globalization and accompanying corporate power, and in which societies are riven by the resulting divisions of wealth, heightened levels of migration, and intensified nationalisms, how are these events played out within film? Such an approach is nothing new. In *American Film and Society since 1945*, Leonard

Quart and Albert Auster set out their belief "in film's historical and social significance,"[29] and asserted Hollywood film was worth watching as "an important barometer of America's dreams and desires and of changes in its cultural and social values."[30] In a book on British cinema in the 1980s, John Hill insisted the study of film was important "not simply because of its 'intrinsic' value but also because of its socio-cultural character, its relationship to larger concerns about how we live."[31] He felt these films were already presenting a strong sense of discord within British society. British films in the 1980s, "in contrast to wartime dramas which celebrated a nation pulling together to win the war," he said, set out "not to project a world of unity and community, but rather to suggest a world of increasing social differences, divisions and conflicts."[32]

The fundamental contention of these sorts of investigations is that films are not created in isolation from whatever socio-economic and political events may be happening during the period in which they are made; that they are produced by particular societies at particular moments of history and bear the traces of the specific time and place of their genesis. As cultural products, films cannot conjure up anything wholly new, they can only reconfigure, recombine, reshape, and re-present ideas and possibilities already in circulation within society. Like all other aspects of social life, film registers issues at play within the contemporary arena.[33] If we hope to gain some understanding of an era, surveying a range of films from the period may permit some insights to occur.[34] In viewing the films, we should see them as "determinedly exploring, purposefully commenting upon, or unwittingly reflecting issues relevant to their particular socio-historical moment," although we should also view them as "being continually reframed and reconstituted by their reception at different times."[35] In other words, this book, like similar investigations, unashamedly views the theoretical position much as Robert Fiske described it over thirty years ago:

> Every text and every reading has a social and therefore political dimension, which is to be found partly in the structure of the text itself and partly in the relation of the reading subject to that text.[36]

We may inhabit a post-truth world in which, as James Ball explains it, because we trust in nothing and believe in nothing, "public discourse" becomes simply "a clash of competing narratives," a contest that "can then be won by the side willing to make the boldest plays toward emotion and mass-appeal,"[37] but in this postmodern world of which post-truth is a part, it remains the case that "reflecting critically on our situation is part of our situation."[38] In viewing films, we are able to inhabit other potential identities and, perhaps, to some degree rework our sense of self. At the same time, films do not merely reflect social norms but work to actively assist in the construction of audience identities; and identities are also necessarily ideologies. As spectators we are able to "try on" identities (and ideologies), and to accept them, reject them, or negotiate in relation to what is on offer. And this may be an active process of engagement, or it may be a passive or a semi-conscious process.

The postmodern digital experience of the world has undoubtedly cast a shadow over the full range of critically important contexts for this book—the historical, the political, the cultural, and the social. Most clearly, the continuous present of the ever-online experience has obfuscated the previously uncontested linearity of history. At the same time, the celebration of celebrity and the movement into a realm of post-truth has muddied the waters of political debate, while the atomization of the digital audience and the accompanying celebration of the individual has obscured earlier much clearer notions of what we might mean by "society." On the other hand, it is also the case that in recent decades such theoretical confusions have been accompanied by a very concrete, on-the-streets, real-world revival of right-wing politics and the gentrification of radical politics into liberal reformism. What we have seen within mainstream UK cinema may have been, generally (although not exclusively),[39] a chattering classes' restatement of liberal politics, but there is at least some evidence of a more confrontational left-wing politics that is prepared to square up to neo-liberalism's widening of divisions of class and wealth.

**Notes**

1. David Cameron, "Full text of David Cameron's speech: The Tory leader's conference address in full," *The Guardian*, 8 October 2009. Available at https://www.theguardian.com/politics/2009/oct/08/david-cameron-speech-in-full (accessed 15 January 2021). We might note the deliberate repetition of the word "together" employed in this speech.
2. Pat Thane, *Divided Kingdom: A History of Britain, 1900 to the Present* (Cambridge: Cambridge University Press, 2018), p. 7.
3. Ibid.
4. Ibid., p. 4.
5. Lester Friedman (ed.), *Fires Were Started: British Cinema and Thatcherism* (London and New York: Wallflower Press, 2006/1993), p. xiv.
6. Ibid., p. 472.
7. Ibid.
8. Arun Advani, George Bangham, and Jack Leslie, *The UK's Wealth Distribution and Characteristics of High-Wealth Households*, Resolution Foundation, December 2020,

p. 10. Available at https://www.resolutionfoundation.org/publications/the-uks-wealth-distribution-and-characteristics-of-high-wealth-households/ (accessed 14 January 2021),
9. Ibid., p. 3.
10. Shoshana Zuboff, *The Age of Surveillance Capitalism: The Fight for a Human Future at the New Frontier of Power* (London: Profile Books, 2019), p. vii. In historical terms, this would seem a gross overstatement but it does reveal a real belief that the current global experience is one in which improvements in equality of opportunity and real-life experience have been reversed.
11. Margaret Thatcher, "Interview for *Woman's Own* ('no such thing as society')," Margaret Thatcher Foundation, 23 September 1987. Available at https://www.margaretthatcher.org/document/106689 (accessed 20 January 2021). "I think we have gone through a period when too many children and people have been given to understand 'I have a problem, it is the Government's job to cope with it!' or 'I have a problem, I will go and get a grant to cope with it!' 'I am homeless, the Government must house me!' and so they are casting their problems on society and who is society? There is no such thing!"
12. Thane, *Divided Kingdom: A History of Britain, 1900 to the Present*, p. 474. On the same page, Thane also implicates the British media in this, claiming the public was "encouraged to reject social responsibility by the government and by an increasingly right-wing, strident popular press—another significant change of the late twentieth century."
13. Zuboff, *The Age of Surveillance Capitalism: The Fight for a Human Future at the New Frontier of Power*, p. 9.
14. Ibid.
15. Slavoj Žižek, *Against the Double Blackmail: Refugees, Terror and Other Troubles with the Neighbours* (London and New York: Penguin, 2017), pp. 15–16.
16. Ibid.
17. Theodore Martin, *Contemporary Drift: Genre, Historicism, and the Problem of the Present* (New York: Columbia University Press, 2017), p. 2.
18. Ibid., p. 197.
19. Ibid.
20. Bobby Duffy, Kirstie Hewlett, Julian McCrae, and John Hall, *Divided Britain? Polarisation and Fragmentation Trends in the UK* (London: The Policy Institute at King's College, 2019), p. 28.
21. Ibid., p. 66.
22. Ibid.
23. Ibid.
24. Thane, *Divided Kingdom: A History of Britain, 1900 to the Present*, p. 474.
25. Ibid., p. 53.
26. In the background there is also a strong sense of the split between England and various continental powers.
27. Simon Schama, "History is better served by putting the Men in Stone in museums," *Financial Times*, 12 June 2020.

28. Ibid.
29. Leonard Quart and Albert Auster, *American Film and Society since 1945* (London: Macmillan, 1984), p. 6.
30. Ibid., p. 140.
31. John Hill, *British Cinema in the 1980s* (Oxford: Clarendon Press, 1999), p. xiv.
32. Ibid., p. 137.
33. Bearing in mind we should be alert not only to what films are directly "about" but also what is not there, the gaps and omissions, elements excluded or marginalized.
34. We could just as easily consider a range of art exhibitions curated during the period (or some other array of media or cultural outputs).
35. Sarah Barrow, Sabine Haenni, and John White (eds.), *The Routledge Encyclopedia of Films* (London and New York: Routledge, 2015), p. xx.
36. Robert Fiske, "British Cultural Studies and Television Criticism," in Robert Allen (ed.), *Channels of Discourse: Television and Contemporary Criticism* (London: Methuen, 1987), p. 273.
37. James Ball, *Post-Truth: How Bullshit Conquered the World* (London: Biteback, 2017), p. 278.
38. Terry Eagleton, *After Theory* (London and New York: Penguin Books, 2004), p. 60.
39. In fact, as John Hill suggested in the preface to *British Cinema in the 1980s*, "there is a degree of ideological tension in the way in which these films both question and reinforce conventional social and cultural divisions" (p. xii).

# Bibliography

Acheson, R. J., *Radical Puritans in England, 1550–1660* (London and New York: Routledge, 1994).
Achilleos-Sarll, Columba and Benjamin Martill, "Toxic Masculinity: Militarism, Deal-Making and the Performance of Brexit," in Moira Dustin, Nuno Ferreira, and Susan Millns (eds.), *Gender and Queer Perspectives on Brexit* (London: Palgrave Macmillan, 2019).
Adam, Rudolf G., *Brexit: Causes and Consequences* (Berlin: Springer, 2020).
Addison, Paul, "Churchill and Social Reform," in Robert Blake and William Roger Louis (eds.), *Churchill* (Oxford: Oxford University Press, 2002), pp. 77–8.
Advani, Arun, George Bangham, and Jack Leslie, *The UK's Wealth Distribution and Characteristics of High-Wealth Households*, Resolution Foundation, December 2020. Available at https://www.resolutionfoundation.org/publications/the-uks-wealth-distribution-and-characteristics-of-high-wealth-households/ (accessed 14 January 2021).
Aitken, Robbie and Eve Rosenhaft, *Black Germany: The Making and Unmaking of a Diaspora Community, 1884–1960* (Cambridge: Cambridge University Press, 2013).
Alcoff, Linda Martin, Michael Hames-Garcia, Satya P. Mohanty, and Paula M. L. Moya (eds.), *Identity Politics Reconsidered* (New York and London: Palgrave Macmillan, 2006).
Anderson, Benedict, *Imagined Communities: Reflections on the Origin and Spread of Nationalism* (London and New York: Verso, 1991/1983).
Anderson, Benedict, "Introduction," in Gopal Balakrishnan (ed.), *Mapping the Nation* (London and New York: Verso, 2012/1996).
Andrew, Dudley, "Cinema and Culture," *Humanities*, 6 (4), August 1985, pp. 24–5.
Anon., "Beautiful but with serious deprivation: Scale of West Somerset rural poverty laid bare," *Somerset County Gazette*, 22 October 2015. Available at https://www.somersetcountygazette.co.uk/news/13886398.beautiful-but-with-serious-deprivation-scale-of-west-somerset-rural-poverty-laid-bare/ (accessed 21 November 2020).
Anon., "Challenges Facing Farmers: A report into upland farming and farming families in Teesdale," Upper Teesdale Agricultural Support Services and Rose Regeneration (London: Oxfam, n.d.).
Anon., "Combating violence against women: United Kingdom," European Institute for Gender Equality, 2016. Available at eige.europa.eu/publications/combating-violence-against-women-united-kingdom (accessed 20 April 2020).
Anon., "*Daphne*," *Box Office Mojo*. Available at https://www.boxofficemojo.com/release/rl1038648321/weekend/ (accessed 30 October 2020).
Anon., "Dealing with TB in your herd. What happens if TB is identified in your herd?" Animal Health and Veterinary Laboratories Agency, 2014. Available at https://assets.publishing.

service.gov.uk/government/uploads/system/uploads/attachment_data/file/347050/TBYHS-03.pdf (accessed 21 November 2020).

Anon., "*Dunkirk* (2017)," *The Numbers*. Available at https://www.the-numbers.com/movie/Dunkirk(2017)#tab=international (accessed 3 November 2020).

Anon., *Elitist Britain 2019: The educational backgrounds of Britain's leading people*, The Sutton Trust/Social Mobility Commission (London: Sutton Trust, 2019).

Anon., "EMP17: People in employment on zero hours contracts," Office for National Statistics, 11 August 2020. Available at https://www.ons.gov.uk/employmentandlabourmarket/peopleinwork/employmentandemployeetypes/datasets/emp17peopleinemploymentonzerohourscontracts (accessed 20 December 2020).

Anon., "EU Referendum Results," BBC News. Available at https://www.bbc.co.uk/news/politics/eu_referendum/results (accessed 21 November 2020).

Anon., "EU Roma strategic framework for equality, inclusion and participation for 2020–2030," European Commission, 7 October 2020. Available at https://ec.europa.eu/info/sites/info/files/union_of_equality_eu_roma_strategic_framework_for_equality_inclusion_and_participation_en.pdf (accessed 2 December 2020).

Anon., "Government sets out key measures to tackle violence against women and girls," GOV.UK, 6 March 2019. Available at https://www.gov.uk/government/news/government-sets-out-key-measures-to-tackle-violence-against-women-and-girls> (accessed 28 April 2020).

Anon., "How Britain voted in the 2016 EU referendum," Ipsos MORI, 5 September 2016. Available at https://www.ipsos.com/ipsos-mori/en-uk/how-britain-voted-2016-eu-referendum (accessed 20 December 2020).

Anon., "How to start a cinema—Understanding audiences—Different films, different people," Independent Cinema Office. Available at https://www.independentcinemaoffice.org.uk/advice-support/how-to-start-a-cinema/understanding-audiences/ (accessed 2 November 2020).

Anon., "Josie Rourke Diversity Casting *Mary Queen of Scots*," *Focus Features*, 12 November 2018. Available at https://www.focusfeatures.com/article/josie-rourke-diversity_casting_mary-queen-of-scots (accessed 20 April 2020).

Anon., "More than one agricultural worker in UK commits suicide a week, figures show," *Farming UK*, 14 February 2018. Available at https://www.farminguk.com/news/more-than-one-agricultural-worker-in-uk-commits-suicide-a-week-figures-show_48613.html (accessed 21 November 2020).

Anon., "Opening Our Eyes: How film contributes to the culture of the UK," BFI/Northern Alliance/Ipsos MediaCT, July 2011. Available at https://www.bfi.org.uk/sites/bfi.org.uk/files/downloads/bfi-opening-our-eyes-2011-07_0.pdf (accessed 5 April 2020).

Anon., "Partition, in pictures," *Hindustan Times*, n.d. Available at https://www.hindustantimes.com/static/partition/gallery/ (accessed 22 July 2020).

Anon., *State of the Nation 2017: Social Mobility in Great Britain*, Social Mobility Commission, November 2017.

Anon., "Talent Abroad: A Review of Romanian Emigrants," OECD (OECD Publishing: Paris, 2019), p. 82. Available at https://doi.org/10.1787/bac53150-en (accessed 2 December 2020).

Anon., *The Remonstrance of the Suffering People of God, called Quakers: Clearing their Innocency from the many False Aspersions, Slanders and Suggestions, which are lately come Abroad in the Nation* (London, 1665).

Anon., "*The Sense of an Ending* (2017)," *The Numbers*. Available at https://www.the-numbers.com/movie/Sense-of-an-Ending-The#tab=box-office (accessed 30 October 2020).

Anon., "The social situation concerning homophobia and discrimination on grounds of sexual orientation in Romania," Danish Institute for Human Rights, March 2009. Available at https://fra.europa.eu/sites/default/files/fra_uploads/389-fra-hdgso-part2-nr_ro.pdf (accessed 2 December 2020).

Anon., "The struggle for democracy: Getting the vote," National Archives, n.d. Available at http://www.nationalarchives.gov.uk/pathways/citizenship/struggle_democracy/getting_vote.htm (accessed 6 March 2020).

Anon., "Violence against women and girls and male position," GOV.UK, Home Office, 2019. Available at homeofficemedia.blog.gov.uk/2019'03/07/violence-against-women-and-girls-and-male-position-factsheets (accessed 16 September 2020).

Armstrong, Stephen, *The New Poverty* (London and New York: Verso, 2017).

Ashby, Justine and Andrew Higson (eds.), *British Cinema, Past and Present* (London and New York: Routledge, 2000).

Baker, Philip, "Rhetoric, Reality, and Varieties of Radicalism," in John Adamson (ed.), *The English Civil War: Conflicts and Contexts, 1640–49* (London and New York: Palgrave Macmillan, 2009), pp. 202–24.

Ball, James, *Post-Truth: How Bullshit Conquered the World* (London: Biteback, 2017).

Bamford, Samuel, *Passages in the Life of a Radical and Early Days: Volume II* (London: T. Fisher Unwin, 1905).

Bandyopadhyay, Sekhar, *From Plassey to Partition: A History of Modern India* (New Delhi: Orient Longman, 2004).

Barnes, Julian, *The Sense of an Ending* (London: Jonathan Cape, 2011).

Barrenechea, Jon, "British Arthouse Cinemas," in Emma Bell and Neil Mitchell (eds.), *Directory of World Cinema: Britain* (Bristol and Chicago: Intellect, 2012), pp. 184–7.

Barron, Hester, *The 1926 Miners' Lockout: Meanings of Community in the Durham Coalfield* (Oxford: Oxford University Press, 2010).

Barrow, Sarah, Sabine Haenni, and John White (eds.), *The Routledge Encyclopedia of Films* (London and New York: Routledge, 2015).

Bassnett, Susan, *Ted Hughes* (Liverpool: Liverpool University Press, 2009).

Bates, Crispin, "The Hidden Story of Partition and its Legacies," BBC, 3 March 2011. Available at http://www.bbc.co.uk/history/british/modern/partition1947_01.shtml (accessed 18 July 2020).

Beauman, Fran, *The Pineapple: King of Fruits* (London: Vintage, 2006).

Belton, John (ed.), *Movies and Mass Culture* (London: Athlone Press, 1996).

Bhopal, Kalwant, *White Privilege: The Myth of a Post-Racial Society* (Bristol: Policy Press, 2018).

Bhutto, Fatima, "Fatima Bhutto on Indian partition film *Viceroy's House*: 'I watched this servile pantomime and wept,'" *The Guardian*, 3 March 2017. Available at https://www.theguardian.com/film/2017/mar/03/fatima-bhutto-viceroys-house-watched-servile-pantomime-and-wept (accessed 15 July 2020).

Blackwell, Anna, *Shakespearean Celebrity in the Digital Age: Fan Cultures and Remediation* (London: Palgrave Macmillan, 2018).

Bolton, Paul, "Education: Historical Statistics," House of Commons, 27 November 2012, p. 19. Available at researchbriefings.files.parliament.uk>documents/SN04252/SN04252.pdf (accessed 30 October 2020).

Bonomi, Patricia U., *The Lord Cornbury Scandal: The Politics of Reputation in British America* (Chapel Hill, NC: University of North Carolina Press, 1998).

Bordwell, David, "The Art Cinema as a Mode of Film Practice," *Film Criticism*, 4 (1), 1979, pp. 56–64. Available at JSTOR, www.jstor.org/stable/44018650 (accessed 24 October 2020).

Bottero, Wendy, *Sense of Inequality* (London and New York: Rowman & Littlefield, 2020).
Bourke-White, Margaret, *Portrait of Myself* (Simon & Schuster, 1963).
Bourke-White, Margaret, "The Great Migration: Five Million Indians Flee for Their Lives," *Life Magazine*, 3 November 1947.
Bowman, Verity, "Clap For Our Carers: How Britons thanked NHS with nationwide round of applause," *The Telegraph*, 27 March 2020. Available at https://www.telegraph.co.uk/news/2020/03/27/thank-nhs-clap-carers/ (accessed 30 March 2020).
Boyce, Travis D. and Winsome M. Chunnu (eds.), *Historicizing Fear: Ignorance, Vilification and Othering* (Louisville: University Press of Colorado, 2019).
Boyd, Kelly, "Moving Pictures? Cinema and Society in Britain," *Journal of British Studies*, 34 (1), January 1995, pp. 130–5.
Bradshaw, Peter, "*The Sense of an Ending* review—an upscale bit of Britfilm hardback cinema," *The Guardian*, 6 April 2017. Available at https://www.theguardian.com/film/2017/apr/06/the-sense-of-an-ending-review-jim-broadbent-julian-barnes (accessed 30 October 2020).
Bradshaw, Peter, "*Daphne* review—Emily Beecham takes a stylish plunge into sex, drugs and drink," *The Guardian*, 28 September 2017. Available at https://www.theguardian.com/film/2017/sep/28/daphne-review-emily-beecham-geraldine-james-pete-mackie-burns (accessed 30 October 2020).
Bradshaw, Peter, "*Sorry We Missed You* review—Ken Loach's superb swipe at zero-hours Britain," *The Guardian*, 16 May 2019. Available at theguardian.com/film/2019/may/16/sorry-we-missed-you-review-ken-loach (accessed 20 December 2020).
Bulajewski, Mike, "Getting a Grip on Slavoj Žižek (with Slavoj Žižek)," 27 June 2018, JSTOR Daily. Available at https://daily.jstor.org/getting-a-grip-on-slavoj-zizek-with-slavoj-zizek/ (accessed 1 November 2020).
Burke, Edmund, *A Philosophical Inquiry into the Origin of Our Ideas of the Sublime and Beautiful* (New York: Harper, 1860).
Busby, Mattha, "Government reduces minimum salary for migrants to settle in UK," *The Guardian*, 24 October 2020. Available at https://www.theguardian.com/world/2020/oct/24/migrants-to-uk-now-need-to-earn-only-20480-after-home-office-climbdown (accessed 2 December 2020).
Butler, C. Violet, *Domestic Service: Inquiry by the Women's Industrial Council* (London: G. Bell, 1916).
Cameron, David, "Full text of David Cameron's speech: The Tory leader's conference address in full," *The Guardian*, 8 October 2009. Available at https://www.theguardian.com/politics/2009/oct/08/david-cameron-speech-in-full (accessed 15 January 2021).
Campt, Tina M., *Other Germans: Black Germans and the Politics of Race, Gender, and Memory in the Third Reich* (Ann Arbor: University of Michigan Press, 2004).
Cant, Callum, *Riding for Deliveroo: Resistance in the New Economy* (Cambridge: Polity Press, 2020).
Carlyle, Thomas, *On Heroes, Hero-Worship, and the Heroic in History*, 1840. Available at http://www.gutenberg.org/files/1091/1091-h/1091-h.htm#link2H_4_0007 (accessed 21 July 2020).
Carson, Rachel, *Silent Spring* (London and New York: Penguin, 2000/1962).
Chadha, Gurinder, "My film has been wilfully misrepresented as anti-Muslim," *The Guardian*, 3 March 2017. Available at https://www.theguardian.com/film/filmblog/2017/mar/03/gurinder-chadha-defends-viceroys-house-film-fatima-bhutto (accessed 14 July 2020).
Chambers, Marlene, "1. Thomas' The White Giant's Thigh," *The Explicator*, 19 (1), October 1960, pp. 1–3. Available at DOI: 10.1080/00144940.1960.11482139 (accessed 30 October 2020).

Chow, Broderick and Alex Mangold (eds.), *Žižek and Performance* (London: Palgrave Macmillan, 2014).
Christie, Christopher, *The British Country House in the Eighteenth Century* (Manchester and New York: Manchester University Press, 2000).
Clay, C. G. A., *Economic Expansion and Social Change: England 1500–1700, Volume 1: People, Land and Towns* (Cambridge: Cambridge University Press, 1984).
Cole, G. D. H. and Raymond Postgate, *The Common People, 1746–1946* (London: Methuen, 1938/1961).
Collier, Paul, *Exodus: How Migration Is Changing Our World* (Oxford: Oxford University Press, 2013).
Collins, Larry and Dominique Lapierre, *Freedom at Midnight* (London: Collins, 1975).
Collins, Patricia Hill and Sirma Bilge, *Intersectionality* (Cambridge: Polity, 2016).
Coss, Edward J., *All for the King's Shilling: The British Soldier Under Wellington, 1808–1814* (Norman: University of Oklahoma Press, 2010).
Cox, Pamela, *Servants: The True Story of Life Below Stairs, Part 1: Knowing Your Place*, BBC4, 5 April 2017.
Cox, Pamela, *Servants: The True Story of Life Below Stairs, Part 2: Class War*, BBC4, 12 April 2017.
Cox, Pamela, *Servants: The True Story of Life Below Stairs, Part 3: No Going Back*, BBC4, 19 April 2017.
Davidoff, Leonore, *Worlds Between: Historical Perspectives on Gender and Class* (Cambridge: Polity Press, 1995).
Dearden, Lizzie, "Online hate blamed as researchers find homophobia is increasing among young people in UK," *The Independent*, 15 October 2019. Available at https://www.independent.co.uk/news/uk/home-news/homophobia-lgbt-hate-crime-young-people-gay-trans-poll-research-a9157111.html (accessed 28 April 2020).
De Haas, Hein, Stephen Castles, and Mark J. Miller, *The Age of Migration: International Population Movements in the Modern World*, 6th edn. (London: Red Globe Press, 2020).
Delap, Lucy, "Housework, Housewives, and Domestic Workers: Twentieth-Century Dilemmas of Domesticity," *Home Cultures*, 8 (2), July 2011, pp. 189–209.
Delap, Lucy, *Knowing Their Place: Domestic Service in Twentieth-Century Britain* (Oxford: Oxford University Press, 2011).
Devasundaram, Ashvin Immanuel, "*Viceroy's House* is very watchable—but its account of Indian independence is limited," Queen Mary, University of London, 3 March 2017. Available at https://www.qmul.ac.uk/media/news/2017/hss/viceroys-house-is-very-watchable--but-its-account-of-indian-independence-is-limited.html (accessed 8 July 2020).
Dickson Leach, Hope, "Writer Director's Statement," *The Levelling* DVD cover, Peccadillo Pictures, 2016.
Disraeli, Benjamin, *Sybil, or the Two Nations* (London: Wordsworth Editions, 1995/1845).
Donnelly, Catherine W. (ed.), *The Oxford Companion to Cheese* (Oxford and New York: Oxford University Press, 2016).
Dorling, Danny, "Brexit: the decision of a divided country," *The BMJ*, 2016, p. 354. DOI: https://doi.org/10.1136/bmj.i3697.
Dresser, Madge and Andrew Hann (eds.), *Slavery and the British Country House* (Swindon: English Heritage, 2013.)
Dubal, Yash, "Migrant workers will be critical to the UK's economic rebirth," 2 June 2020, *Personnel Today*. Available at https://www.personneltoday.com/hr/migrant-workers-will-be-critical-to-the-uks-economic-rebirth/ (accessed 2 December 2020).

Duda-Mikulin, Eva A., *EU Migrant Workers, Brexit and Precarity: Polish Women's Perspectives from Inside the UK* (Bristol: Policy Press, 2019).

Duffy, Bobby, Kirstie Hewlett, Julian McCrae, and John Hall, *Divided Britain? Polarisation and fragmentation trends in the UK* (London: The Policy Institute at King's College, 2019).

Eagleton, Terry, *After Theory* (London and New York: Penguin Books, 2004).

Eldridge, C. C., *The Imperial Experience: From Carlyle to Forster* (London: Macmillan, 1996).

Ellis, Hugh and Kate Henderson, *Rebuilding Britain: Planning for a Better Future* (Bristol: Policy Press, 2014).

Engels, Friedrich, *The Condition of the Working-Class in England in 1844* (New York: Cosimo, 2008/1892).

Erizanu, Paula, "'A whole sheep for £18': how live exports are hurting farmers in Romania," *The Guardian*, 22 January 2020. Available at https://www.theguardian.com/environment/2020/jan/22/a-whole-sheep-for-18-how-live-exports-are-hurting-farmers-in-romania (accessed 2 December 2020).

Evans, Elizabeth, *The Politics of Third Wave Feminisms: Neoliberalism, Intersectionality and the State in Britain and the US* (London and New York: Palgrave Macmillan, 2015).

Evans, Eric J., *The Great Reform Act of 1832* (London and New York: Routledge, 1983/2000).

Everett, Wendy, "Ken Loach and the Geographies of Class," in Nicole Cloarec, David Haigron, and Delphine Letort (eds.), *Social Class on British and American Screens: Essays on Cinema and Television* (Jefferson, NC: McFarland, 2016), pp. 167–82.

Fiske, Robert, "British Cultural Studies and Television Criticism," in Robert Allen (ed.), *Channels of Discourse: Television and Contemporary Criticism* (London: Methuen, 1987).

Flemmen, Magne and Mike Savage, "The politics of nationalism and white racism in the UK," *The British Journal of Sociology*, 68 (1), 2017. Available at: http://eprints.lse.ac.uk/87229/1 (accessed 31 August 2020).

Florczak, Izabela and Marta Otto, "Precarious work and labour regulation in the EU: current reality and perspectives," in Jeff Kenner, Izabela Florczak, and Marta Otto (eds.), *Precarious Work: The Challenge for Labour Law in Europe* (Cheltenham and Northampton, MA: Edward Elgar, 2019), pp. 2–21.

Ford, Rob, "Britain's new political landscape: what the voting numbers tell us," *The Observer*, 15 December 2019. Available at https://www.theguardian.com/politics/2019/dec/15/britains-new-political-landscape (accessed 31 March 2019).

Francis, Sam, "Call for law change over increases in homophobic hate crimes in London," BBC News, 10 January 2020. Available at https://www.bbc.co.uk/news/uk-england-london-51049336 (accessed 28 April 2020).

Friedman, Lester (ed.), *Fires Were Started: British Cinema and Thatcherism* (London and New York: Wallflower Press, 2006/1993).

Friedman, Sam and Daniel Laurison, *The Class Ceiling: Why It Pays to Be Privileged* (Bristol: Policy Press, 2019).

Fudge, Judy and Petra Herzfeld-Olsson, "The EU Seasonal Workers Directive: When Immigration Control Meet Labour Rights," *European Journal of Migration and Law*, 16 (4), 2014, pp. 439–66. Available at https://kar.kent.ac.uk/44227/1/FudgeandHerzfeldOlssonSeasonalWorkersDirectiveFinal%2028%20Sept.pdf (accessed 2 December 2020).

Fulbrook, Mary, "Myth-Making and National Identity: The Case of the GDR," in Geoffrey Hosking and George Schöpflin (eds.), *Myths and Nationhood* (London and New York: Routledge, 1997).

Fuller, Thomas, *A Pisgah-sight of Palestine and the Confines thereof, with the Historie of the Old and New Testament acted thereon* (London: Tegg, 1650/1869).

Gamble, Andrew and Tony Wright (eds.), *Britishness: Perspectives on the British Question* (Malden, MA and Oxford: Wiley-Blackwell, 2009).

Garnett, Mark and Philip Lynch, *Exploring British Politics*, 4th edn. (London and New York: Routledge, 2016).

Geraghty, Christine, *British Cinema in the Fifties: Gender, Genre and the "New Look"* (London and New York: Routledge, 2000).

Gilbert, Martin, *Winston Churchill: Companion Documents*, 5 (3) (London: Heinemann, 1982).

Gill, Rosalind, "Postfeminist Media Culture: Elements of a Sensibility," *European Journal of Cultural Studies*, 10 (2), 2006, pp. 157–66.

Gillborn, David, *Racism and Education: Coincidence or Conspiracy?* (London and New York: Routledge, 2008).

Gilroy, Paul, *There Ain't No Black in the Union Jack: The Cultural Politics of Race and Nation* (London and New York: Routledge, 2002/1987).

Goldstein, Robert J., *Political Repression in 19th Century Europe* (London and New York: Routledge, 1983/2010).

Grater, Tom, "The Winding Journey of Puritan Western *Fanny Lye Deliver'd*: On-set Flooding, Three Years in Post, and a Determined Director," *Deadline*, 8 October 2019. Available at https://deadline.com/2019/10/inside-story-uk-drama-fanny-lye-deliverd-flooding-three-years-post-determined-director-1202753825/ (accessed 14 September 2020).

Greene, Larry A., "Race in the Reich: The African American Press on Nazi Germany," in Larry A. Greene and Anke Ortlepp (eds.), *Germans and African Americans: Two Centuries of Exchange* (Jackson: University Press of Mississippi, 2011), pp. 70–87.

Gregg, Edward, *Queen Anne* (New Haven, CT and London: Yale University Press, 2001/1980).

Gurney, John, *Brave Community: The Digger Movement in the English Revolution* (Manchester and New York: Manchester University Press, 2007).

Hajari, Nisid, *Midnight's Furies: The Deadly Legacy of India's Partition* (Boston and New York: Houghton Mifflin Harcourt, 2015).

Hall, Stuart, "The Future of Identity," in Sean P. Hier and B. Singh Bolaria (eds.), *Identity and Belonging: Rethinking Race and Ethnicity* (Toronto: Canadian Scholars' Press, 2006), pp. 249–69.

Harland, John, *Ballads and Songs of Lancashire, Ancient and Modern* (London: George Routledge, 1875).

Harris, John, "Britain is in the midst of a working-class revolt," *The Guardian*, 17 June 2016. Available at theguardian.com/comentisfree/2016/jun/17/Britain-working-class-revolt-eu-referendum (accessed 20 December 2020).

Harvey, Elizabeth D., *Ventriloquized Voices: Feminist Theory and English Renaissance Texts* (London and New York: Routledge, 1992).

Harvey, James (ed.), *Nationalism in Contemporary Western European Cinema* (London: Palgrave Macmillan, 2018).

Hastings, Max, "Churchill was a racist, but he still deserves respect," *The Sunday Times*, 14 June 2020, p. 21.

Hawkins, Jamie, "Coronavirus: Britain comes to standstill as millions join Clap for Our Carers," *Daily Mirror*, 26 March 2020. Available at https://www.mirror.co.uk/news/uk-news/breaking-coronavirus-britain-comes-standstill-21761321 (accessed 30 March 2020).

Helleiner, Eric, *The Status Quo Crisis: Global Financial Governance after the 2008 Meltdown* (Oxford and New York: Oxford University Press, 2014).

Heyes, Cressida, "Identity Politics," *The Stanford Encyclopedia of Philosophy*, Fall 2020, Edward N. Zalta (ed.). Available at https://plato.stanford.edu/archives/fall2020/entries/identity-politics/ (accessed 24 August 2020).

Hicks, Lady Pamela, *Daughter of Empire: My Life as a Mountbatten* (New York and London: Simon & Schuster, 2012).

Hickson, Kevin, *Britain's Conservative Right since 1945: Traditional Toryism in a Cold Climate* (London: Palgrave Macmillan, 2019).

Higson, Andrew, *Waving the Flag: Constructing a National Cinema in Britain* (Oxford: Oxford University Press, 1995).

Higson, Andrew, "Re-presenting the National Past: Nostalgia and Pastiche in the Heritage Film," in Lester Friedman (ed.), *British Cinema and Thatcherism* (London: UCL Press, 1996), pp. 109–29.

Higson, Andrew, *English Heritage, English Cinema: Costume Drama Since 1980* (Oxford: Oxford University Press, 2003).

Hill, Christopher, *The World Turned Upside Down: Radical Ideas During the English Revolution* (London: Viking Press, 1972).

Hill, Christopher, *The Century of Revolution, 1603–1714* (London: Van Nostrand Reinhold, 1980).

Hill, John, *British Cinema in the 1980s* (Oxford: Clarendon Press, 1999).

Hilliard, Robert L., *Hollywood Speaks Out: Pictures That Dared to Protest Real World Issues* (Chichester: Wiley-Blackwell, 2009).

Hitler, Adolf, *Mein Kampf* (New York: Houghton Mifflin, 1943).

Hobsbawm, Eric, "Identity Politics and the Left," Barry Amiel & Norman Melburn Trust Lecture, Institute of Education, London, 2 May 1996. Available at http://banmarchive.org.uk/articles/1996%20annual%20lecture.htm (accessed 31 August 2020).

Hoskins, W. G., *The Making of the English Landscape* (Toller Fratrum: Little Toller Books, 2013/1955).

Howkins, Alun, "The Discovery of Rural England," in Robert Colls and Philip Dodd (eds.), *Englishness: Politics and Culture, 1880–1920* (London: Croom Helm, 1986).

Humes, James C., *Churchill: The Prophetic Statesman* (Washington, DC: Regnery, 2012).

Hutchinson, Pamela (ed.), *30-Second Cinema* (London: Ivy Press, 2019).

Ignatieff, Michael, *Blood and Belonging* (London: Vintage, 1994).

Ignatieff, Michael, "Is identity politics ruining democracy?" *Financial Times*, 5 September 2018. Available at https://www.ft.com/content/09c2c1e4-ad05-11e8-8253-48106866cd8a (accessed 22 August 2020).

Irigaray, Luce, *This Sex Which Is Not One*, trans. Catherine Porter and Carolyn Burke (Ithaca, NY: Cornell University Press, 1985).

Jack, Ian, "*The Viceroy's House* version of India's partition brings fake history to the screen," *The Guardian*, 18 March 2017. Available at https://www.theguardian.com/commentisfree/2017/mar/18/the-viceroys-house-version-of-indias-partition-brings-fake-history-to-screen (accessed 14 July 2020).

Jack, Ian, "*Dunkirk* and *Darkest Hour* fuel Brexit fantasies—even if they weren't meant to," *The Guardian*, 27 January 2018. Available at https://www.theguardian.com/commentisfree/2018/jan/27/brexit-britain-myths-wartime-darkest-hour-dunkirk-nationalist-fantasies (accessed 16 June 2020).

Jalal, Ayesha, *The Sole Spokesman: Jinnah, the Muslim League and the Demand for Pakistan* (Cambridge and New York: Cambridge University Press, 1994/1985).

Jeffreys-Jones, Rhodri, *We Know All About You: The Story of Surveillance in Britain and America* (Oxford: Oxford University Press, 2017).

Jinnah, Quaid-e-Azam Muhammad Ali, presidential address to the Constituent Assembly of Pakistan, 11 August 1947. Available at http://www.pakistani.org/pakistan/legislation/constituent_address_11aug1947.html (accessed 21 July 2020).

Jones, Daniel (ed.), *Dylan Thomas: The Poems* (London: Dent, 1971).
Jones, Jonathan, "Whistlejacket, George Stubbs (1762)," *The Guardian*, 22 April 2000. Available at theguardian.com/culture/2000/apr/22/art1 (accessed 16 June 2020).
Jones, Owen, *Chavs: The Demonization of the Working Class* (London and New York: Verso, 2020/2011).
Jones, Tobias, "The harsh lives of the forgotten rural poor," *The Guardian*, 24 February 2013. Available at https://www.theguardian.com/commentisfree/2013/feb/24/rural-poverty-invisible (accessed 21 November 2020).
Katz, David, "Review: *Fanny Lye Deliver'd*," 14 October 2019. Available at https://cineuropa.org/en/newsdetail/379745/ (accessed 14 September 2020).
Kaufman, Stephen, "Blacks in Germany During the Third Reich: Star of David Not Required," in Kevin Reilly, Stephen Kaufman, and Angela Bodino (eds.), *Racism: A Global Reader* (New York and London: M. E. Sharpe, 2003), pp. 270–2.
Keegan, Paul (ed.), *Ted Hughes: Collected Poems* (London: Faber & Faber, 2012).
Kelby, Rosamund, "*Fanny Lye Deliver'd*," *The Upcoming*, 11 October 2019. Available at https://www.theupcoming.co.uk/2019/10/11/london-film-festival-2019-fanny-lye-deliverd-review/ (accessed 14 September 2020).
Kenner, Jeff, Izabela Florczak and Marta Otto (eds.), *Precarious Work: The Challenge for Labour Law in Europe* (Cheltenham and Northampton, MA: Edward Elgar, 2019).
Kenny, Michael, *The Politics of English Nationhood* (Oxford: Oxford University Press, 2014).
Kermode, Frank, *The Sense of an Ending: Studies in the Theory of Fiction* (with a New Epilogue) (Oxford and New York: Oxford University Press, 2000).
Kermode, Mark, "*Viceroy's House* review—gripping political drama with a populist edge," *The Guardian*, 5 March 2017. Available at https://www.theguardian.com/film/2017/mar/05/viceroys-house-review-gurinder-chadha-gillian-anderson-hugh-bonneville (accessed 8 July 2020).
Kermode, Mark, "*The Levelling* review—a tremendous debut from Hope Dickson Leach," *The Observer*, 14 May 2017. Available at https://www.theguardian.com/film/2017/may/14/the-levelling-review-mark-kermode-somerset-hope-dickson-leach (accessed 15 November 2020).
Kesting, Robert, "The Black Experience during the Holocaust," in Michael Berenbaum and Abraham J. Peck (eds.), *The Holocaust and History: The Known, the Unknown, the Disputed and the Re-examined* (Bloomington and Indianapolis: Indiana University Press, 2002), pp. 358–66.
Kezar, Adrianna, Tom DePaola, and Daniel T. Scott, *The Gig Academy: Mapping Labor in the Neoliberal University* (Baltimore, MD: Johns Hopkins University Press, 2019).
Kirk, John, Andrew Noble, and Michael Brown (eds.), *United Islands? The Languages of Resistance* (London and New York: Routledge, 2016).
Klenotic, Jeffery, "The Place of Rhetoric in 'New' Film Historiography: The Discourse of Corrective Revisionism," in *Film History*, 6 (1), 1994, pp. 45–58.
Lambert, Rob and Andrew Herod, *Neoliberal Capitalism and Precarious Work: Ethnographies of Accommodation and Resistance* (Cheltenham and Northampton, MA: Edward Elgar, 2016).
Lansley, Stewart and Joanna Mack, *Breadline Britain: The Rise of Mass Poverty* (London: Oneworld, 2015).
Larkin, Philip, "Aubade," *The Times Literary Supplement*, 23 December 1977, p. 1491.
Laybourn, Keith, *The General Strike of 1926* (Manchester and New York: Manchester University Press, 1993).
Lee, Ken, "Foreword," in Ian Hancock, *We Are the Romani People* (Hatfield: University of Hertfordshire Press, 2002).

Leigh, Jacob, *The Cinema of Ken Loach: Art in the Service of the People* (London: Wallflower Press, 2002).

Lethbridge, Lucy, *Servants: A Downstairs History of Britain from the Nineteenth Century to Modern Times* (New York and London: W. W. Norton, 2013).

Lewis-Stempel, John, "Foreword," in Ruth Janette Ruck, *Along Came a Llama* (London: Faber & Faber, 2020/1978).

Lind, Michael, *Up From Conservatism* (New York and London: Simon & Schuster, 1997).

Lipscomb, Suzannah, "A Modern Queen of Scots," *History Today*, 69 (2), February 2019. Available at https://www.historytoday.com/archive/making-history/modern-queen-scots (accessed 20 April 2020).

Lobley, Matt, Michael Winter, and Rebecca Wheeler, *The Changing World of Farming in Brexit UK* (London and New York: Routledge, 2019).

Loughrey, Clarisse, "*Mary Queen of Scots*: How historically accurate is it?" *The Independent*, 15 January 2019. Available at https://www.independent.co.uk/arts-entertainment/films/news/mary-queen-of-scots-historical-accuracy-meet-queen-elizabeth-margot-robbie-saoirse-ronan-a8666266.html (accessed 20 April 2020).

Lusane, Clarence, *Hitler's Black Victims: The Historical Experiences of Afro-Germans, European Blacks, Africans, and African Americans in the Nazi Era* (London and New York: Routledge, 2003).

Magelssen, Scott, *Living History Museums: Undoing History Through Performance* (Lanham, MD: Scarecrow Press, 2007).

Major, John, "I'm a Conservative. But it is time to vote with your head as well as your heart," *The Guardian*, 6 December 2019. Available at theguardian.com/commentisfree/2019/dec/06/john-major-conservative-general-election-vote-head-heart (accessed 1 June 2020).

Makovsky, Michael, "Being Winston Churchill," *The New Republic*, 8 December 2010. Available at https://newrepublic.com/article/79718/winston-churchill-life-battle-britain (accessed 17 June 2020).

Marino, Stefania, Judith Roosblad, and Rinus Penninx, *Trade Unions and Migrant Workers: New Contexts and Challenges in Europe* (Cheltenham and Northampton, MA: Edward Elgar, 2017).

Marmot, Michael, Jessica Allen, Tammy Boyce, Peter Goldblatt, and Joana Morrison, *Health Equity in England: The Marmot Review 10 Years On (2020)*. Available at http://www.instituteofhealthequity.org/resources-reports/marmot-review-10-years-on/the-marmot-review-10-years-on-executive-summary.pdf (accessed 31 March 2020).

Marsili, Lorenzo, "Ken Loach: If We Don't Understand Class Struggle, We Don't Understand Anything," *Political Critique*, 30 October 2018. Available at http://politicalcritique.org/world/uk/2018/ken-loach-class-struggle/ (accessed 20 December 2020).

Martin, Theodore, *Contemporary Drift: Genre, Historicism, and the Problem of the Present* (New York: Columbia University Press, 2017).

Masham, Damaris Cudworth, *Occasional Thoughts In Reference to a Vertuous or Christian Life* (1705), The Project Gutenberg. Available at https://www.gutenberg.org/cache/epub/13285/pg13285.html (accessed 30 May 2020), n.p.

Massaquoi, Hans J., *Destined to Witness: Growing Up Black in Nazi Germany* (New York: Perennial, 2001).

Matera, Marc, *Black London: The Imperial Metropolis and Decolonization in the Twentieth Century* (Oakland: University of California Press, 2015).

McCann, Philip, *The UK Regional–National Economic Problem: Geography, Globalisation and Governance* (London and New York: Routledge, 2016).

McIntosh, Charles, *The Orchard: Including the Management of Wall and Standard Fruit Trees, and the Forcing Pit* (London: Orr, 1839).

McKenzie, Kirsten, *A Swindler's Progress: Nobles and Convicts in the Age of Liberty* (Cambridge, MA: Harvard University Press, 2010).

McKenzie, Kirsten, *Imperial Underworld: An Escaped Convict and the Transformation of the British Colonial Order* (Cambridge: Cambridge University Press, 2016).

McNay, Lois, *Foucault and Feminism* (Cambridge: Polity Press, 1992).

Mears, Steven, "*Sorry We Missed You*," *Film Comment*, 56 (2), March/April 2020, p. 70.

Meehan, Diana, *Ladies of the Evening: Women Characters of Prime-Time Television* (Metuchen, NJ: Scarecrow Press, 1983).

Milton, Sybil H., "'Gypsies' as Social Outsiders in Nazi Germany," in Robert Gellately and Nathan Stoltzfus (eds.), *Social Outsiders in Nazi Germany* (Princeton, NJ and Oxford: Princeton University Press, 2001), pp. 212–32.

Mingay, G. E., *English Landed Society in the Eighteenth Century* (London and New York: Routledge, 2007/1963).

Monbiot, George, "Dredging rivers won't stop floods. It will make them worse," *The Guardian*, 13 January 2014. Available at https://www.theguardian.com/commentisfree/2014/jan/30/dredging-rivers-floods-somerset-levels-david-cameron-farmers (accessed 21 November 2020).

Monk, Claire, "The British 'heritage film' and its critics," *Critical Survey*, 7 (2), 1995, pp. 116–24.

Monk, Claire and Amy Sargeant (eds.), *British Historical Cinema: The History, Heritage and Costume Film* (London and New York: Routledge, 2002).

Mooney, Gerry, "'Remoralizing' the Poor?: Gender, Class and Philanthropy in Victorian Britain," in Gail Lewis (ed.), *Forming Nation, Framing Welfare* (London and New York: Routledge, 1998/2017).

Moraru, Adela, "Social perception of homosexuality in Romania," *Procedia—Social and Behavioral Sciences*, 5 (2), 2010, pp. 45–9. Available at https://www.researchgate.net/publication/232415423_Social_perception_of_homosexuality_in_Romania (accessed 2 December 2020).

Morgan, Alison, *Ballads and Songs of Peterloo* (Manchester: Manchester University Press, 2018).

Morgan, George and Pariece Nelligan, *The Creativity Hoax: Precarious Work and the Gig Economy* (London and New York: Anthem Press, 2018).

Morris, Christopher, *The Tudors* (London: Fontana, 1966).

Morton, Timothy, *Ecology without Nature: Rethinking Environmental Aesthetics* (Cambridge, MA: Harvard University Press, 2007).

Mouffe, Chantel, *On the Political (Thinking in Action)* (London and New York: Routledge, 2005).

Mountbatten, Pamela, *India Remembered: A Personal Account of the Mountbattens During the Transfer of Power* (London: Pavilion, 2007).

Nail, Thomas, *Theory of the Border* (Oxford and New York: Oxford University Press, 2016).

Najam, Adil, "How a British royal's monumental errors made India's partition more painful," *The Conversation*, 16 August 2017. Available at https://theconversation.com/how-a-british-royals-monumental-errors-made-indias-partition-more-painful-81657 (accessed 16 July 2020).

Nehru, Jawaharlal, "Tryst with Destiny" speech, 15 August 1947. Available at https://soundcloud.com/university-of-cambridge/tryst-with-destiny (accessed 21 July 2020).

Nica, Felicia and Madalina Moraru, "Diaspora Policies, Consular Services and Social Protection for Romanian Citizens Abroad," in Jean-Michel Lafleur and Daniela Vintila (eds.), *Migration and Social Protection in Europe and Beyond (Volume 2): Comparing Consular Services and Diaspora Policies*, IMISCOE Research Series (Cham, Switzerland: Springer Nature, 2020) pp. 409–26. Available at https://doi.org/10.1007/978-3-030-51245-3 (accessed 2 December 2020).

Niță, Delia-Luiza, "ENAR Shadow Report 2008: Racism in Romania," European Network against Racism (ENAR), October 2009, p. 3. Available at http://cms.horus.be/files/99935/MediaArchive/national/Romania%20-%20SR%202008.pdf (accessed 2 December 2020).

O'Leary, Brendan, "Partition," in Thomas M. Wilson and Hastings Donnan (eds.), *A Companion to Border Studies* (Malden, MA: Wiley-Blackwell, 2016), pp. 29–47.

Olsen, Kirstin, *Daily Life in 18th Century England* (Westport, CT and London: Greenwood Press, 1999).

Pandey, Bishwa Mohan, "An Attempt to Revive Imperialist Assumptions: A Historiographical Study of the Writings of P. N. S. Mansergh," *Proceedings of the Indian History Congress*, Vol. 61, 2000, pp. 605–11. Available at www.jstor.org/stable/44148133 (accessed 6 July 2020).

Parkinson-Bailey, John J., *Manchester: An Architectural History* (Manchester and New York: Manchester University Press, 2000).

Pattie, Charles J. and Ron J. Johnston, "Changing Geographies of Prosperity and Representation: The Role of the Local State," in Richard T. Harrison and Mark Hart (eds.), *Spatial Policy in a Divided Nation* (London: Jessica Kingsley, 1993) pp. 37–63.

Paulin, Tom, *Thomas Hardy: The Poetry of Perception* (London: Macmillan, 1986/1975).

Perkins, Anne, *A Very British Strike: 3 May–12 May 1926* (London: Macmillan, 2006).

Petley, Julian, "The Englishness of British Cinema: Beyond the Valley of the Corn Dollies," in John Hill (ed.), *A Companion to British and Irish Cinema* (Chichester: Wiley-Blackwell, 2019) pp. 463–89.

Pettigrew, William A., "Free to Enslave: Politics and the Escalation of Britain's Transatlantic Slave Trade, 1688–1714," *The William and Mary Quarterly*, 64 (1), 2007, pp. 3–38. Available at www.jstor.org/stable/4491595 (accessed 14 June 2020).

Poole, Robert, *The English Uprising: Peterloo* (Oxford: Oxford University Press, 2019).

Powell, Margaret, *Below Stairs: The Bestselling Memoirs of a 1920s Kitchen Maid* (London: Pan Books, 2011/1968).

Powell, Margaret, *Climbing the Stairs: Further Tales of a 1920s Kitchen Maid* (London: Pan Books, 2011/1969).

Powell, Zachary Michael, "The Form of the White Ethno-State: *Dunkirk* (2017) Omits Indian Soldiers for White Vulnerable Bodies," in Clementine Tholas, Janis L. Goldie, and Karen A. Ritzenhoff (eds.), *New Perspectives on the War Film* (London: Palgrave Macmillan, 2019).

Prassl, Jeremias, *Humans as a Service: The Promise and Perils of Work in the Gig Economy* (Oxford: Oxford University Press, 2018).

Proctor, Robert N., *Racial Hygiene: Medicine under the Nazis* (Cambridge, MA and London: Harvard University Press, 2002/1988).

Quart, Leonard, "A Fidelity to the Real: An Interview with Ken Loach and Tony Garnett," *Cinéaste*, 10 (4), Fall 1980, pp. 26–9.

Quart, Leonard and Albert Auster, *American Film and Society since 1945* (London: Macmillan, 1984).

Ramchand, Ken, "Interviews with C. L. R. James," September 1980. Available at http://www.clrjames.uk/wp-content/uploads/2015/10/Interviews-with-C.L.R.-James-by-Ken-Ramchand.pdf (accessed 17 June 2020).

Read, Donald, *Peterloo: The "Massacre" and Its Background* (Manchester: Manchester University Press, 1958).

Rebanks, James, *The Shepherd's Life: A Tale of the Lake District* (London and New York: Penguin, 2016).

Rebanks, James, *English Pastoral: An Inheritance* (London and New York: Allen Lane, 2020).

Reed, Rex, "*The Sense of an Ending* Is a Powerful, Moving Portrait of Memories Past," *The Observer*, 14 March 2017. Available at https://observer.com/2017/03/sense-of-an-ending-movie-review-jim-broadbent/ (accessed 30 October 2020).

Reger, Jo, *Everywhere and Nowhere: Contemporary Feminism in the United States* (Oxford and New York: Oxford University Press, 2012).

Rhodes James, Robert (ed.), *Winston S. Churchill: His Complete Speeches, 1897–1963, Volume 5: 1928–1935* (New York: Chelsea House, 1974).

Richards, Jeffrey, "Film and Television: the moving image," in Sarah Barber and Corinna M. Peniston-Bird (eds.), *History Beyond the Text* (London and New York: Routledge, 2009).

Riding, Jacqueline, *Peterloo: The Story of the Manchester Massacre* (London: Head of Zeus, 2018).

Roberts, Andrew, *Churchill: Walking with Destiny* (London: Penguin, 2019).

Robertson, Geoffrey, "Introduction," in Philip Baker (ed.), *The Putney Debates: The Levellers* (London and New York: Verso, 2018).

Romocea, Oana, "Facets of migrant identity: ethical dilemmas in research among Romanian migrants in the UK," in Ulrike Ziemer and Sean P. Roberts (eds.), *East European Diasporas, Migrations and Cosmopolitanism* (London and New York: Routledge, 2013), pp. 123–37.

Rosario, Kennith, "*Viceroy's House* review: A soapy political saga," *The Hindu*, 17 August 2017. Available at https://www.thehindu.com/entertainment/movies/viceroys-house-review-a-soapy-political-saga/article19510228.ece (accessed 14 July 2020).

Roscoe, E. S., *Robert Harley, Earl of Oxford, Prime Minister, 1710–14: A Study of Politics and Letters in the Age of Anne* (London: Methuen, 1902).

Rose, Steve, "The *Dunkirk* spirit: how cinema is shaping Britain's identity in the Brexit era," *The Guardian*, 20 July 2017. Available at https://www.theguardian.com/film/2017/jul/20/dunkirk-spirit-british-film-brexit-national-identity-christopher-nolan (accessed 16 June 2020).

Rosenhaft, Eve, "Translator's Preface," in Theodor Michael, *Black German: An Afro-German Life in the Twentieth Century* (Liverpool: Liverpool University Press, 2017).

Rosenstone, Robert A., *History on Film/Film on History* (Harlow: Pearson, 2006).

Ruck, Ruth Janette, *Place of Stones* (London: Faber & Faber, 1961).

Ryle, Martin, "The Historical Novel?: Novel, History and the 'End of History,'" in Garin Dowd, Lesley Stevenson, and Jeremy Strong (eds.), *Genre Matters: Essays in Theory and Criticism* (Bristol: Intellect, 2006).

Sabine, George H. (ed.), *The Works of Gerrard Winstanley: With an Appendix of Documents Relating to the Digger Movement* (Ithaca, NY: Cornell University Press, 1941).

Sarila, Narendra Singh, *The Shadow of the Great Game—The Untold Story of India's Partition* (London: Constable, 2005).

Sathyamurthy, T. V., "Victorians, socialisation and imperialism: consequences for post-imperial India," in J. A. Managan (ed.), *Making Imperial Mentalities: Socialisation and British Imperialism* (London and New York: Routledge, 2012/1990).

Schama, Simon, "History is better served by putting the Men in Stone in museums," *Financial Times*, 12 June 2020.

Scheck, Raffael, *Hitler's African Victims: The German Army Massacres of Black French Soldiers in 1940* (Cambridge and New York: Cambridge University Press, 2006).

Schwartz, Laura, *Feminism and the Servant Problem: Class and Domestic Labour in the Women's Suffrage Movement* (Cambridge: Cambridge University Press, 2019).

Schwartz, Laura, "Karl Marx and Domestic Servants: A historical overview of Marx's and Marxist thinking on domestic workers, reproductive labour and class struggle," 2019. Available at https://www.academia.edu/42641042/Karl_Marx_and_Domestic_

Servants_A_historical_overview_of_Marxs_and_Marxist_thinking_on_domestic_workers_reproductive_labour_and_class_struggle (accessed 13 October 2020).

Scott, Peter and Anna Spadavecchia, "Did the 48-hour week damage Britain's industrial competitiveness?" *Economic History Review*, 64 (4), 2011, pp. 1266–88.

Scrivener, Michael, *Poetry and Reform: Periodical Verse from the English Democratic Press 1792–1824* (Detroit, MI: Wayne State University Press, 1992).

Seymour, Susanne and Sheryllynne Haggerty, "Slavery Connections of Bolsover Castle (1600–1830)," Report for English Heritage, July 2010. Available at https://historicengland.org.uk/images-books/publications/slavery-connections-bolsover-castle/slavery-connections-bolsover-castle/ (accessed 15 June 2020).

Sinngh, Amritjit, Nalini Iyer, and Rahul K. Gairola (eds.), *Revisiting India's Partition: New Essays on Memory, Culture and Politics* (Lanham, MD and London: Lexington Books, 2016).

Smith, Nigel, *A Collection of Ranter Writings: Spiritual Liberty and Sexual Freedom in the English Revolution* (London: Pluto Press, 2014/1983).

Sobchack, Thomas and Vivian C. Sobchack, *An Introduction to Film* (Glenview, IL and Boston: Scott, Foresman, 1987).

Spencer, Ian R. G., *British Immigration Policy Since 1939: The Making of Multi-Racial Britain* (London and New York: Routledge, 1997).

Staiger, Janet, *Interpreting Films: Studies in the Historical Reception of American Cinema* (Princeton, NJ: Princeton University Press, 1992).

Standing, Guy, *The Precariat: The New Dangerous Class* (London and New York: Bloomsbury Academic, 2016/2011).

Stark, Cameron, "Suicide in rural areas," in Stephen Palmer (ed.), *Suicide: Strategies and Interventions for Reduction and Prevention* (London and New York: Routledge, 2008), pp. 48–68.

Street, Sarah, *British National Cinema* (London and New York: Routledge, 2009/1997).

Street, Sarah, *British Cinema in Documents* (London and New York: Routledge, 2000).

Suarez-Orozco, Marcelo M. (ed.), *Humanitarianism and Mass Migration: Confronting the World Crisis* (Oakland: University of California Press, 2019).

Sutherland, Claire, *Nationalism in the Twenty-First Century: Challenges and Responses* (London: Palgrave Macmillan, 2012).

Swire, John, "More than one farmer a week in the UK dies by suicide," *Farm Business*, 15 February 2018. Available at http://www.farmbusiness.co.uk/news/more-then-one-farmer-a-week-in-the-uk-dies-by-suicide-2.html (accessed 21 November 2020).

Szeman, Ioana, *Staging Citizenship: Roma, Performance and Belonging in EU Romania* (New York and Oxford: Berghahn, 2018).

Tennyson, Alfred, *Poems, Volume I* (Boston: William D. Ticknor, 1842).

Thane, Pat, *Divided Kingdom: A History of Britain, 1900 to the Present* (Cambridge: Cambridge University Press, 2018).

Tharoor, Shashi, "The Partition: The British game of 'divide and rule': Before leaving India, the British made sure a united India would not be possible," *Aljazeera*, 10 August 2017. Available at https://www.aljazeera.com/indepth/opinion/2017/08/partition-british-game-divide-rule-170808101655163.html (accessed 16 July 2020).

Tharoor, Shashi, *Inglorious Empire: What the British Did to India* (London: Penguin, 2017).

Thatcher, Margaret, "Interview for *Woman's Own* ('no such thing as society')," Margaret Thatcher Foundation, 23 September 1987. Available at https://www.margaretthatcher.org/document/106689 (accessed 20 January 2021).

Tholas, Clementine, Janis L. Goldie, and Karen A. Ritzenhoff (eds.), *New Perspectives on the War Film* (London: Palgrave Macmillan, 2019).

Thomason, George, *Catalogue of the Pamphlets, Books, Newspapers, and Manuscripts Relating to the Civil War, The Commonwealth, and Restoration, Collected by George Thomason, 1640–1661, Vol. I, 1640–1652* (London: William Clowes, 1908). Available at https://www.bl.uk/collection-guides/thomason-tracts (accessed 16 September 2020).

Thompson, E. P., *The Making of the English Working Class* (Harmondsworth: Penguin, 1980).

Thompson, Julian, *Dunkirk: Retreat to Victory* (London: Pan Macmillan, 2009).

Thwaite, Anthony (ed.), *Philip Larkin: Collected Poems* (Victoria and London: The Marvell Press and Faber & Faber, 2003).

Tileaga, Cristian, *The Nature of Prejudice: Society, Discrimination and Moral Exclusion* (London and New York: Routledge, 2016).

Townsend, Mark, "Homophobic attacks in UK rose 147% in three months after Brexit vote," *The Observer*, 8 October 2016. Available at theguardian.com/society/2016/oct/08/homophobic-attacks-double-after-brexit-vote (accessed 2 December 2020).

Toye, Richard, *Churchill's Empire: The World That Made Him and the World He Made* (London: Macmillan, 2010).

Trandafoiu, Ruxandra, *Diaspora Online: Identity Politics and Romanian Migrants* (New York and London: Berghahn, 2013).

Trevelyan, George Macaulay, *A Shortened History of England* (Harmondsworth: Penguin, 1965/1942).

Turner, Graeme, *Film as Social Practice* (London and New York: Routledge, 1993/1988).

Uberoi, Elise, "UK Dairy Industry Statistics," House of Commons Library Briefing Paper, No. 2721, 1 May 2020.

Underwood, Doug, *Literary Journalism in British and American Prose: An Historical Overview* (Jefferson, NC: McFarland, 2019).

Vincent, Andrew, *Modern Political Ideologies* (Oxford and Malden, MA: Wiley-Blackwell, 2010/1992).

Vlandas, Tim and Daphne Halikiopoulou, "What is new and what is nationalist about Europe's new nationalism? Explaining the rise of the far right in Europe," *Nations and Nationalism*, 25 (2), April 2019, pp. 409–34.

Walker, Alexander, *Hollywood England: The British Film Industry in the Sixties* (London: Harrap, 1974/1986).

Walsh, Joseph, "Director Clio Barnard on *Dark River* and the drama of rural life," *Financial Times*, 16 February 2018. Available at https://www.ft.com/content/2aed47a8-f48d-11e7-a4c9-bbdefa4f210b (accessed 15 November 2020).

Ward, Paul, *Britishness Since 1870* (London and New York: Routledge, 2004).

Webster, Wendy, *Mixing It: Diversity in World War Two in Britain* (Oxford: Oxford University Press, 2018).

Welfens, Paul J. J., *An Accidental Brexit: New EU and Transatlantic Economic Perspectives* (London: Palgrave Macmillan, 2017).

Wheale, Nigel, *Writing and Society: Literacy, Print and Politics in Britain, 1590–1660* (London and New York: Routledge, 1999).

White, E. A., "The Diggers' Song," *Journal of the English Folk Dance and Song Society*, 4 (1), December 1940, pp. 23–30. Available at www.jstor.org/stable/4521172 (accessed 11 September 2020).

White, Jerry, *A Great and Monstrous Thing: London in the Eighteenth Century* (Cambridge, MA: Harvard University Press, 2013).

White, John, "Defending Home, Defending Homeland: *Jane Got a Gun* (2016)," in John White, *The Contemporary Western: An American Genre Post-9/11* (Edinburgh: Edinburgh University Press, 2019).

White, John, *European Art Cinema* (London and New York: Routledge, 2017).

Whitman, James Q., *Hitler's American Model: The United States and the Making of Nazi Race Law* (Princeton, NJ and Oxford: Princeton University Press, 2018).

Wiarda, Howard J., *Political Culture, Political Science, and Identity Politics: An Uneasy Alliance* (London and New York: Routledge, 2016).

Wigger, Iris, *The "Black Horror on the Rhine": Intersections of Race, Nation, Gender and Class in 1920s Germany* (London: Palgrave Macmillan, 2017).

Williams, A. Susan, *Colour Bar: The Triumph of Seretse Khama and His Nation* (London: Allen Lane, 2006).

Winlow, Simon, Steve Hall, and James Treadwell, *The Rise of the Right: English Nationalism and the Transformation of Working-Class Politics* (Bristol: Policy Press, 2017).

Wolpert, Stanley, *Shameful Flight: The Last Years of the British Empire in India* (Oxford and New York: Oxford University Press, 2006).

Wood, Ellen Meiksins and Neal Wood, *A Trumpet of Sedition: Political Theory and the Rise of Capitalism, 1509–1688* (London: Pluto Press, 1997).

Wood, Robin, *Hollywood From Vietnam to Reagan and Beyond* (New York: Columbia University Press, 1986/2003).

Wrigley, Chris, *Churchill* (London: Haus, 2006).

Wroughton, John, *Seventeenth-Century Britain* (London: Macmillan, 1980).

Zane, Damian, "Being black in Nazi Germany," BBC News, 22 May 2019. Available at https://www.bbc.co.uk/news/world-africa-48273570 (accessed 22 August 2020).

Ziegler, Philip, *Mountbatten: The Official Biography* (New York: Fontana, 1986).

Žižek, Slavoj, *Living In the End Times* (London and New York: Verso, 2011).

Žižek, Slavoj, *The Year of Dreaming Dangerously* (London and New York: Verso, 2012).

Žižek, Slavoj, *Against the Double Blackmail: Refugees, Terror and Other Troubles with the Neighbours* (London and New York: Penguin, 2017).

Zuboff, Shoshana, *The Age of Surveillance Capitalism: The Fight for a Human Future at the New Frontier of Power* (London: Profile Books, 2019).

# Index

*49th Parallel*, 3
*1917*, 85

Achilleos-Sarll, Columba, 117
Addison, Paul, 119n
*Aguirre, Wrath of God*, 117n
Alcoff, Linda Martin, 132
Allen, Jessica, 6
Anderson, Benedict, 5, 11
Anderson, Lindsay, 83n
Andrew, Dudley, 7
anti-gypsyism *see* racism
aristocracy *see* class
art-house cinema *see* genre
Asante, Amma, 14, 121, 122, 127; *see also A United Kingdom, Where Hands Touch*
Ashby, Justine, 10
Attlee, Clement, 106, 139
Auster, Albert, 226–7

Baldwin, James, 126
Bamford, Samuel, 65, 80–1n, 82n
Bandyopadhyay, Sekhar, 140, 143, 146
Barnard, Clio, 192, 193, 194, 196, 197; *see also Dark River*
Barnes, Julian *see Sense of an Ending, The* (novel)
Barrenechea, Jon, 161
Bassnett, Susan, 199–200n
Bates, Crispin, 140, 144, 147
Batra, Ritesh, 169n; *see also Sense of an Ending, The*
Beauman, Fran, 61
Bechuanaland, 127
Beecham, Emily, 167

Belton, John, 8
Bhopal, Kalwant, 136n
Bhutto, Fatima, 141
Bilge, Sirma, 8
Black Lives Matter, 106, 129, 148
Blackwell, Anna, 114
borders, 6, 7, 14, 16, 109, 140, 142, 175
Bordwell, David, 159–60
Bottero, Wendy, 214n
Bourke-White, Margaret, 128, 151–2n
Boyce, Travis, 174, 184n
Boyd, Kelly, 8
Bradshaw, Peter, 161, 165, 206
Brexit *see* EU referendum (2016)
British Empire, 15, 59–60, 112, 114, 117, 123, 138, 148, 149n
Britishness, 5, 12, 91, 93–4, 105–6, 184
Broadbent, Jim, 163–4, 168n
Burke, Edmund, 107–8
Burns, Peter Mackie *see Daphne*
Butler, Violet, 89

Cameron, David, 218, 220
Campt, Tina, 125, 130, 134n, 135n
Cant, Callum, 209
capitalism, 54, 67, 79, 99, 206, 209, 213, 219, 221
Carlile, Richard, 82n
Carlyle, Thomas, 148
Carson, Rachel, 196
Chadha, Gurinder, 141, 142, 143, 146; *see also Viceroy's House*
Charles I, 13, 32, 43, 46n
*Chavs: The Demonization of the Working Class see* Jones, Owen

Christian religion, 35, 41, 43
  Catholic, 31, 34n, 50, 222
  King James Bible, 37, 169n
  Quakers, Society of Friends, 42, 45, 46n
  radical sects, 42–3, 46n
Chunnu, Winsome, 174, 184n
Churchill, Winston, 104, 106, 107, 108, 111, 112, 114, 115, 116, 117, 118n, 119n, 120n, 223, 224
  Partition, 140, 141, 143, 150n
  racism, 114, 119n
*Churchill*, 2, 14, 104–6, 114, 115–17
Clarkson, Laurence, 42–3
Clay, Christopher, 62n
Clay, Thomas *see Fanny Lye Deliver'd*
class, 2, 9, 43–4, 67, 69, 78, 79–80, 81n, 82n, 88, 91–2, 93–4, 145, 203, 206, 222, 223, 225
  aristocracy, 51, 60, 68, 69, 89, 144–5, 223
  servant class, 17n, 51, 61, 89, 92–3, 94, 95, 97–8, 99, 144, 223
  upper class, 49–51, 59, 60, 61, 80, 91, 94
  white working class, 6, 127, 136n, 173, 203–4, 225
  working class, 4, 14, 69, 70–2, 74, 76, 77, 79, 80, 96, 119n, 174, 177–8, 184, 203, 204, 205, 206, 211, 214n, 223, 224
Collins, Larry, 152n
Collins, Patricia Hill, 8
Collier, Paul, 13
colonialism, 115, 123, 125, 127–8, 138, 141, 142, 143, 145
"coming-of-age" film *see* genre
commodification, 221
Congress Party, 139, 146
Conservative Party, 4, 5–6, 51–2, 76, 218, 220
Conservatism, 5, 10, 87–9, 90, 92–3, 220
Corbyn, Jeremy, 220
Corn Laws, 82n
Coss, Edward J., 81n
counter-cinema *see* genre
country houses, 17n, 62n, 63–4n, 90, 91–3, 97–8
Covid-19, 3, 142
Cox, Brian, 115
Cox, Pamela, 97, 98
Cromwell, Oliver, 38, 44
Crown, the, 88, 89, 90–1, 223

*Daphne*, 15, 157–9, 160–1, 162, 165–7, 225
*Dark River*, 15, 189–99, 225
*Darkest Hour*, 2, 14, 104–15, 116, 117, 223, 224
David, Jacques-Louis, 107, 118n
Davidoff, Leonore, 99, 102n
Delap, Lucy, 99, 102n
Deliveroo, 209–10
DePaola, Tom, 209, 216n
Devasundaram, Ashvin Immanuel, 140
Diggers/True Levellers, 36, 42, 46n
Disraeli, Benjamin, 4, 87–8
Disraelian conservatism *see* one-nation Conservatism
documentary style, 108, 109
domestic service, 99–100, 102n
Dorling, Danny, 214n
*Downton Abbey*, 14, 87–100, 223
*Downton Abbey* (TV series), 87
Dresser, Madge, 63–4n
Duda-Mikulin, Eva, A., 180, 181
*Dunkirk* (1958), 1–2
*Dunkirk* (2017), 2, 14, 104–6, 114, 117, 160
Dunkirk evacuation, 1–2, 16n, 104, 106

Elizabeth I, 23, 34n
*Empire Windrush*, 123
enclosure laws, 72
Engels, Friedrich, 4
Engler, Michael *see Downton Abbey*
English Civil War, 32, 36, 44, 46n
*English Pastoral: An Inheritance see* Rebanks, James
Englishness, 10, 91, 93–4, 105, 106
ethnic diversity *see* race
EU referendum (2016)/Brexit, 5, 6, 15, 18n, 52, 76, 105, 106, 114–15, 117, 132, 136n, 174, 177, 180, 181, 183–4, 199, 203–4, 214n, 220, 222
Europe, 12, 14, 32, 109, 110, 114, 175, 176, 182, 208, 224
European Union, 52, 110, 174–5, 185n
Evans, Elizabeth, 34n
Evans, Eric J., 82n
Everett, Wendy, 217n

*Fanny Lye Deliver'd*, 13, 35–45, 222, 226
*Favourite, The*, 13–14, 49–61, 222–3, 226

feminism, 24, 29–30, 30–31, 34n, 54, 55, 57, 136n
Fifth Monarchists, 42
financial crisis (2007–8), 209, 216n, 220
Fiske, Robert, 227
Flemmen, Magne, 136n
Florczak, Izabela, 208, 216n
Ford, Rob, 6
franchise *see* voting rights
French Revolution, 68, 74
Friedman, Lester, 218–19
Friedman, Sam, 167
Fudge, Judy, 187n
Fulbrook, Mary, 4, 5
Fuller, Thomas, 118n

Gairola, Rahul K., 147, 149n
Gallipoli landings, 115
Gamble, Andrew, 12
Gandhi, Mahatma, 139
Garnett, Mark, 4
gay romance *see* genre
gender, 13, 30, 39, 131, 221, 222
　representation of women, 10, 25–32, 36–9, 39–41, 45, 47n, 48n, 49–50, 52–5, 56, 57–9, 63n, 77, 96, 97, 102n, 148, 165–6, 190–1, 222–3, 225
General Strike, 96–7, 98
genre
　art-house cinema, 15, 157–62
　"coming-of-age" film, 122–3
　counter-cinema, 161
　gay romance, 173, 177
　heritage films, 10–11, 87, 91, 97, 100, 102n
　historical drama, 9–11, 14, 23–5, 44, 48n, 115, 143, 223
　"upstairs-downstairs," 138, 145
gig economy, 207–8, 213, 225
Gill, Rosalind, 30
Gillborn, David, 176, 185n
Gilroy, Paul, 11, 12
globalization, 11, 16, 142, 178, 179, 180, 193, 206, 209, 220, 225, 226
*God's Own Country*, 15, 172–84, 225
Goldstein, Robert, 80n
*Gosford Park*, 87
Grater, Tom, 48n

Great Britain/United Kingdom, 18n, 62n
Greene, Larry A., 125, 134–5n
Gregg, Edward, 62n

Habeas Corpus Act, 67, 68
Hajari, Nisid, 140
Halikiopoulou, Daphne, 7
Hall, Steve, 173, 177–8, 183–4
Hall, Stuart, 11
Hames-Garcia, Michael, 132
Hann, Andrew, 63–4n
Harland, John, 83n
Harris, John, 203–4
Harvey, James, 6
Hastings, Max, 114, 119n
hate crime, 25, 33n, 181, 182, 187n
Helleiner, Eric, 216n
heritage films *see* genre
Herod, Andrew, 206, 212, 216n
Herzfeld-Olsson, Petra, 187n
Heyes, Cressida, 136n
Hicks, India, 151n
Hickson, Kevein, 88–9
Higson, Andrew, 10, 91, 94, 97
Hill, Christopher, 36, 42–3, 44, 48n, 64n
Hill, John, 227, 230n
Hilliard, Robert, 8
historical drama *see* genre
history, 1, 9–11, 15, 32, 44, 67, 68, 113–14, 117, 148, 223
　cultural representation of the past, 2–3, 131
　historical accuracy, 23–5, 44, 48n, 110–11, 112, 116, 143
　historical interpretation, 50, 79–80, 91–2, 100, 115, 141, 143, 224
Hitler, Adolf, 134n
Hobsbawm, Eric, 132
homosexuality *see* sexuality
homophobia, 15, 25, 173, 181, 182, 183
Hoskins, W. G., 72
Howkins, Alun, 94
Hughes, Ted, 199–200n
Hunt, Henry, 74, 82n

identity, 121, 122, 129–33, 165–6, 224, 226, 227–8
identity politics, 25, 130, 131–3, 136n

Ignatieff, Michael, 11, 131
immigration, 7, 12, 105, 110, 111–12, 123, 128, 184, 184n, 186–7n
   migrant labour, 100, 173, 176–9, 180, 187n
   migration, 12–13, 112, 178, 180–1, 182, 183
imperialism, 16, 24, 114, 128, 148, 223, 226
Independent Cinema Office, 159
India, 113, 147–8, 149n
   aristocracy, 145
   independence, 15, 138
   Partition, 15, 139, 140, 141–2, 143–4, 146–7, 148, 149n
   Second World War, 138
Irigaray, Luce, 31–2
Iyer, Nalini, 147, 149n

Jack, Ian, 105, 110, 141
Jalal, Ayesha, 144
James I, 32
James, C. L. R., 112, 118–19n
jazz, 135n
Jeffreys-Jones, Rhodri, 75–6
Jinnah, Muhammad Ali, 139, 140, 147
Johnson, Boris, 51, 220
Johnston, Ron, 4
Jones, Jonathan, 107
Jones, Owen, 204

Katz, David, 44
Kaufman, Stephen, 133n
Kelby, Rosamund, 44, 45
Kenner, Jeff, 216n
Kermode, Frank, 170n
Kermode, Mark, 141, 200n
Kesting, Robert, 125
Kezar, Adrianna, 209, 216n
*King Lear*, 115–16, 120n
Knox, John, 34n

Labour Party, 76, 106, 123, 220
Lambert, Rob, 206, 212, 216n
Lanthimos, Yorgos, 223; *see also Favourite, The*
Lapierre, Dominique, 152n
Larkin, Philip, 163–4, 169n, 170n
Laurison, Daniel, 167
Laverty, Paul, 205, 206, 208, 209, 211–12

Laybourn, Keith, 97
*Lays of Ancient Rome see* Macaulay, Thomas Babington
Leach, Hope Dickson, 189, 192, 193, 199, 200n; *see also Levelling, The*
Lee, Francis, 15, 172, 173, 184; *see also God's Own Country*
Lee, Ken, 175
Leigh, Jacob, 208, 217n
Leigh, Mike, 66, 68, 69, 74, 75, 77, 79, 80, 83n; *see also Peterloo*
Lethbridge, Lucy, 92, 100
Levellers, 42
*Levelling, The*, 15, 189–99, 225
Lewis-Stempel, John, 196
LGBT+, 25, 27, 187
liberal values, 31, 97, 114, 128, 221, 222, 224
Lind, Michael, 88
*Lion Has Wings, The*, 3
Lipscomb, Suzannah, 23, 25
Loach, Ken, 15–16, 203, 204, 205, 206, 208, 209, 210, 211, 212, 213–14, 215n, 217n; *see also Sorry We Missed You*
Lobley, Matt, 198
Loughrey, Clarisse, 33n
Luddites, 68, 73
Lusane, Clarence, 124, 125, 135n
Lynch, Philip, 4

Macaulay, Thomas Babington, 112–14, 117
   Macaulayism, 113
*Macbeth*, 106–7, 120n
McCann. Philip, 76–7
MacKay, George, 130
McKenzie, Kirsten, 81n
Magelssen, Scott, 100
Major, John, 52, 62n
*Making of the English Landscape, The see* Hoskins, W. G.
Makovsky, Michael, 114
"March of the Blanketeers," 66
Marlborough, Duke of, 55, 63n
Marmot, Michael, 6
Marsili, Lorenzo, 203, 205
Martill, Benjamin, 117
Martin, Theodore, 211
*Mary Queen of Scots*, 13, 23–32, 222
Masham, Damaris Cudworth, 63n

Massaquoi, Hans J., 124
Matera, Marc, 112
media representations, 3
Meehan, Diana, 58
*Mein Kampf*, 128
migrant labour *see* immigration
migration *see* immigration
Miners' Strike (1984–5), 208
Mingay, Gordon, 62n
miscegenation, 110, 122, 129
Mohanty, Satya P., 132
monarchy, 90, 91
Monbiot, George, 199
Monk, Claire, 9, 10
Mooney, Gerry, 4
Moraru, Adela, 181
Moraru, Madalina, 178
Morgan, Alison, 82n
Morgan, George, 207, 208, 213
Morris, Christopher, 34n
Morton, Timothy, 196
Mouffe, Chantel, 16
Mountbatten, Lord Louis ("Dickie"), 138, 139, 140, 141, 143–5, 149n, 151n
Mountbatten, Pamela, 145, 149n
Moya, Paula M. L., 132
Muslim League, 139, 140, 147

Nadin, Joseph, 82n, 83n
Nail, Thomas, 142
Najam, Adil, 144
narration, 1, 2, 35, 38, 41, 44–5, 164–5
nationalism, 7, 11, 15, 16, 101n, 105–6, 107, 114, 117, 136n, 180, 223, 225
  and national heritage, 95–6
  and national identity, 7, 123, 131–2
  and nationhood, 4–5, 11–12, 93–4
  and racism, 11, 12
  and regionalism, 20n, 76
Nazism *see* Third Reich
Nehru, Jawaharlal, 139, 146, 147, 148, 152–3n
Nelligan, Pariece, 207, 208, 213
neo-liberalism, 16, 206, 209, 211–12, 213, 218, 220, 221, 225, 226, 228
Nica, Felicia, 178
*Night Mail*, 87
nobility, 90, 95

"North–South divide," 20n, 76, 69, 214n
Northern Rock, 208, 209, 216n
nostalgia, 6, 9, 10, 87, 95, 97, 98, 99, 105, 117, 179

Office for National Statistics, 216n
O'Leary, Brendan, 149n
Oliver (government spy), 66–7, 81n
Olsen, Kirstin, 50
one-nation Conservatism *see* Conservatism
Organisation for Economic Co-operation and Development, 186–7n
Otto, Marta, 208, 216n

Padmore, George, 112
Pakistan, 15, 138, 140, 146, 147, 152n, 153n
Pandey, Bishwa Mohan, 143
Parkinson-Bailey, John J., 83n
parliamentary democracy, 49–50, 65, 73, 74–5
Partition *see* India
*Partition: 1947 see Viceroy's House*
patriarchy, 13, 21, 26–8, 30, 31, 32, 37, 40, 45, 50, 54, 57, 58, 61, 96, 196, 222, 223, 224, 225–6
Pattie, Charles, 4
Paulin, Tom, 101n
performance, 166–7
personal identity *see* identity
Peterloo, 65–6
*Peterloo*, 14, 65–80, 223, 224
Petley, Julian, 10
Pettigrew, William, 60
Picturehouse (cinema chain), 161
pineapples, 60–1, 64n
Pitt, William (the Elder), 108
Poole, Robert, 65, 80n
post-imperial racism *see* racism
post-truth, 227, 228
postcolonialism, 24
postmodernism, 24, 79
Powell, Enoch, 12
Powell, Margaret, 98
Powell, Zachary Michael, 114
Prassl, Jeremias, 207–8
precarious work, 206, 210, 212, 213, 215n, 216n, 217n, 225
  precariat, 208, 209

*Pride*, 80
Proctor, Robert, 126

Quakers/Society of Friends, 42, 45, 46n
Quart, Leonard, 226–7
Queen Anne, 49, 53, 57, 59, 61–2n, 62n

race, 101n, 105, 114, 126–7, 128, 131, 132–3, 144, 148, 176, 224
 and ethnic diversity, 23, 110, 111–12
 and Hitler's Germany, 121, 122–3, 124–6
 and post-war Britain, 122
racism, 11, 12, 111, 117, 121, 122, 123, 124–5, 125–9, 136n, 173, 174–5, 176, 182, 185n, 226
 anti-gypsyism, 173, 174, 176
 post-imperial racism, 173
 xenophobia, 15, 174, 175, 176
Ranters, 42–3
Read, Donald, 81n
Reagan, Ronald, 208
Rebanks, James, 192–3, 196
Reed, Rex, 162
Reger, Jo, 54
*Remains of the Day, The*, 87
"Rhineland bastards," 124, 125, 134n, 135n
Richards, Jeffrey, 24
Roberts, Andrew, 116, 120n
Roma, 174–5, 185n
Roman Catholicism *see* Christian religion
Romania, 174–5, 178–9, 180, 181–2
Romocea, Oana, 178
Rosario, Kennith, 141, 146, 149
Roscoe, Edward Stanley, 61
Rose, Steve, 105
Rosenhaft, Eve, 134n
Rosenstone, Robert A., 23–4
Rourke, Josie, 23, 30, 33n; *see also Mary Queen of Scots*
Royal African Company, 60
Ruck, Ruth Janette, 196
rural poverty, 193–5, 202n, 225
rural suicide, 198
Ryle, Martin, 24–5

Sargeant, Amy, 9
Sarila, Narendra Singh, 140
Savage, Mike, 136n

Schama, Simon, 224
Scheck, Raffael, 125
Schwartz, Laura, 89, 99, 100
Scott, Daniel T., 209, 216n
Scott, Leonard, 226–7
Scott, Peter, 99
Scrivener, Michael, 66
Second World War, 3, 14, 17n, 104–17, 122 125, 138, 223
*Sense of an Ending, The*, (film), 15, 157–8, 160–5, 167, 225
*Sense of an Ending, The*, (novel), 162, 165, 169n
servant class *see* class
Seven Years War, 108
sexuality, 13, 25, 27, 31, 32, 33n, 54, 181–2, 187n, 221–2, 225
*Silent Spring see* Carson, Rachel
Sinngh, Amritjit, 147, 149n
slave trade, 59–60, 61, 64n, 223
Smith, Adam, 212
Smith, Nigel, 43
"social contract," 213, 217n
social inequality, 6, 67, 68, 69–72, 75, 76–7, 78–9, 93, 94, 100, 167, 218, 219–20, 223
Social Mobility Commission, 167, 194
Somerset Levels, 189, 191, 199
*Sorry We Missed You*, 15–16, 203–14, 224, 225
South Africa, 127–8
Spadavecchia, Anna, 99
Spencer, Ian, 111
Staiger, Janet, 100
Standing, Guy, 209
Stark, Cameron, 198
sterilization, 124, 125
Street, Sarah, 9, 91
Stubbs, George, 107–8
Suarez-Orozco, Marcelo, 12
suicide *see* rural suicide
surveillance, 68, 75–6, 219, 221
Sutherland, Claire, 12
*Sybil, or the Two Nations*, 88

Teesdale, 193
Tennyson, Alfred, 90, 101n
Teplitzky, Jonathan *see Churchill*
Thane, Pat, 218, 219, 220, 221–2, 229n
Tharoor, Shashi, 142, 145, 148

Thatcher, Margaret, 4, 10, 208, 218–19, 220, 229n
*They Shall Not Grow Old*, 85
Third Reich, 121, 133n, 134n, 136n
Thomas, Dylan, 162–3, 169n, 169–70n
Thompson, E. P., 66, 80
Thompson, Julian, 1–2
Townsend, Mark, 187n
Toye, Richard, 114, 119n
Trandafoiu, Ruxandra, 174–5, 178, 179, 183
Treadwell, James, 173, 177–8, 183–4
Trevelyan, George Macaulay, 34n
Tyndale, William, 47n

UK election (2019), 5–6, 51–2, 76, 220
UK Film Council, 161
Underwood, Doug, 113
*United Country, A*, 14–15, 121–3, 127–8, 129, 130, 131, 132–3, 224
United States, 7, 123, 124, 125, 126, 127, 128, 131, 134–5n, 176, 208
university education in UK, 158, 167, 168n, 171n
upper class *see* class
"upstairs-downstairs" *see* genre

*Viceroy's House*, 15, 138–49, 224–5
Vincent, Andrew, 88
Vlandas, Tim, 7
voluntary living wage, 201n
voting rights, 50, 65, 66, 73

Walsh, Joseph, 200n
Ward, Paul, 12

Waterloo, Battle of, 69
Webster, Wendy, 110, 111
Welfens, Paul, 5
Wellington, Duke of, 69, 81n
West Somerset, 195
Wheale, Nigel, 34n, 46n, 47n
Wheeler, Rebecca, 198
*Where Hands Touch*, 14–15, 121–33, 224
white working class *see* class
Whitman, James, 128
Wiarda, Howard J., 123, 130, 132
Wigger, Iris, 124, 125
Williams, A. Susan, 123, 127, 128
Winlow, Simon, 173, 177–8, 183–4
Winstanley, Gerrard, 46n, 47n
Winter, Michael, 198
Wolpert, Stanley, 144
Wood, Ellen Meiksins, 44
Wood, Neal, 44
Wood, Robin, 7
working class *see* class
working conditions, 66, 89, 98–9, 127, 178
Wright, Joe *see Darkest Hour*
Wright, Tony, 12
Wrigley, Chris, 119n

xenophobia *see* racism

Yorkshire Dales, 192

Zane, Damian, 133n
Ziegler, Philip, 144
Žižek, Slavoj, 165–7, 170n
Zuboff, Shoshana, 219–20

EU representative:
Easy Access System Europe
Mustamäe tee 50, 10621 Tallinn, Estonia
Gpsr.requests@easproject.com

www.ingramcontent.com/pod-product-compliance
Lightning Source LLC
Chambersburg PA
CBHW071834230426
43671CB00012B/1962